Master Chian Zettnersan

Taoist Bedroom Secrets

Tao Chi Kung
Sexual-Therapeutic Exercises
for Enjoyment, Health, and Rejuvenation
Energetic Chi Kung Exercises
for Strengthening the Sexual Power,
Optimizing Health, and Prolonging Life

Translated by Christine M. Grimm

T0169281

LOTUS PRESS
SHANGRI-LA

First English Edition 2002
© by Lotus Press, Box 325
Twin Lakes, WI 53181, USA
The Shangri-La Series is published in cooperation with Schneeloewe Verlagsberatung, Federal Republic of Germany
© 2000 by Windpferd Verlagsgesellschaft mbH, Aitrang, Germany
All rights reserved
Translated from German by Christine M. Grimm
Cover design by Kuhn Graphik, Digitales Design, Zurich
(using illustrations by Wolfgang Juenemann [dragon and tiger])
Illustrations by Daniel Muschalik
Production: Schneeloewe, Aitrang, Germany

ISBN 0-914955-71-3
Library of Congress Control Number 2002103996
Printed in USA

Table of Contents

Pine and plum twigs, as well as narcissus in the vase:
"Evergreen life, love, happiness, and peace"
to all the readers
from Master Chian Zettnersan

Nine Wise Taoist Sayings

1 Eternal and harmonious peace on earth is based on successful nations.

2 A flourishing society is based on a successful nation.

3 A successful and healthy society is based on harmonious and happy families.

4 A happy and reliable family is based on an unlimited marriage.

5 A happy and successful marriage is based on a happy sexual life in the partnership.

6 So the method of Taoist sexuality is the complete and indispensable wisdom and love since the reproductive secretions contain the unceasing growth of nature.

7 Only in the orgasm are we human beings "one" with ourselves, "one" with the partner, "one" with the entire Creation, and "one" with God, the universal energy of all life. There is no past and no future, there is only the present: the "eternal here and now." At this point, the human being stops breathing. His spirit becomes completely empty and relaxes; new and true love, divine joy, and enlightened bliss develop from this void.

8 The ancient Taoist masters considered love, food, and the breathing and chi kung exercises to be the "three pillars" that support the life of a human being. These three pillars determine whether someone reaches ripe old age.

9 One of the worst things that people can do to their bodies is overeating. It would be better for us to spend less time at the table and more time in the love nest.

ACKNOWLEDGEMENTS

In order to move something big in life, we must first set a high goal: Only those who aim at the moon hit the eagle in flight: This is the philosophy of the ancient Taoist sages. We must therefore often begin our efforts where other people give up. This not only requires hard work but also endurance, discipline, and courage, as well as helpful people who give us assistance and support in difficult situations.

Through courage and discipline, I have had to develop the necessary endurance and strength time and again, as well as the vitality and health, so I could continue to study and learn. The courage of the people who have been helpful to me has made it possible for me to draw on the strength to survive even difficult situations. We can only reach the goal of our lives through our actions.

I want to especially thank my partner in life, Gudrun Zettner, our son Marcel, our dear Dr. Ingrid Huther-Thor, Petra Maeuer, and Monika Juenemann, as well as our mutual friend Alberto Dal Fabbro, Dr. Juergen A. Machat, Stephan and Sabine Glaser, Gerhard Volkmann, and the many other helpful friends—whose names are too numerous to be included here. These people stand like powerful pillars in my life. They have encouraged, cautioned, respectfully criticized, and effectively activated me. And they always did this just when my strength was threatening to wane and I thought I couldn't complete this book because of the abundance of the material. I also received additional support and encouragement from the students of my feng shui and chi kung training seminars 1 to 5 in Germany and Austria (1992-1999).

I would also like to thank certified designer Axel Duckstein for helpfully using his abilities to assist me in translating my ideas into manuscript form, especially in connecting the text and illustrations.

And, last but not least, I thank the entire team of the Windpferd publishing house for their commitment, expertise, and inspiration. I would like to specifically mention my editor, Sylvia Luetjohann, who has contributed much with her devotion to detail and extensive knowledge. I would also like to thank the Marx graphic team for the successful layout and text design, as well as the artist Daniel Muschalik, who interpreted the sketches with sensitive strokes. I am also grateful to my publisher, Monika Juenemann, for her gentle way of inspiring a challenge.

However, I alone am responsible for any remaining errors in this book.

GENERAL NOTES

The ancient Chinese diagnostic and therapy process in this book, which serves the health and longevity of human beings, has been compiled and copyrighted by the chi kung and feng-shui Master Chian Zettnersan.

For more than 30 years, all of the information in this handbook has been carefully compiled, examined, and exclusively selected according to the ancient Chinese diagnosis and therapy procedures of traditional Taoist medicine. Because of laws and certain regulations, as well as the various scientific studies of Western and Eastern medicine, it is inevitable that there will be changes that may alter the medicinal-gymnastic activities of Taoist chi kung in relation to the five phases of change: breath—movement—nutrition—sexuality—meditation.

Please understand that because of the ancient Chinese characters and their translation into modern informal speech, we cannot assume any liability for the correctness and completeness of the text.

ADDITIONAL PRACTICAL NOTES

The length of the exercises and number of repetitions of all the ancient Chinese diagnosis and therapy procedures depends on the age, sex, and constitution of the person practicing them.

It should be expressly noted that none of the ancient Chinese therapy procedures are meant to replace a physician, medication, or course of treatment at a spa. Instead, they should be understood as therapeutic accompanying measures in agreement with the prescribed medical measures. The therapeutic chi kung exercises promote the healing process and serve both prevention and rehabilitation.

Practice only under the direction of an experienced chi kung teacher or therapist who can correctly impart the ancient Chinese diagnosis and therapy procedures to you.

PREFACE

The Taoist erotic arts call sexuality the original source of all being—the power that produces every phenomena of life: from infinitely great joy to utmost pain. Invisible and always present, this sexual energy permeates our daily life. We can use its unlimited power to prolong and enrich our lives.

Even though the principles of the Taoist erotic arts were first formulated in words and symbols about 6000 years ago in ancient China, sexuality is considerably older than what we know of human civilization. It transcends all the boundaries of time and space, as well as race and culture, since the deep sexual wisdom of loving is the universal and enduring essence of nature.

Thanks to the Taoist sages, who established the oldest and most lasting civilization in the world, it became possible for the deeper sexual truth between man and woman to develop. It is more than a philosophy of life. It is an all-encompassing lifestyle and the only possibility for achieving enjoyment of love's delights is by practicing these forms of the sexual-therapeutic exercises. Fortunately, the ancient Taoist sages have left us an abundance of records on the path of sexual longevity in the form of ancient Chinese bedroom secrets, the so-called "Taoist Pillow Books."

In our modern stress-plagued age, with an increasing health consciousness and the constantly growing expenses of the health-care system, there is a general need for suitable therapy and healing procedures that can increase energy and performance in the long run, as well as counteract libido disorders and the development of sexual diseases. An increasing significance is being attributed to health in the sexual area, so that this aspect meets with more and more interest, even in Western medicine and pharmacology.

The Taoist tradition of the eight ancient Chinese diagnosis, therapy, and healing procedures takes into account the changing quality and quantity of the relationship between matter and energy, body and mind, breath and movement, as well as sexuality and nutrition. This book concentrates on the three practical aspects and is based on the following pillars of the ancient Chinese diagnosis, therapy, and healing procedures, which have always been of great interest to men and women throughout the entire world:

Health through the chi kung breathing and movement exercises

 Sexuality that includes the energetic chi kung exercises for strengthening the libido

 Longevity through nutrition and balance of the acid-alkali equilibrium.

All three aspects have a close connection with each other and together form the foundation for a happy human life.

My remarks in this book are largely based on the evaluation of authentic ancient Chinese sources from Japanese, Korean, and Chinese masters of the healing and martial arts, as well as professors of Western and Eastern medicine. I would also like to point out that I have been personally practicing all of the exercise forms described here for more than 30 years and also teach them in our German-Chinese Chi Kung and Feng Shui Academy and Rheumatism Health Center in Nuremburg. This book is therefore based on experiences that I have had personally or that have been had by patients who I have taught or provided with therapy, as well as the scientific basis of Taoism and the eight ancient Chinese diagnosis, therapy, and healing procedures for health and longevity.

May it bring spiritual, mental, and physical enrichment to the readers and help them activate the energy source that is necessary for advancing on the path of the Tao and harvesting its fruits.

GENERAL INTRODUCTION TO THE EIGHT ANCIENT CHINESE DIAGNOSIS AND THERAPY PROCEDURES OF TAOIST MEDICINE

Before we begin with the energy exercises themselves, I would like to briefly describe the eight pillars of Taoist medicine. The symbol of the ancient Chinese diagnosis and therapy procedure results from the eight trigrams, which were first depicted in the world's oldest book of wisdom—the I Ching from the Middle Kingdom. These trigrams, which are arranged in the form of an octagon around the yin/yang symbol, represent the pillars of Taoism. They symbolize the eight pillars of the sky, the eight directions, the eight mountains, and the eight gates of the energetic and cosmic forces through which the rain clouds enter and which cause the eight winds.

The great storm comes from the south, the hot wind from the southeast, the roaring wind from the east, and the flaming wind from the northeast (yang energy circulates counterclockwise). The cool wind comes from the southwest, the lasting wind from the west, the sharp wind from the northwest, and the cold wind from the north (yin energy circulates clockwise).

1. **The Tao of philosophy, psychology, religion, mythology, and meditation** of the Traditional Chinese Medicine (TCM) in theory and practice.

2. **The Tao of revitalization, concentration, and meditation, yin and yang breathing, the large and small energy cycle.**
Inner exercises and medical-gymnastic activity of the ancient Chinese healing wisdom for prevention and rehabilitation.

3. **The Tao of the balanced diet**
(Strengthening of the defensive energies)
Yin and yang energy of drinks and food, the five taste qualities of sour, bitter, sweet, spicy, and salty, as well as classification with the five phases of change: wood, fire, earth, metal, and water.

**4. The Tao of the forgotten medicinal plants
(Strengthening of the immune response)**
Medicinal plant and herb therapy, such as ginseng, ginger, and angelica root according to the cycle of the organs and meridians.

**5. The Tao of the healing arts / martial arts
(Activation of the powers of resistance = yin/yang)**
Pulse diagnosis, acupuncture, acupressure, moxa therapy, tuina massage, meridian-organ-clock therapy, the five phases of change and eight trigrams, chiropractic, and self-defense.

**6. The Tao of sexual wisdom and love
(Harmonious partnership)**
Energetic exercise forms with breath therapy for strengthening sexual power and endurance, control of the semen energy, elimination of sexual disharmonies between man and woman, as well as rejuvenation exercises.

7. The Tao of self-discipline, numerology, astrology, and the I Ching, as well as the 108 strategies
Law of cause and effect through mental and physical actions, numerology according to the magical Lo-Shu square of the heavenly turtle Hi and Chinese astrology. Numerological opinions and dispositions for the private, family, professional, and social area in idea-related, material, and financial competition.

8. The Tao of the formed destiny, geomancy, feng shui
Feng shui consultation with pulse diagnosis / numerology and I Ching. Law of cause and effect in the art of placement and recognition of the healthy life, living and working, color design, renovation, design of new buildings and landscapes, harmonious interior design and architecture, and advertising and design.

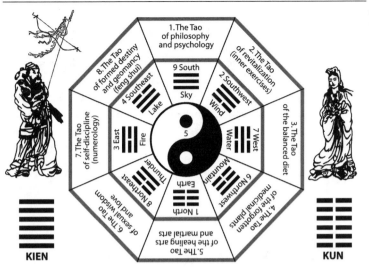

The eight trigrams as a symbol of the ancient Chinese diagnosis and therapy procedure

For thousands of years, many teachings of the ancient Chinese diagnosis and therapy procedure were kept secret. Even today, the foundation of this Taoist therapy procedure is still a philosophically and psychologically oriented perspective of how human beings live and act in their environment. Starting with the opposing and yet complementary polarity of the yin and yang phenomena, which flows through all things and forces, the Taoist healing arts were carried out beyond China's boundaries into the entire world. According to this millennia-old viewpoint, every manifested form of life—including the individual human being—is composed of these opposing forces, the receptive and begetting force (yin) and the creative and exploding force (yang). On one hand, they act in opposition to each other; on the other hand, they complement each other in order to form a mutual and complete whole.

All medical forms from the East follow this idea. They consider not only the disturbed relationship with one individual organ as requiring treatment, but also connect it with the entire system and look at its inclusion in the surrounding world as the main task: The cause and not the effect is the focus of the therapy measure.

One form of advanced medical development became the Taoist chi kung, which aims to strengthen the self-healing and strength of the organism. This therapeutic chi kung developed as an independent discipline of the ancient Chinese diagnosis and therapy procedure. Its goal is refining the energies of the body in order to achieve the higher spiritual levels of transcendental knowledge through meditation and inner visions.

WHAT IS TAO CHI KUNG?

 TAO

Nothing is constant in the universe. Everything is ebb and flow, every form that is born contains within its bosom the seed of change. Tao actually means the path or gate through which all things pass. Those who progress with the Tao find themselves in a "state of grace," an expression borrowed from the Christian terminology. Conduct in harmony with the Tao can be compared to water that flows incessantly and boundlessly. It fills up all the hollow places, overcomes every form of resistance, persists in order to fill up the deep places, and then continues its flow. It always remains true to its nature and moves in harmony with the forces of the cosmos. Only when we move with the Tao can we find our place in the cosmos, live with it in harmony, and actually exercise our free will. When we know the Tao of changes and alterations, we know the work of the gods. The Tao is a science and philosophy of health and longevity, following the ceaseless and unlimited growth of nature: the perfect and natural organizing principle of life and action. The polarity of yin and yang results in the Tao, the unity of body, mind, and soul. It leads to health and longevity.

CHI

Many Western people think that chi is a part of occultism, esotericism, or some other form of mysticism that is open only to a few initiates. This viewpoint can be easily refuted when we remember that chi has been something completely obvious and used for inner and outer advancements by the entire Chinese population for about 8,000 years now. Meng-Dse (371-289 B.C.) already said: "Anyone who develops his chi will find the right path. This chi is the greatest and strongest energy that there is. Chi is everything and always present." In the big nation of Chi-na, there is much chi energy. "Chi = energy" and "na = the big country" is what the ancient sages of the East called it, specifically implying the healing arts of China.

Consequently, chi lives in all things and beings. It is also your energy, your motor, and your life force. It is the most natural and liveliest force, and is in everything that you touch or eat every day. Above all, chi circulates in sexuality. It is in you and around you and allows life to be created. If you would like to create a stronger connection between your own chi and the chi that surrounds you, we recommend studying the traditional Taoist Deer Exercise.

The word "chi" means the dynamic, inexhaustible, electromagnetic force—that invisible vital energy that animates the coarse, molecular portions of every body. It is a cosmic energy cycle that forms a network of 72,000 circuits. Chi is the absolute energy and foundation for all forms of life and matter in the universe. It permeates the atomic structures of all things, including the atmosphere that surrounds us. Chi is the key and the inexhaustible source of a long, vital, and productive life. Human beings absorb it from the endless expanse of the universe through movement, breath, nutrition, meditation, and sexuality.

功 KUNG This term describes medical-gymnastic therapy procedures, the so-called "inner exercises." This is an extensive and holistic system of the ancient Chinese diagnosis and therapy procedure's mental and physical movement and breath culture. It is an excellent therapeutic measure for prevention and rehabilitation in order to optimize health and prolong life.

THREE LEGENDARY EMPERORS AND TEN PHYSICIANS OF THE ANCIENT CHINESE DIAGNOSIS AND THERAPY PROCEDURE

The forefathers of Taoist medicine

The three rulers on this picture are the legendary emperors Fu-Hsi, Shen Nong, and Huang Ti. Together with the physicians who followed them, they are said to have served the people in many ways. These included the discovery of medicinal plants, the invention of stone needles for acupuncture, and the compilation of valuable medical works.

The ten physicians are Qi Bo and Lei Gong (from the Huangdi governing period, 26-22 B.C.), Bian Que (from the period of the Feuding Kingdom, 475-221 B.C.), Chunyu Yi and Zhang Zhongjing (Hang Dynasty, 206 B.C.-220 A.D.), Hua Tuo (Staat Wei, 220-265), Wang Shue, Huangfu Mi, and Ge Hong (Jin Dynasty), 265-420), as well as Li Jinghe (Tang Dynasty, 619-907).

Later physicians of traditional Taoist medicine, as well as the simple folk, worshipped them as gods. Furthermore, practitioners of the healing arts gathered on the 28th day of the 4th month according to the Moon Calendar to burn paper horses as a sacrifice for Sun Simiao, who lived during the Tang Dynasty and was considered the King of Medicine.

LIST OF THERAPEUTIC INDICATIONS

To support the physician's treatment for preventive and rehabilitation measures

Functional headache and facial pain
Vasomotor headache—migraine—stromatitis—discopathy of the jaw joint—myofacial pain syndrome

Disorders of the Respiratory System
Tuberculosis (to support the physician's treatment)—bronchial asthma—pulmonary emphysema—cystic fibrosis—chronic sinusitis—vasomotor rhinitis—pneumonia

Eye Diseases
Glaucoma, cataract—blepharitis—myopia and hypertropia (far-sightedness)

Neuralgic Pain
Rheumatism—dizzy spells, rotary vertigo, trigeminal neuralgia—paresis of the facial nerve—phantom pain and other neuralgiform complaints

Disorders of the Digestive Tract
Gastritis—liver and gallbladder function disturbance—non-specific diarrhea—constipation—irritable colon—colitis—diabetes—vomiting—stomach complaints—ulcer—overacidified stomach (hyperpepsia) —hemorrhoids

Disorders of the Supporting Apparatus and Locomotor System
Arthritis—bursitis—sciatica—lumbago—tendopathy—chronic polyarthritis—slipped or lacerated disk —lumbar mylagia—iliac/sacral pain

Cardiovascular Disorders
Functional heart complaints—hyperkinetic heart syndrome—high blood pressure—low blood pressure—hypercholesteremia—arteriosclerosis

Stress Disorders
Disorders of the autonomic nervous system—tinnitus (ringing in the ears)—general irritability, nervousness, and sleep disorders—psychosomatic disorders—cellulite-regenerative weakness—sensitivity to changes in the weather—nephritis—retention of urine

Male Abdominal Disorders
Prostatism—impotence—spermatorrhea—lack of drive—sterility—complaints related to penis—bedwetting—incontinence

Female Abdominal Disorders
Menstrual disorders—pruritus of the vulvae—leucorrhea (the whites)—amenorrhea (absence of menstruation)—dysmenorrhea—menstrual pain—cystitis—enuresis—incontinence—menopausal complaints—frigidity

This list of indications is intended to serve your orientation: It makes no claims of completeness. Not every individual afflicted with one of the above-mentioned problems can be successfully treated with the medical chi kung system. This list of indications was compiled according to the guidelines of WHO (World Health Organization) and published by Professor Dong Haiquan, M.D., Professor Stephen T. Chang, M.D., and Professor Liu Gui Zhen, M.D.

INTRODUCTION TO THE TAOIST BEDROOM SECRETS

On the Deep Wisdom of Loving

"There is nothing more constant in the universe than yin and yang. Everything is ebb and flow, every form that is born bears within its bosom the seed of change."

In contrast to the Indian Kamasutra and all of the Western books on sex, which are very popular and concentrate solely on sexual intercourse, the traditional Taoist "Pillow Books" are designed for the study of sexual health and longevity. They discuss how sexual relationships can be designed so that:

- They promote the health and longevity of the male and female body and mind.

- The love play occurs in a manner that is attractive and pleasurable for both parties.

In addition, the Taoist "Pillow Books" contain information on:

- Special partner massages, thrust techniques, and control of ejaculation.

- Exercises for maintaining and strengthening the sexual organs in order to promote sexual power and endurance, as well as strengthening the nervous system and lymphatic glandular system.

- Instructions on how to reverse sexual energy and orgasm and return them to the brain.

This wealth of experience related to using sexual energy for promoting health and prolonging life is one of the most original and valuable contributions of the Taoist culture to the knowledge of sexual equilibrium between man and woman and for the benefit of all humanity.

When the West discovered China approximately 800 years ago, it was unfortunate that arrogance, prudery, and prejudices prevented a serious study of the "traditional Taoist bedroom secrets" (Fang-Shu). Otherwise, these would be as popular throughout the world today as Chinese medicine or cookery. In traditional Taoist households, every bedroom had several of the erotic "Pillow Books," which could be consulted before and during the sexual act. They were called "pillow books" because they rested on a pillow near the bed so that they could quickly be reached, if necessary.

The role of the "Pillow Books" in the sex life of the ancient Chinese culture is illustrated by the following excerpt from a poem by Zeng Hing (78-139 B.C.):

"I have cleaned the pillow and bed mat and filled the burner with precious incense.
Let us now lock the double door with its golden lock and light the lamp to fill our room with its brilliance.
I shed my robes and remove my paint and powder, and roll out the picture scroll by the side of the pillow.
The Plain Girl I shall take as my instructress, so that we can practice all the variegated postures, those that an ordinary husband has but rarely seen, such as taught by Tian-Lao (the "Plain Girl") to the Yellow Emperor."

This poem contains an abundance of information about sexual life in ancient China:

 The first line addresses the importance of hygiene, while the second suggests the Taoist custom of creating a special atmosphere by perfuming the room and bed sheets with precious incense.

 In addition, the need for seclusion is discussed, the practice of abandoning oneself to love play by the light of a lamp.

 Moreover, there are references to the role of the "Pillow Books," the "Plain Girl (Tian-Lao) as the teacher in sexual matters, practicing the various positions, and strengthening the sexual organs through the therapy of the five elements.

All of these references were not reserved solely for the Taoist adepts. Instead, they were practiced in this way by the entire Chinese population—even by the most conservative Confucian bureaucrats! Unfortunately, these accomplishments are no longer accessible to the modern-day Chinese people since there are only a few remaining Taoist masters who pass on this knowledge of sexual equilibrium to their students.

POETRY AND AESTHETICS IN THE EXPRESSION OF THE SEXUAL ORGANS

Some of the most imaginative and aesthetically appealing aspects of the Taoist bedroom secrets are the poetic terms of the sexual organs and the various sexual activities. Contrary to the Western use of language, which is either characterized by clinical-objective or vulgar terms, the poetic-erotic expressions of Taoist informal speech awakens associations of romanticism and innocence. The pictorial language has a very positive effect on the atmosphere in which the love play takes place. Moreover, this informal language makes it possible for Chinese poets and writers to describe sexual events in great detail without upsetting sensitive readers or religious organizations, or violating literary conventions.

As an example, the various phrases in connection with the expression "clouds and rain," which are poetic paraphrasing for the love act in Chinese, are listed below:

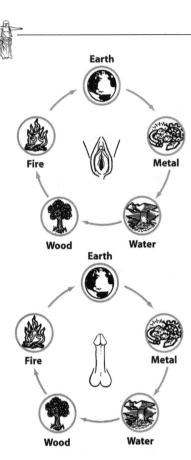

The positive cycle of the five elements

- The "clouds" symbolize the concentrating storm of the feminine essence

- The "rain" represents the ejaculation of the male semen

- The "clouds" gathered, but no "rain" came

- After the "rain" had fallen, the "clouds" dispersed

- A light "dripping," a "heavy shower," etc.

For those people who have a feeling for pictorial language and the aesthetic components of sexuality, the Taoist formulations may be helpful when they wish to speak with their partner about this "taboo topic" and enjoy the sexual act.

When awakening the erotic stimulus, it is very helpful to use positive and loving expressions when talking about the sexual organs. Accordingly, lovers throughout the world use tender terms of endearment when speaking about each other's sexual organs. When a couple creates individual personalities for the partners' sexual organs, this contributes to the intimacy of the love relationship and brings them into deeper communication with their own places of desire.

In the Taoist tradition, the male sexual organ, the penis, is called the "jade stem" or "yang sequence"—the embodiment of cosmic creativity, which is approached with respect. Since the male sexual organ is external and changes its appearance depending on the mood of the moment. It can be imagined to have a character of its own.

The female sexual organ, the vagina, is called the "jade gate" or "yin sequence"—the entrance to the original "holy palace of life," the embodiment of conception. The couple can only bring creativity and harmony into the "palace of joy and life" and worship God, the creator of all things, within it when they do so together.

ADDITIONAL CLASSIFICATIONS
OF THE MALE SEXUAL ORGAN

Jade rod, jade stalk, positive peak, mountain pinnacle, yang pagoda, carmine bird, unicorn, jade scepter, weapon of love, diplomat, ambassador, messenger, general, tiger, snake, frog, young rooster, turtle head, boy, vassal, experienced warrior, brave hero, lonely monk, adept, flute, jade shaft, jade tool, yang peak, and yang weapon.

> A man can communicate with his jade stem as if it were a separate, independent individual. This is a way of communicating with his "ambassador" and will help him achieve conscious control over his body and its functions.

ADDITIONAL CLASSIFICATIONS
OF THE FEMALE SEXUAL ORGAN

Jade gate, jade chamber, jade door, cinnabar cave, the inch square, little stream, deep valley, hidden place, path of yin, heavenly palace, valley of loneliness, golden ravine, jade vein, cinnabar chamber, honey pot, pleasure grotto, shady valley, noble gate, jade room, mysterious room, purple chamber, anemone, grotto of the white tiger, valley of joy, cinnabar chasm, secret cabinet, golden furrow, corn-shaped cave, melting pot, oyster, pearl, lotus, open melon, peace, opening the most secret knot, hidden shell, lyre, and phoenix.

> In a similar manner, a woman can do this with her jade gate and create a connection with the inner functions of her melting pot. Then she will be able to receive information about the most secret wishes from her hidden place in order to become conscious of her "linear cycles" and better understand how she can control her "path of yin."

English Names of the Sexual Organs	Taoist Correlations of the Sexual Organs
Sexual intercourse	Love play with clouds and rain, firing the canons, friendly relations
Homosexuality between men	Dragon-yang relationship, splitting the peach
Homosexuality between women	Polishing the mirror
Orgasm (male ejaculation)	Losing the essence, flowing out, surrendering, dying, coming and going
Orgasm (female)	Flood, tide peak, flood of yin
Penis	Jade stem, jade rod, jade shaft, jade tool, jade sword, yang peak, yang weapon, turtle head, the ambassador
Penis (erect)	Excitement, anger, explosive
Penis (flaccid)	Motionless, powerless, dead
Ureteritis	Gate of various diseases
Vagina (entrance)	Jade gate, jade door, cinnabar cave, one inch square
Vagina (middle part)	Deep valley, hidden place, arrow of yin
Vagina (upper part)	Heavenly palace, valley of loneliness
Cervix	Inner door
Clitoris	Jade terrace, precious pearl, seed-corn, yin bean
Frenulum (bundle of the clitoris)	Lute strings
Fold of the clitoris	Divine field
Cunnilingus (licking the female sexual organs for sexual arousal)	Drinking at the immense source
Fellatio (inserting the male organ into the mouth)	Blowing the flute
Mount of Venus (fatty cushion of the front pubic region with characteristic female pubic hair)	Sedge hill
Vestibule of the vagina	Little stream

Vulva (upper part, outer female genitals)	Jade vein
Uterus	Children's palace, North Pole, cinnabar chamber

This list of poetic expressions clearly shows that:

 The Taoist and Chinese philosophers, poets, and physicians pay much more attention to the female anatomy than to the male and that their attention was always focused on the mysterious and magical portal of the "one-inch square," which they lovingly called the "jade door."

 The goal of the Taoist bedroom arts is to extend "the visit of the ambassador to the heavenly palace" as long as possible by teaching the man the official proper behavior and equipping him with the correct references of a "master lover."

Most men are much too fixated on the size and form of their penis while paying too little attention to how to properly handle their jade stem. Below is a dialog between the "Yellow Emperor" and the "Plain Girl" describing how more importance must be placed on the skillful use of the yang weapon than its size.

THE LONGEST POSSIBLE PATH IS THE GOAL

Yellow Emperor: *"Do the various characteristics that a man's phallus can have influence the desire that a woman feels during the sexual act?"*

Plain Girl: *"Their phallic variations related to size and strength are purely external and have no significance. The true beauty and pleasure of communion are inner feelings. They can only be achieved by harmonizing the yin jade door and the yang jade stem on the highest level."*

Yellow Emperor: *"What about the difference in long and short, hard and soft phalli?"*

Plain Girl: *"A long tool that is not completely hard is not as suitable as a short one that is as hard as iron. A short,*

29

> *hard tool that is used roughly and without consideration of the woman's feelings is not nearly as suitable as one used with expertise and careful observation of the woman's reactions. As in all things, a man should also strive for the path of the golden mean when it comes to achieving harmony between the yin jade door and the yang jade stem."*

Yellow Emperor: *"I have heard that men of great antiquity lived over two-hundred years. And men of middle antiquity lived up to be one hundred and twenty years. But men of our time often die before they reach the age of thirty. So few men are relaxed and at peace with themselves these days and many of them are suffering from disease. What do you think is the reason for this?"*

Plain Girl: *"The reason that men often die young today is that they do not know the secret of the Tao of Love."*

Taoist adepts almost never give information about their actual age because they consider facts like this to be unimportant. Instead of counting birthdays, Taoists measure their life in breaths, heartbeats, and—in so far as they are men—ejaculations. They believe that human lives on the earth end when we have used up the number of heartbeats and breaths intended for us. This is why they attempt to slow down the tempo of life in order to lengthen the lifetime. People who try to squeeze as much activity as possible into every minute of their lives in the waking state will not even reach the normal human life expectancy of one-hundred years.

One of the most amazing cases of longevity is the Chinese herbalist and Taoist Li Jing-yuen, who maintained youthful strength, sexual potency, and complete health during his entire long and active life. Master Li Jing-yuen died in the year 1933, shortly after he married his 24th wife. In China, it is considered a historical fact that he was born in 1677. If this is true, then he was 256 years old at the time of his death. When he died, he still had his own teeth and hair. People who knew him said that he still looked like 50 even when he was already 200 years old.

Master Li Jing-yuen left behind concrete advice for those who intend to follow his example. He followed these three main rules:

1. Never hurry in life

Do everything at a leisurely pace. Take it easy and allow yourself the time that you need. He instructed his students to always be sure that the heart remains calm, to sit as still as a turtle, to walk as sprightly as a bird, and to sleep as soundly as a dog.

2. Avoid extreme emotions

Vehement emotional outbursts should be avoided, especially when you are older. Nothing robs the body of its energy as quickly, and nothing disturbs the functional harmony of the inner organs, as much as vehement emotional outbursts. The three detoxification stations—kidneys, liver, and lungs—become congested as a result.

3. Practice chi kung every day

Practice chi kung exercises on a regular basis. The length and intensity of such therapeutic programs are less important than the regularity in so far as a chi kung master selects the exercises. In particular, the Deer, Crane, and Turtle exercises are outstanding Taoist chi kung exercises.

In addition, Li Jing-yuen gave three more specific instructions related to nutrition:

• Don't eat too much on hot summer evenings because this causes a stagnation of the blood and energy.

• Eat large amounts of nourishing foods on cold winter days because this supplies the body with the essence and energy that it needs to keep itself warm in cold weather.

• Eat a vegetarian diet for the most part and also take life-prolonging herbs.

The herbs that Master Li Jing-yuen recommended almost exclusively were ginseng, a root for longevity, and a rather unknown plant called Hydrocotyle Aratica minor, a modest member of the marsh pennywort family that grows in the tropical marshes of Asia. It contains a strong alkaloid, which has an intensely vitalizing effect on the nervous system, the brain cells, and the endocrine system.

The theory of the "four seasons" can help us adapt our diets to the rhythm of spring, summer, autumn, and winter:

The energy moves upward in spring (wood, wind, mild): peach, pear, almond, spring onion, leek, chives, parsley, banana, plum, apple, carrot, apricot, gooseberry, raspberry, strawberry, blackberry, etc.

The energy moves outward in summer (fire, heat, cool): melon, peppermint, ginger, basil, zucchini, eggplant, coriander, lettuce, tomato, radish, garlic, grapefruit, Chinese cabbage, spinach, asparagus (until June 21st), coconut.

The energy moves downward in autumn (metal, dryness, moist): orange, bean, crystal sugar, potato, onion, lemon, grape, red beet, rice, peas.

The energy moves inward in winter (water, cold, hot): chestnut, peanut, pepperoni, chili, pepper, sesame oil, lamb, honey, lychee.

RULES FOR THE TAOIST SEXUAL ACT

"Birds of a feather like to flock together.
But in sexuality it is also true that opposites attract."

Since traditional Taoist medicine promotes human health and longevity in all areas, an entire series of rules and prohibitions has been established for sexual contact between man and woman within the scope of the ancient Chinese diagnosis and therapy procedure. These rules determine when, if possible, either no sexual contact or reduced sexual contact should occur under specific circumstances. These recommendations serve not only the physical and mental/emotional well-being of the respective couple but also the energy potential given to the child produced by their union on its path in life.

1. Chain-Smokers

Not only are the nerves of the central and autonomic nervous system considerably damaged in chain-smokers, but also the entire endocrine system with its "seven glands." These "seven glands" regulate our well-being, as well as the health and longevity of our organs and meridians. Children of smokers are often small and have overly sensitive autonomic nervous systems, which can lead to major nervous problems in the course of their lifetime.

2. Intoxication or Alcoholism

In case of intoxication, the affected individual is already so over-stimulated in terms of the nervous system that a further stimulation through the sexual act can become dangerous for the entire body (circulatory collapse, heart attack, stroke). Children of alcoholics or children conceived by people in an intoxicated state are often born with deformities or severe nerve damage. These nervous disturbances are usually evident after the third or fourth year of life. Liver damage and heart disorders also frequently occur as late symptoms.

3. Under the Influence of Drugs or Medication

Drugs and medication create not only a physical and mental imbalance, but also change the personality of an individual. When these substances affect either men or women, they suffer considerable damage through the energy deficiency that develops, together with the influence of the medication. If sexual activities lead to conception, the child may suffer from nervous disorders or deformations as a result.

4. Diseases in General

In case of a serious illness, there should be no sexual contact between a man and a woman for the same reasons as listed under No. 2. In addition, the kidney energy is weakened in this situation. In particular, flu infections and cardiovascular disorders are considered unfavorable preconditions for sexual contact.

In the traditional Taoist medicine, if a physician determined that a man suffered from cardiac insufficiency, he was prohibited from assuming any sexual position with his face pointing downward because this increases pressure on the heart, stomach, and lungs. The result would be a worsening of his heart problems. For the same reasons, he also should not engage in the sexual act while laying on his left side. These rules naturally also apply to women.

5. **Extreme Fatigue**

When men or women are extremely tired or exhausted, their energy is primarily focused on their genitals during the sexual act. This impairs the overall experience. However, if there is already an energy deficiency, the sexual act will reduce the overall physical and mental energy level. As a result, vital energies will be taken from the rest of the body when they are actually required for maintaining the organs and supporting cell renewal.

A sex drive that is too strong reduces the rate of cell renewal and produces a skin color that ranges from pale to sallow, dark circles around the eyes that appear almost black, and similar symptoms. If a child is conceived in this situation, throughout its entire lifetime it may suffer from a lack of drive, reckless behavior, and ventures that are not completed.

6. **Venereal Disease**

Refrain from every form of sexual intercourse in cases of venereal disease or liver disorders such as hepatitis since both are contagious through sexual contact. Even a condom offers no absolute protection in these situations. A body that has been weakened by venereal disease or liver infection requires the vital healing energy of the endocrine system's "seven glands" to be restored to health. The liver and gallbladder are very unstable during illness, so sexual intercourse not only transmits the disease-causing germs but also weakens the body's healing energy.

7. **After an Operation**

After an operation, a man or woman should wait 90 days before becoming sexually active again since the body needs this time for regenerating its powers of self-healing. As we know, the sexual act takes vital healing energies from the body that are very important for a patient's healing process.

8. **After an Acupuncture Treatment**

Refrain from sexual contact after an acupuncture treatment since the acupuncture is intended to restore the disturbed energy equilibrium of the afflicted organs in the body.

9. **During Pregnancy**

During pregnancy, sexual intercourse can agitate the baby or even injure the fetus in its state of repose in the uterus. Unfortunately, not all pregnant women know that coitus can have an earthquake-like effect on the body and even produce later nervous disorders. It may even lead to miscarriages.

Some babies are born with bruises and severe nervous disorders because of hard thrusts by the man's jade stem. It is therefore absolutely necessary, at least during the last three months of the pregnancy, to refrain from sexual intercourse. The parents should also practice abstinence during the first and second month following birth while the woman's body heals and regenerates after pregnancy.

10. During Menstruation

During menstruation, the uterus is like an "open wound" that has very sensitive reactions and requires time to heal. The transmission of disease-causing germs is especially possible during menstruation.

Sexual contact should also be avoided when a woman experiences unexplained bleeding, spotting in the middle of the monthly cycle or inter-cyclic bleeding caused by hormonal disorders, vaginal discharge, or uterine polyps.

11. Anger and Annoyance

Sexual activities in a state of anger and annoyance cause an increased heart frequency, as well as respiratory complaints. They also release toxins in the body, which especially endangers the equilibrium of the endocrine system in the area of the liver and gallbladder.

Hyperactive children are one example of the consequences that such a state of parental emotional imbalance during the conception of the child can have.

12. After Showering, Bathing, or the Visiting the Sauna

After showering, bathing, or visiting the sauna, sex is an additional stimulator. It leads to a state of over-stimulation and an imbalance of the entire nervous system. In addition, particularly after a sauna in an unfamiliar environment, bacteria have the greatest opportunity of growing because of the state of imbalance within the body. This could also lead to weakening the partner.

In this case, wait for at least 24 hours before engaging in the next sexual act. By then, the intruders (which prefer to enter the genital area through hot water or humidity) have no more chances of survival because of the body's own immune defense, in so far as an individual has an intact endocrine glandular system. Children conceived directly after a hot bath or visit to the sauna are also particularly susceptible in the area of the central and autonomic nervous system.

13. Directly After a Meal

Sexual intercourse directly after a meal, especially in the time between 11 a.m. and 1 p.m. (heart problems) and between 9 p.m. and 11 p.m. (circulatory problems), can create an intense imbalance of your nervous and digestive system. The energy that the body requires for the digestion of the food in the stomach is drawn away by the sexual act. This prevents proper digestion and leads to weight gain. Sexual intercourse after meals not only promotes stomach complaints but also diaphragmatic hernia. Because of the pressure on the stomach, which is pressed into the chest area as a result, obstructions of the heart and lungs may occur.

> Between 11 a.m. and 1 p.m., meaning around noon, the heart is particularly endangered—especially when lunch is eaten at this time. The strain caused by the full stomach can also have an effect when a child is conceived during this time period since it could later develop problems related to the heart and small intestine.

> Between 9 p.m. and 11 p.m., the stability of the circulatory system decreases. The entire circulatory system works at a reduced rate, as well as the "triple warmer," which guarantees the three-part division of the circulation, and the lymph-gland system, which is the detoxification channel of the body. Most cardiovascular patients are especially endangered by heart attacks and strokes during this time period and many deaths occur. The male genes are also particularly weak and therefore susceptible between these hours, so a child should not be conceived during this time period.

14. Shortly After Male Urination

Shortly after urination, it is easily possible that the man's jade stem could leave pathogens from the urine in the woman's jade gate. In addition, the jade stem is particularly irritated during urination by the emptying of the bladder, which causes the urethra to react sensitively to an erection. The partners should therefore wait for at least 30 minutes after male urination before engaging in the sexual act.

15. While Observing

Important vital energy is constantly lost through the eyes, the "windows of the soul." This applies particularly to the sexual act and primarily to the man: he should keep his eyes closed during the entire sexual act. His eyes should be focused inward to the lower Dantien (a hand's width below the navel). Especially during orgasm, the man risks an additional loss of energy—equal to "three days of heavy physical labor"—with open eyes.

16. While Traveling in the Car, Train, Airplane, or on a Ship

The ancient Taoist sages already know that sexuality on trips or generally in all types of means of locomotion covering longer stretches can become a problem for the endocrine system of the "seven glands." This could have particularly severe consequences when a child is conceived since it would give it a weak nervous system.

17. In Temples and Churches, at Cemeteries, on Holy Mountains, or Other Sacred Places

According to the beliefs of traditional Taoist medicine, the protectors or spirits of these holy places are jealous of any couple performing the act of physical love in their surroundings. Even if we consider this a superstition, many couples who didn't obey this rule have been surprised by major problems. Why should we tempt the anger of the gods?

18. In War or General Fighting

Sexual activities should not be engaged in during war or other fighting actions since the very chaotic and hostile environment infects the respective couple with this energy. Children conceived under such circumstances not only have over-stimulated nervous systems and are aggressive and fearful, but also have an antagonistic attitude without knowing the actual reason for it. For both the mother and child, rape leads to a lifetime of fearing the opposite sex and negative disorders

19. During Intense Storms, Thunder, and Lightening

During intense storms, thunder, or lightening, the prevailing energy in the atmosphere is also stormy and chaotic. No sexual acts between man and woman should take place under such circumstances since this unrestrained energy penetrates the bodies of the couple and creates a major imbalance in the endocrine system of the "seven glands." The dangers of a circulatory collapse and "not being able to let go" are also possible consequences.

20. On Special Days in the Cycle of the Year

According to the traditional Taoist rules, the sexual act should also not take place on special days like summer and winter equinoxes, as well as eclipses of the sun and moon.

21. Auspicious Times

In contrast to the multitude of "prohibited times" within the scope of the ancient Chinese diagnosis and therapy procedures, particularly auspicious times for the sexual life of a man and a woman are recommended. Examples of these are:

- Two weeks before a woman's menstruation
- One week after a woman's menstruation
- Early mornings between 5 a.m. and 7 a.m.
- Evenings between 7 p.m. and 9 p.m.

We have consciously listed only a selection of these types of prohibitions that can easily be followed by those of us who live in the West. All of these regulations and recommendations can be generally explained by the terms of "energy balance," which corresponds with the Taoist term of "harmony between yin and yang." Human health and longevity are dependent on the energetic equilibrium between our organs and meridian paths.

Sexuality practiced in a balanced manner has an effect on the organism that is very stimulating and increases its energy. However, inadequate attention is often paid to the idea that any type of sexual activity remains concentrated on the vital force of the sexual glands and the entire lower body while energy is taken from the remaining parts of the body: This creates an imbalance of the organs and meridians. In the case of various physical and mental conditions such as illness, tiredness, or disinterest, sexual union between a man and a woman can additionally weaken the bodies of both when they are already suffering from an energy lack. It can also make them more susceptible to disease-causing influences.

Our organism can only absorb healing energies from the cosmos when its endocrine system (sexual glands, adrenal glands, pancreas, thymus gland, thyroid gland, pituitary gland, and pineal gland) are healthy and efficient. Consequently, it is important to know that the sexual act between a man and woman can have very negative effects at certain times and under specific conditions, creating an imbalance in the body.

EROTIC PARTNER MASSAGE

"In the relationship between man and woman, we see the best and liveliest example for harmonious partnership relationships in sexuality and the reciprocal influence of things upon each other."

When a couple desires to make love, it is very beneficial for the process of the love play to observe a certain sequence of stimulating the partner's erogenous zones. The first important precondition is that the man harmonize his mood with the feelings of his partner; only then will his jade stem stand up, meaning that he will have an erection.

THE EROGENOUS BODY ZONES FOR THE MAN AND THE WOMAN

1. The primary erogenous body zones (yin energy) include:

 Lips, labia, tongue, nipples

The nipples radiate subtle energy and inhale the vital energy of chi in order to give it to the thymus gland, the "house of the heart." When the breast is gently stimulated, the Third Eye (in the middle of the forehead between the eyebrows) opens. This leads to the activation of the small energy cycle.

For a woman, the clitoris in particular is the key to the autonomic nervous system. For a man, the glans (tip of the penis) contains the heart reflex zone.

2. The secondary erogenous body zones (yang energy) include:

 The earlobes: They stimulate the sexual glands. First massage the right earlobe in order to let the energy flow, then the left.

 The nape of the neck, especially the seventh cervical vertebra (GV 14): firmly but gently massage 72 times in a clockwise direction, then gently 72 times in a counterclockwise direction (opens all of the yang meridians).

 The most certain stimulation point is located where the sacrum and the lumbar vertebrae meet: Massaging here benefits the sexual and adrenal glands and sparks a pleasant reaction in the genitals.

 The buttocks (the point where the legs turn into the hips): This is where the sexual glands are most strongly stimulated.

 The inner side of the thighs: Light stroking in an upward direction to the genitals opens the adrenals and contracts the testicles upward.

 The hollow of the knees: Lightly stroking the hollow of the knees stimulates the kidneys, the source of immune defense, and is experienced as extremely pleasurable.

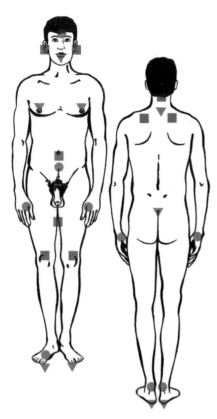

Right side of the body
Yin form = receptive force

Please note:
The right side of the man's body is most sensitive.

▼ 1. Primary erogenous body zones = yin energy

■ 2. Secondary erogenous body zones = yang energy

● 3. Tertiary erogenous body zones = neutral energy between yin and yang

In special sexual rites, the individual erogenous zones ▼ are massaged, kissed, caressed, rubbed with aromatic oils, and admired with the eyes in a clockwise direction—and the ■ zones in a counterclockwise direction—until the entire body has become one single erogenous zone in its energy field.

The partner's greatest erogenous stimulation can be achieved by:
• beginning with a massage of the secondary erogenous body zones
• moving to the primary erogenous body zones immediately afterward
• and massaging the tertiary erogenous body zones in conclusion.

3. The tertiary erogenous body zones = neutral energy

These are normally found in a resting state until they are stimulated through activation of the secondary and primary erogenous zones. These tertiary zones include:

    The sides of the small finger (heart and small intestine): Tender stroking sends thrills of delight to the spinal column.

    The palms of the hand (heart-circulation/sexuality): They are very receptive to circular, gentle stroking.

    The navel (collection point for the 14 main meridians in the radius from the pubic bone to the solar plexus): Gently stroke 72 times in a clockwise direction and 72 times in a counterclockwise direction. This massage opens and cleanses, heals and strengthens the influx of energy.

Left side of the body
Yang form = creative force

Please note:
The left side of the woman's body is the most sensitive.

▼ 1. Primary erogenous body zones = yin energy

■ 2. Secondary erogenous body zones = yang energy

● 3. Tertiary erogenous body zones = neutral energy between yin and yang

When all of these erogenous zones have been awakened, concentrate on the zones that create the greatest receptivity in your partner.

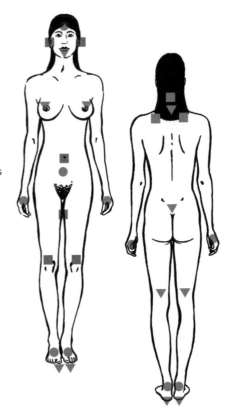

The anus (rectum) represents a direct connection to the "first house of the sexual glands" and gives unusual pleasure.

The nostrils: Stroking, nibbling, or licking the nostrils has an intensely erogenous effect.

The ear openings (kidneys, liver): Blowing strongly into the ears can end a state of trance.

Soles of the feet (kidney meridian): Massaging the soles of the feet activates sexuality and general performance.

Sucking on the large toe can cause some people to experience an orgasm.

Acupuncture points on the hands and feet

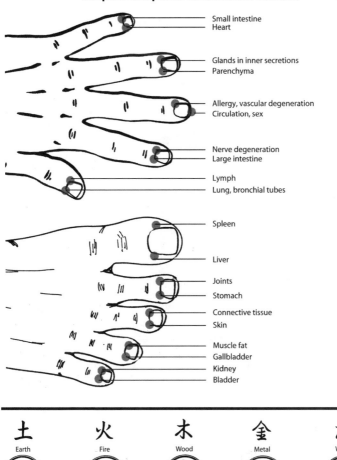

Small intestine
Heart

Glands in inner secretions
Parenchyma

Allergy, vascular degeneration
Circulation, sex

Nerve degeneration
Large intestine

Lymph
Lung, bronchial tubes

Spleen

Liver

Joints
Stomach

Connective tissue
Skin

Muscle fat
Gallbladder
Kidney
Bladder

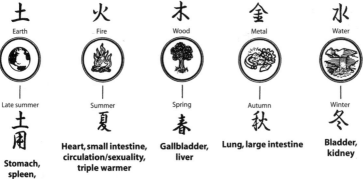

土	火	木	金	水
Earth	Fire	Wood	Metal	Water
Late summer	Summer	Spring	Autumn	Winter
土用	夏	春	秋	冬
Stomach, spleen, pancreas	Heart, small intestine, circulation/sexuality, triple warmer	Gallbladder, liver	Lung, large intestine	Bladder, kidney

The relationship between the five elements and the organs

45

THE EROTIC PARTNER MASSAGE OF THE JADE STEM

The erogenous zones listed here are stimulated through the penis and supply the body with subtle energy.

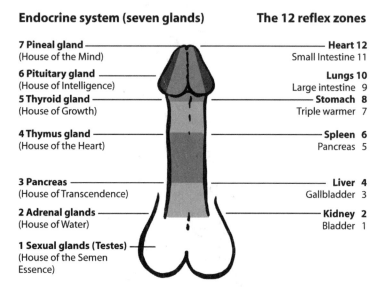

Endocrine system (seven glands)	The 12 reflex zones
7 Pineal gland (House of the Mind)	**Heart 12** / Small Intestine 11
6 Pituitary gland (House of Intelligence)	**Lungs 10** / Large intestine 9
5 Thyroid gland (House of Growth)	**Stomach 8** / Triple warmer 7
4 Thymus gland (House of the Heart)	**Spleen 6** / Pancreas 5
3 Pancreas (House of Transcendence)	**Liver 4** / Gallbladder 3
2 Adrenal glands (House of Water)	**Kidney 2** / Bladder 1
1 Sexual glands (Testes) (House of the Semen Essence)	

The erotic partner massage of the jade stem

This mushroom shape is considered the "most desirable form of the jade stem." It can only be achieved with the method of milking and squeezing the penis and desensitizing it, as well as practicing the male Deer Exercise (contractions of the sphincter muscle and pelvic floor). Any man can achieve this with regular practice. This method is also absolutely free of side effects and keeps the prostate gland healthy as well.

According to the Taoist sequence of erotic partner massage, the jade stem is tenderly kissed and blown on. Although this sequence should not become a rigid series of caresses, each step leads to an almost unbelievable level of sexual stimulation. Once a man has experienced this on his own body, he will hardly want to miss it in the future.

When all of these erogenous zones have been awakened, the woman should concentrate on those points to which the partner has shown the greatest receptivity.

THE EROTIC PARTNER MASSAGE OF THE JADE GATE

The erogenous zones listed here are stimulated through the vagina and supply the body with subtle energy.

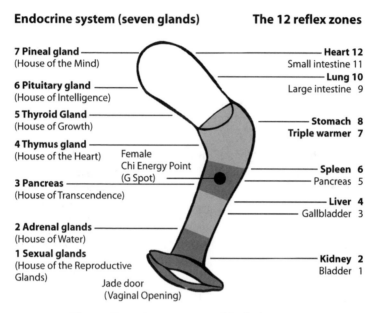

Endocrine system (seven glands)

7 **Pineal gland**
(House of the Mind)

6 **Pituitary gland**
(House of Intelligence)

5 **Thyroid Gland**
(House of Growth)

4 **Thymus gland**
(House of the Heart)

Female
Chi Energy Point
(G Spot)

3 **Pancreas**
(House of Transcendence)

2 **Adrenal glands**
(House of Water)

1 **Sexual glands**
(House of the Reproductive Glands)

Jade door
(Vaginal Opening)

The 12 reflex zones

Heart 12
Small intestine 11
Lung 10
Large intestine 9

Stomach 8
Triple warmer 7

Spleen 6
Pancreas 5

Liver 4
Gallbladder 3

Kidney 2
Bladder 1

The erotic partner massage of the jade gate

According to the Taoist sequence of erotic partner massage, the jade gate is tenderly kissed and blown on. The statements in the corresponding sentence under "Jade Stem" also apply here. However, the woman reacts more sensitively on the left side of her body (yang energy). This energy rises up from below.

 During the erotic massage, the right side of the man's body (yin energy) reacts most sensitively. This energy falls down from above.

THE MASSAGE OF THE JADE TERRACE (LABIA)

The massage of the labia

Stimulation Points of the Labia from Point 1 to 12

Massage 81 times clockwise	Massage 81 times counterclockwise
1 = Liver	Gallbladder = 12
2 = Lung	Triple warmer = 11
3 = Large intestine	Circulation = 10
4 = Stomach	Kidney = 9
5 = Spleen/pancreas	Bladder = 8
6 = Heart	Small intestine = 7
7 = Small intestine	Heart = 6
8 = Bladder	Spleen/pancreas = 5
9 = Kidney	Stomach = 4
10 = Circulation	Large intestine = 3
11 = Triple warmer	Lung = 2
12 = Gallbladder	Liver = 1

The Dragon Ring is considered a stimulation aid for activating the vaginal clock and extending the duration of the erection. It should not be used for more than 20 minutes. The Dragon Ring is pulled over the erect jade stem and pressed onto the vaginal clock through deep penetration into the vagina.

The following massage should be done by the woman 2 x 81 times in the early morning and late evening, both clockwise (cleansing and detoxification) and counterclockwise (supplying of energy):

1. Inhale through the mouth and tense the muscles of the vagina and the anus, as if you wanted to close both openings. Then try to pull the rectum into your body and upward by tensing the sphincter muscles even more intensely. If you do this exercise right, you will feel like you are sucking air into your intestines and vagina. Hold the muscles tensed as long as you can without feeling unwell in the process, but for at least 7 seconds, without breathing (7 seconds = one second for each of the 7 glands of the endocrine system).

2. Exhale and relax, then repeat the tensing of the anal sphincter and pelvic floor 49 times without becoming cramped in the process.

Note:
- While you do this, you can insert a finger into the vagina to test the strength of the contractions there.
- The labia are sensitive and should be massaged and stimulated during the Deer Exercise. The heel or ball of the foot can be used for this purpose. You can also use your fingers for the massage; but it is important to massage the labia and press them on the points shown in the illustration. Do this in a clockwise direction, starting with Point 1. Your partner can also massage your vagina; this will feel especially good since the energy that comes through your partner's hands flows into your body. (Conversely, the woman can also take her partner's testes in her hands and gently squeeze them 49 times during the male Deer Exercise).

THE DEEPLY HIDDEN VALLEY: FOREPLAY

Foreplay is important and necessary in order to satisfy a woman. The active partner can create feelings of delight in the passive partner, who receives the caresses in the deep hidden valley. This is the beginning of "friendly relations."

At the same time, foreplay is also a preventive measure against widespread problems like inadequate lubrication of the jade door and inadequate male erection before the sexual act, which the Taoists call "clouds and rain":

- The clouds symbolize the gathering storm of the feminine yin essence.

- The rain represents the ejaculation of the male semen.

It is also reported that the lubrication of the jade gate and the swelling of the jade stem are the first basic signs for the interplay of yin and yang before the two sexual organs meet each other directly.

Foreplay also prepares the body's energy system for the following intensive stimulation through the partner massage. The instructions below were written in a Taoist discourse on sexuality:

In order to "heat the pot of water on the stove" (= feminine energy), it is necessary to have a "big fire in the stove" (= masculine energy). Foreplay should first begin at the extremities of the body and not on the genitals (see the related illustrations on pages 43 and 44 for the partner massage).

Moreover, the acupuncture point San-yin-jiao—the "meeting place of the three yin"—has proved to be an extremely effective stimulation point for women. It is located directly behind the shinbone, about 3 inches above the inner side of the ankle bone and has a particularly stimulating effect on the female sexual organs. The area of the back, the spinal column, and the inner side of the arms and legs are sensitive and erogenous energy zones for both the man and the woman.

In the first half of the foreplay, the man dedicates himself to the area around the eyes. Later, he strokes along the stomach meridian down to the groin region: He embraces the woman with his left hand and, with the four fingers of his right hand, rubs and squeezes the vaginal opening and clitoris with small, circular motions. At the same time, he dedicates himself to the area around her eyes for a while, covers her with tender kisses, licks and gently breathes on her. He continues these caresses and then gradually turns to her cheeks, her mouth, ear, nape of the neck, and shoulder blades, etc. When he reaches her breasts, he gently kisses the nipples and licks the breast in circular motions. From the breast, he moves to the belly until he finally reaches her sexual organs. After the foreplay on one side of the body is completed, he follows the stomach meridian on the other side.

The second half of the foreplay begins at the foot. It follows the course of the kidney meridian and ends at the face. While the man kisses, licks, and breathes on his partner's individual acupuncture points, he simultaneously massages and strokes these places with one hand. With the other hand, he stimulates the woman's genitals.

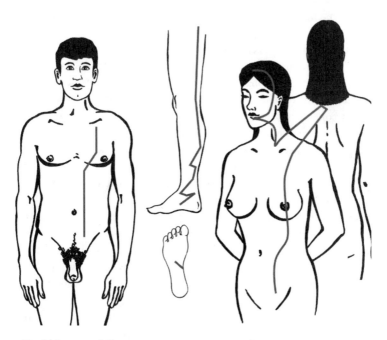

The kidney meridian   **The stomach meridian**

MASTURBATION

RENEWAL AND STRENGTHENING OF THE ERECTION

For hundreds of years, masturbation has primarily been damned by the Western religions and cultures. Even during the first portion of the 20th century, an open discussion about it was taboo.

Masturbation has been described as "playing with yourself," the "lonely vice," "self-gratification," or even "self-abuse." Children, especially teenagers in the puberty phase, had to listen to sermons on the moral and health hazards related to this practice. The imparted feelings of sin and guilt frequently became the trigger for later neurosis. In the meantime, the former "vice" has now even been elevated to a therapy, a variation of foreplay, and thereby an important component for sexually liberated lovers.

In the unhealthy form of male masturbation, a portion of the jade stem is stimulated to the point that semen escapes. The result is a loss of nutrients, energy, and other valuable qualities of the semen. When a boy, whose body is still in the growth phase, masturbates and discharges semen, he is in danger of losing his vitality. If he continues to do this on a regular basis, he risks weakening his body. This applies particularly up to 16 years of age since the male sexuality is only fully developed after this time. The parents should tell their child about the technique of the jen-mo point in order to avoid him experiencing a further loss of energy. The same principle applies to the son as to the adult male: Additional negative stimulation can be produced through false masturbation of the jade stem's reflex zones.

People who are familiar with foot reflex-zone massage know that the nerves and meridians are located in the soles of the feet: Various points on the feet are related to certain areas of the body. When these reflex zones are specifically massaged, energy is supplied to the various organs. The jade stem also has reflex zones that correlate with specific organs (cf. illustration on page 46).

For example, the heart zone, which correlates with the tip of the glans, is most easily stimulated. Although this type of massage is pleasant for the man since he quickly reaches orgasm with it, the tip of the glans is not only most quickly excited but also the most sensitive part of the jade stem. A one-sided masturbation technique can cause certain organs—above all, the heart—to be over-stimulated. Especially when semen is also discharged, the non-participating organs are also undersupplied with energy. This creates an inner imbalance.

From the Taoist perspective, the one-sided excitement of the jade stem is harmful since over-excitation of the glans over-stimulates the lungs and the heart. It also shortens the breath, leads to an acceleration of the heartbeat, and a stroke or heart attack could occur. The critical hours for this are between 11 a.m. and 1 p.m. (the heart period) and in the evening between 9 p.m. and 11 p.m. (period of the major circulatory weakness). The usual type of masturbation, in which most men concentrate in a one-sided manner on a certain place on the jade stem that they feel to be especially enjoyable, should therefore be avoided.

When a specific reflex zone is excessively stimulated, this excites and over-excites a certain part of the body, which in turn over-stimulates the reflex zone. This is why the man should include the entire jade stem when he masturbates. If, for example, he avoids the seminal discharge through the Deer Exercise or jen-mo technique, he can masturbate without causing any type of harm to himself.

Masturbation with a loss of semen has an effect on all of the physical, emotional, and mental/spiritual aspects of a man. As we already know, vital substances and energies are lost through ejaculation. The physical reserves are emptied without creating the possibility of filling them up again. According to the teachings of Taoist medicine, there is no compensation through the absorption of a partner's vital fluids or energies. Ecstasy occurs only for a very brief time, and the support of a deeper, mutual experience is lacking. Masturbation creates a special type of psychological influence, which remains limited to the area of sensation in the sexual region. When the "raw" semen energy leaks out through masturbation, there is no ascent or transformation since all Seven Glands of the man are emptied.

Masturbation without a loss of semen can help the man gain willful control over his sexual energies and injaculate. This term means returning the valuable semen energy to the body and becoming aware of the relationship between breathing/thinking and the ejaculation of semen. This contributes considerably to strengthening sexual self-assurance, which is a significant component of a healthy sexual life. Becoming familiar with the phases of excitement before ejaculation can teach a man to gain control over his sexuality. Then he will be appropriately prepared for higher sexual experiences in keeping with the Taoist tradition.

Frequent masturbation usually can be perceived in a very pale to yellowish skin color. The eyes are often cloudy because they are lacking in strength. The person tends to think slowly, has little ambition, is often depressed, and isolates himself. Sexual exhaustion weakens the pituitary gland, which increases memory performance. Circulation, metabolism, and entire physical well-being are also impaired because the endocrine system is exhausted through the loss of semen.

The Eastern teachings are unanimously against the practice of male masturbation with ejaculation. The writings advise that a man who lives apart from women should practice certain chi kung exercises in order to sublimate his sexual energy with the "sexual breath" and transform it in this manner. This also includes activating the jen-mo point and practicing the male Deer Exercise by holding the breath and tensing and relaxing the anal sphincter (PC muscle = pubococcygeal muscle), as well as visualizing how the sexual energy circulates and nourishes the body (minor and major energy cycle).

In addition, the Taoist teachings point out that masturbation with ejaculation is medically acceptable in the following cases:

- When a sublimation is not possible, so that the body does not store "vital essence that has become diseased."

- When the subtle channels of the body are blocked, which can be expressed in extreme lethargy, for example

- When an unhealthy diet or an excess of drugs such as coffee, alcohol, nicotine, hashish, heroin, or designer drugs have de-vitalized the semen that cannot be sublimated.

From the Taoist perspective, only shiny, healthy semen is suitable for increasing energy and for ritual purposes. Such semen is formed, among other things, through a healthy diet and the Taoist inner exercises like the Deer, Crane, and Turtle Exercise, in combination with the "Immortal Breath," the Solar-Plexus Exercise, and the "Return to Springtime," etc.

An intensive sexual pressure can develop in a man who does not engage in sex, to the point that physical relaxation is advisable. Without a doubt, it is unnatural for a man, no matter what his age, to suppress his sexuality. If he does not strive for relaxation through chi kung exercises, masturbation with ejaculation is an emergency solution. However, he should only do this twice a month since serious health strains could otherwise occur.

Since healthy semen contains vital nutrients, vitamins, trace elements, and amino acids in a purified form, sperm should never be carelessly wasted: It is the male life essence. Taoist philosophers write that: "There is no greater stupidity than putting your semen energy "at the roadside" and waiting for a wonderful woman to come and invite you to achieve power and influence with her. If you want to be successful in life, you must control your ejaculation, just like you must watch boiling water in a pot so that it does not evaporate." Because of this respect toward sperm, feng-shui masters also use it for ritual purposes.

In the above-mentioned exceptions for masturbation with semen discharge, Taoist medicine advises that the ejaculated sperm be positively charged through an appropriate spiritual attitude toward it. Ejaculate should be spiritually and ritually classified with the "five phases of change"—wood, fire, earth, metal, and water—in order to use it for magical purposes such as amulets that are meant to give the wearer power, influence, or health. The ancient Taoist customs are also reflected in the squirting of male semen on the fields, under trees, in sacred fire, and on amulets and talismans so that its indestructible life essence can penetrate these objects, giving them unlimited power and influence. The Taoists also believed that preparations mixed with male semen and applied to the body have an astonishing long-term effect and can have therapeutic curative results against skin problems.

When a man masturbates in the Taoist way—which means reversing the ejaculation by means of the jen-mo point or the male Deer Exercise—he can theoretically repeat this as often as he desires in one day without harming himself. This is even good for his body since the massage of the jade stem stimulates the endocrine system and supplies his body with more energy—but only if he avoids any type of semen discharge!

FEMALE MASTURBATION

All of the Eastern teachings see female masturbation as a manifestation that is completely different from male masturbation. The primary difference is that every woman has an unlimited supply of yin essence when compared with the limited yang energy of the man. After completion of each moon cycle, the female body is filled with yin energy. This brings its vital elements back into balance. The "Nine Spirits" of the woman are nourished by the release of erotic energy through the female body. The woman is therefore nourished and protected through her natural harmony by the powers of the moon and completely revitalized in the course of one month.

Women have much more effective methods of self-gratification than men. For example, even simple rocking movements stimulate the sexual center. A woman can even have an orgasm through gentle stimulation of the breasts or the jade gate or through deep, rhythmic breathing. Consequently, masturbation is a possibility for a woman to nourish her own eroticism and simultaneously learn to strengthen the hidden forces in her womb.

In China and Japan, a multitude of sexual aids were developed for female self-gratification. It was also a tradition for wives to have their husband's jade stem imitated in wood, jade, horn, or tortoise-shell and have his name artfully engraved on it. This object was given special care and stored in a box made especially for it. The wife used this substitute for her husband's jade stem, called the harikatu, for masturbation purposes or for sex with the concubines of the household, assuming the masculine role. When the husband and master of the house was gone for longer periods of time, this meant that a means of self-gratification embodying the actual form of his jade stem was available.

As we already know, various male complaints are attributed to "false masturbation," namely a one-sided over-stimulation of a certain reflex zone of the jade stem and therefore the corresponding organ. In women, the intensity of masturbation is focused on the clitoris, while the vaginal canal, the "jade door," is neglected. As shown in the illustration on page 47, the jade door has the same reflex zones as the jade stem. When we look at the vaginal reflex zones, we can see that the kidney and bladder zone is located in the front third of the entrance to the jade door. The liver and gallbladder zone is right behind it, the reflex zones for the stomach and spleen/pancreas are approximately in the middle, the lung and large-intestine zone are in the upper area, and the heart and small-intestine zone are entirely at the upper end before the entrance to the womb.

When the jade stem completely penetrates the jade gate, the zones of heart/small intestine, lung/large intestine, stomach/triple warmer, spleen/pancreas, liver/gallbladder, and bladder/kidney correlate with each other since the jade stem touches the corresponding reflex zones in the jade door. In this way, the two partners mutually stimulate each other and exchange their forces. This is the ideal situation and, in any case, the most pleasant stimulation of the reflex-zone massage since the two bodies unite like yin and yang.

When a woman masturbates in a one-sided manner, without evenly stimulating the jade door, the following complaints may develop: weakness of the bladder and kidneys, high blood pressure, edema in the subcutaneous fatty tissue, irregular menstruation, angina pectoris, overweight, and many other symptoms.

Many women feeling an urge to urinate when they masturbate by stimulating the clitoris. Since this is at the entrance of the jade door, where the reflex zones of the bladder and kidneys are located, stimulating just the clitoris unintentionally also stimulates the bladder and kidneys. Lesbian women, or even women who masturbate very frequently, often unconsciously retain fluids and consequently suffer from "creeping overweight" that cannot be balanced by any diet. Sexual frustration strains the bladder and kidneys, which are then no longer capable of eliminating excess bodily fluids. The result of this is edema in the subcutaneous fatty tissue, which in turn becomes overweight.

HARMONY BETWEEN THE JADE GATE AND JADE STEM

THE VAGINA—THE JADE GATE OF RECEPTIVITY

The jade gate can stretch and contract in its width; but it hardly changes in its length—at most about one inch. The diameter only changes in times of pregnancy and at birth in order to allow the child's head and body to pass through.

An aroused jade stem of about 6 inches has exactly the right length for a jade gate of average length. This measures about 5 inches from the entrance of the jade gate to the cervix. About 1 more inch can be added to this figure when it extends in length, and this distance again for the area around the jade gate. The maximal length of jade gate therefore corresponds quite precisely to the average size of an aroused jade stem. As a result, when a jade stem is too long, it causes only displeasure and pain in a woman, while a jade stem of an average length up to 6 inches unites with all of the sensitive reflex zones when penetrating the jade gate and evenly massages them.

The harmony between the jade gate and the jade stem plays a decisive role when it comes to achieving the "nine steps" of the woman's complete satisfaction. A jade stem or jade door only achieves a state of virtual flawlessness when it perfectly fits the respective counterpart. Such perfect harmony precludes the development of disharmonies in the sexual act from the very start.

Examples:

- If a man has an 8-inch long jade stem and the woman just a 5-inch long jade door, he will inevitably cause her pain. She will therefore hardly be able to experience her orgasmic potential with him.

- If the same man has sexual contact with a woman whose jade gate is just as long, he will be able to make her happier than a woman with a short jade gate.

- If the jade stem is shorter than the woman's jade gate, he cannot penetrate deeply enough to completely satisfy her. However, the same man can make a woman with a jade gate of corresponding length completely happy.

This will hopefully clear away the myth about the size of the jade stem since the only decisive factor is the harmony between the jade stem and the jade gate.

RISKS FOR THE JADE GATE

When a woman who has a long jade door engages in the sexual act with a man who has a short jade stem, both will probably feel unsatisfied afterward.

This also applies in the reverse situation. If a man with a long jade stem penetrates as deeply as possible into a short jade gate, the glans thrusts through the narrow cervix into the uterus. Immediately before and during his orgasm, this is extremely pleasurable for a man, but particularly painful for the woman. The opening of the jade gate is called the "first ring," while the cervix is called the "second ring." If the jade stem penetrates the second ring, it not only causes the woman considerable pain but also transports smegma, urine, bacteria, and other pathogens into the cervix and expands the neck of the uterus. This causes inflammations, herpes, and cytomorphosis (changes in the cells), which can ultimately also lead to cancer. Prostitutes with unusually short jade gates may be very popular with their customers, but this may lead to an early death because of cancer.

A woman should be just as careful about the spiral. It prevents the fertilized egg from implanting in the uterus by causing a constant vibration. This is achieved by the discharge of copper ions or "progesterone secretions" within the uterus. The fertilized egg is also prevented from implanting because of the change in the uterine fluid and mucous membrane that also results from the presence of the spiral. It is also possible for the spiral to slip or wander in the uterus and cause injures as a result.

If the jade stem penetrates too deeply into the uterus during the sexual act, this may cause a prolapsed uterus. This often can cause an imbalance in the energy flow of the sexual

organs and lead to lack of sexual desire, frustration, and
health complaints that can damage the entire glandular and
nervous system.

Solutions for Sexual Disharmonies

When a woman with a short jade gate has sexual intercourse
with a man who has a long jade stem, she should sit on top
of the man so that she can determine how deeply the jade
stem is allowed to penetrate her. She knows best what stimulates her and what causes her pain.

Moreover, the woman can wrap a cotton cloth around the
lower part of the jade stem's shaft so that its full length cannot penetrate the jade gate. This will prevent possible uterine diseases and pain. This method squeezes the shaft of the
jade stem, which enlarges the glans and intensifies the erection.

If the jade stem has already caused inflammatory processes
and injuries of the cervix, the man should use an antibiotic
ointment, which he applies to the tip of the glans before he
penetrates the jade gate and thrusts into the inflamed area;
this will also accelerate the healing of the inflammation. In
order to avoid serious health disorders of the female organs,
all women and men must be aware that the jade stem should
basically never penetrate the cervix through the second ring.

CARE OF THE JADE GATE

Not just many men, but apparently also many women, believe that the
jade gate needs no special care since it cleanses itself in a natural way.
This is not always the case because the jade gate is warm and dark,
making it an ideal breeding ground for bacteria and fungi. The vaginal
flora always contains germs, especially after sexual intercourse. Every
man unknowingly transmits a great variety of pathogens to his partner.
Even just a French kiss transmits thousands of pathogens, which can
multiply through the saliva and vaginal secretions when the jade stem
penetrates the jade gate. Only when a woman is completely healthy and

not confronted with depressions and stress situations can her immune system defend itself against all the germs that are carried into her body during the sexual act.

Thorough cleansing of the jade gate makes it possible for the beneficial vaginal flora to regenerate. Frequent showers, especially after the sexual act, can keep vaginal inflammations in check. A solution made of 1/3 cup of apple-cider vinegar and 2/3 cup of warm water has proved to be particularly effective here. The jade gate should receive just as much attention as the face in order to remain clean, odor-free, and, above all, healthy!

CONTROL OF THE ERECTION

The Angle of the Erection for Determining
the Biological Age

"The living well of sexuality, the source of life:
This is why we see the well of vital energy in sexuality and love,
which is shared by everything and absolutely necessary for life,
the balance of yin and yang."

As we know on the basis of scientific studies, the angle of the man's
erection changes with age. Consequently, by measuring the angle of the
erection, the biological age or health of a man can be studied. The relationship between age and angle of the erection can best be seen by looking at a hand (see illustration on page 45 above). This is how the strength
of the erection can be measured.

For a healthy man at the age of:

15-20 years, the jade stem stands at its highest power and forms about a 45-60° angle to the trunk. This angle of erection corresponds to the hand position of the thumb, which is associated with the lungs and bronchial tubes, as well as the lymphatic glandular system. The corresponding wood phase is the first phase of change in the sign of the Tiger.

20-30 years, the aroused jade stem displays its stronger power and forms about a 60-90° angle to the trunk. This angle of erection corresponds to the hand position of the index finger, which is associated with the large intestine and the nerves. The corresponding phase of fire is the second phase of change in the sign of the Dragon.

30-40 years, the aroused jade stem is in a weaker position and forms about a 90-108° horizontal angle to the body. This angle of erection corresponds to the hand position of the middle finger, which is associated with the circulation and sexuality, allergic reactions, and the blood vessels. The corresponding phase of earth is the third phase of change in the sign of the Bear.

40-50 years, the aroused jade stem is in a weak state of vitality and forms a downward angle of about 108-135° from the center of the body. This angle of erection corresponds to the hand position of the ring finger, which is associated with the system of the seven glands. The corresponding phase of metal is the fourth phase of change in the sign of the Eagle.

50-80 years, the aroused jade stem is in a weakened position and forms a downward angle of about 135-144° from the center of the body. This angle of erection corresponds to the hand position of the little finger, which is associated with the heart and the small intestine. The corresponding phase of water is the fifth phase of change in the sign of the Monkey.

The "five correlations" in the signs of the Tiger, the Dragon, the Bear, the Eagle, and the Monkey represent the willingness of these types of animals to conceive. The ancient Taoist sages applied these to human conditions. There is naturally also no rule without an exception in these experiential values.

The angle of erection in the mirror of the hand

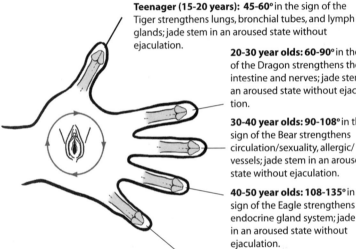

Teenager (15-20 years): 45-60° in the sign of the Tiger strengthens lungs, bronchial tubes, and lymph glands; jade stem in an aroused state without ejaculation.

20-30 year olds: 60-90° in the sign of the Dragon strengthens the large intestine and nerves; jade stem in an aroused state without ejaculation.

30-40 year olds: 90-108° in the sign of the Bear strengthens circulation/sexuality, allergic/vessels; jade stem in an aroused state without ejaculation.

40-50 year olds: 108-135° in the sign of the Eagle strengthens the endocrine gland system; jade stem in an aroused state without ejaculation.

50-80 year olds: 135-144° in the sign of the Monkey strengthens the heart and small intestine; jade stem in an aroused state without ejaculation.

At the time of ejaculation, all of the above-listed organs, the seven glands, and the erection are weakened. The result is a loss of protein, carbohydrates, vitamins, minerals, and amino acids.

Here is an explanation for the "inner effects" of the five fingers:

- Lungs, bronchial tubes, and lymph glands are associated with the thumb

- Large intestine and nerve degeneration are associated with the index finger

- Circulation/sexuality and allergy/vessel degeneration are associated with the middle finger

- The endocrine system and glands with inner secretions are associated with the ring finger

- Heart and small intestine are associated with the little finger

These guidelines can be used to determine a man's actual "biological age" and state of health. The angle of erection corresponding with the above categories shows the actual "biological age"—independent of how old a man's calendar age may be! For example, a 50-year-old man with an erectile strength of 60° corresponds with the erection state of a 20-year-old and will biologically be able to perform like a 20-year-old according to our scale. So the healthier a man's sexual glands are, the higher the erection angle of his jade stem will be.

Weak sexual glands can naturally also regain their strength with the help of chi kung exercises. Daily training is necessary in order to recharge the lost energy reserves of the sexual glands. More information on the meridian massage of the jade stem can be found on the next page.

The angle of erection and the five elements

Heaven chi

Transformation of sexual energy through tensing of PC muscle

Parasympathetic nervous system Energy-saving

Human sexual energy

Transport of chi energy

Ocean of blood

Ascent of sexual energy (kidney energy)

Earth chi

Teenager (15-20 years): 45-60°
Wood energy: house of the mind (pineal gland), house of intelligence (pituitary gland)
20-30 year olds: 60-90°
Fire energy: house of the heart (thymus gland)

30-40 year olds: 90-108°
Earth energy: house of transcendence (pancreas, crossing the physical and mental boundaries)

40-50 year olds: 108-135°
Metal energy: house of growth (thyroid gland)

50-80 year olds: 135-144°
Water energy: house of water (kidneys and adrenals), house of the semen essence (sexual glands)

The Tao of sexual wisdom and love differentiates between five energy types that are required in producing a strong erection and stable angle of erection for the jade stem. These are:

1. Blood energy (stability of heart and circulation)

2. Muscle energy (complaints of the musculature in the body or excessive muscle-power training like bodybuilding can prevent an erection)

3. Nerve energy (nervousness, emotional problems, or some type of distraction can also interrupt an erection)

4. Bone energy (cancer of the bones, weak bones, weak kidneys, arthritis, and arthrosis can stop an erection)

5. Stretching energy (insufficient ability of tendons, ligaments, and muscles to stretch and move blocks the erection).

All of the five energy forces listed here are transferred from the man to the woman during the sexual act. When a man is unable to have an erection, one of these five energies is lacking.

THE MALE DEER EXERCISE

*"The nature of sexuality favors a dynamic equilibrium
between yin and yang, between heaven and earth,
day and night, man and woman, mother and child,
father and child."*

The female and male Deer Exercise, which is also called the "union of sun, clouds, and rain," is responsible for awakening the snake force (highest sexual energy). When this highest sexual energy is directed upward and circulates through the entire body, the psychosomatically caused diseases are replaced by newly acquired spiritual luster and a higher state of well-being.

This is the secret of the male and female Deer Exercise:

 Contract the anal muscle (PC muscle), close the outer and inner vessel, open it and expand it, repeatedly (9 x 9 = 81 repetitions) until the gates of bliss are opened.

INTRODUCTION TO THE MALE DEER EXERCISE

Contraction of the PC Muscle and Pelvis: Strengthening the Chi Energy

Heaven creates things—inhaling is health and strength

The earth stabilizes things—holding the breath restores the equilibrium of energy

Water generates things—exhaling is breathing away illness and weakness (cleansing of the lymphatic glandular system)

A "cosmic energy cycle" is created by tensing the PC muscle. This cycle forms a network of 72,000 circuits and conducts this subtle electromagnetic current to all parts of the physical body, keeping the cells healthy and vital. Tensing the PC muscle corresponds with the meridian system of the ancient Chinese wisdom from the healing and martial arts. This exercise is connected with the nervous, lymphatic glandular, and endocrine system.

The source of youth lies within us! The question of aging is a mental attitude long before it becomes a physical problem. Anyone who wants to live longer and remain younger must use the advantages of nature. Although the number of years can add up within the body, it does not in the brain. In order to reactivate the vitality of the glands and attain more health, beauty, and energy, we must use our minds and practice the Taoist Deer Exercise of the ancient Chinese diagnosis and therapy procedure. Many of the rejuvenation methods from ancient China were consciously kept secret by the masters of the healing and martial arts in our hemisphere until about 1986. One of these secrets is how we can maintain youthful freshness in order to bring new luster to the face and new strength, vitality, and endurance to the body.

In order to counter the aging process through sexuality, we must be "reborn." Within this context, this means the constant increase of vital energy through chi kung exercises in connection with the sexual organs, which are the individual "energy generators" for them. These organs not only contribute to the conception of a child or personal satisfaction of sexual needs, but also to the psycho-physical rebirth of the individual.

The Taoists also call the sexual glands the "stove." "Fire" or sexual energy is produced in the stove. Without the stove, the fire cannot burn properly and cannot be used as a result. Nothing can "cook"—and nothing is kept alive: Many vital bodily functions are dependent upon sexual energy. The terms stove and fire are ancient alchemical terms from the age when such knowledge was kept secret. They describe a portion of the rebirthing process that is still kept from the Chinese population today since rebirth is the equivalent of rejuvenation, health, and longevity.

Water is also an ancient alchemical term for all secretions from the kidneys, bladder, adrenals, lymphatic system, and sexual organs (hormones or sexual fluids). In addition, it also represents all of the organs and glands that eliminate fluids. In the Taoist teachings, it is said that we are born of water and spirit. It is interesting to note that this saying is confirmed time and again in many religions.

For the Taoists, the sexual organs and the brain are "sister" organs. They are both related to the element of water and also have a reciprocal relationship with each other: They either mutually strengthen or weaken each other in a never-ending cycle.

69

THE HISTORY OF THE MALE DEER EXERCISE

Many thousands of years ago, the Taoist sages selected three animals that were legendary for their longevity. One of them was the deer, which stands out because of its enormous quantity of sexual and reproductive power. The Taoist masters very carefully studied the behavior of the deer and noticed how it exercised its anus with the constant wagging of its tail. This principle produces increased sexual stimulation, which they then also applied to human beings. The so-called Taoist Deer Exercise, which can have an invaluable health value for both sexes, was created

Our calendar age, meaning the number of years that we have lived up to now, is an indication of our age. However, the true age is biological age. This is independent of our calendar age since it reflects the body's state of health, as well as possible morphological changes of the skeleton and bone structure.

One of the most important indications of our biological age is the state of the anus, which means the firmness of the anal sphincter. This muscle, which is also connected to the PC muscle (pubococcygeal muscle = rejuvenation or love muscle), belongs to the same energy unit as the sexual glands. If the sexual glands are strong, the PC muscle will also be strong; in the reverse case, an untrained anal sphincter weakens the sexual glands.

With a small child, it is difficult to even insert something as thin as a fever thermometer into the anus. A child's anus remains tight until the need to empty the bowels relaxes it. Otherwise, it remains tightly closed—which is a sign of stable health. On the other hand, the anal sphincter is somewhat weaker in an adult since the contractions of the anus and perineum are no longer trained due to the lack of exercise. The PC muscle slackens as a result. The anus can become so loose and slack that many people even have difficulty in holding back feces when they experience flatulence, cough intensely, or have to sneeze. Further consequences of this are considerable problems related to sexual stimulation, to the point of prolonged potency disorders in men and frigidity in women.

The higher a person's biological age, the slacker the anal muscle, the ability to move, and the concentrated attention. This is why the ancient Taoist sages created the Deer Exercises as a possibility for people to considerably decrease their biological age: We can rejuvenate ourselves by once again persistently activating the PC muscle.

THE EFFECT OF THE MALE DEER EXERCISE ON THE ORGANISM

The Deer Exercise develops the tissue of the sexual organs, expels harmful gases from the body, and contributes to the avoidance of constipation. In addition, it trains the urogenital diaphragm and also massages the prostate gland in men. The formation of hemorrhoids is prevented since the exercise expels the spent blood from both anal sphincters and the muscles connected with them, dissolving the stagnation of energy and blood in these important areas. Furthermore, this exercise helps men gain control over their urogenital canal, which can be very useful for ejaculation control. It also develops deliberate control of the jade gate's love muscle for women. Moreover, this exercise prevents anal prolapse and prolapse of the uterus (hysteropexy). For pregnant women, this is a good opportunity to prepare the muscles and tendons for birth.

Another result of the Deer Exercise is that the vital energy is drawn through six of the seven glands up into the epiphysis (pineal gland). Since this is a hormonal path leading from the prostate gland through the kidneys to the other glands, it also intensifies spirituality. At the same time, blood circulation in the stomach area is increased. In turn, the abrupt congestion of blood transports nutrients and the energy of the semen into the rest of the body. When energy flows into the epiphysis by means of the Deer Exercise, we can feel a type of shiver or tickle spreading upward from the sacrum through the spinal column until it reaches the head—it feels like a little orgasm. With increasing exercise experience, the sensitivity also increases. This can noticeably change the emotional/mental attitude we have toward our body.

A further positive benefit of the Deer Exercise is related to the endocrine system, which dissolves blocked areas on its own. So if one of the seven glands is not functioning properly, the energy current ends there. This indicates a weakness of the endocrine circulation, which ascends from below from the sexual glands to the adrenals, pancreas, thymus gland, thyroid gland, pituitary gland, and pineal gland. The energy current will only ascend to the point of the blocked gland and then remain stuck there until it is able to function again. Such blocks are dissolved by means of the Deer Exercise so that the blocked gland can once again be supplied with oxygen and nutrients. As a result, all of the "seven glands" can function normally once again. Each of us can feel this new current of energy within ourselves.

Probably the most significant and effective type of stimulation that the Deer Exercise provides for the man is the development of his sexual potency and the ability to extend the sexual act as long as he wants, delaying orgasm as long as possible. During normal sexual union—which we can compare to the image of a kettle whose water begins to boil as it hangs just above the fire—the prostate gland swells to its maximum size until just before the seminal discharge. During ejaculation, it squeezes out its contents in a series of contractions like an explosion.

This ends the act, meaning that there is no longer anything there to be emptied, which could cause contractions or maintain the erection. The man is exhausted and cannot continue the sexual act: He has died the so-called "little death."

The act of ejaculation usually lets the man fall into an abyss of exhaustion, emptiness, depression, guilt feelings, anger, or hunger. He becomes nervous and weak, losing a portion of his youth. This is also the reason why women tend to live an average of ten years longer than men.

However, when the man uses the Deer Exercise and learns to release small amounts from the prostate gland—but in the opposite direction, inward and upward into the other glands and the blood vessels—he can not only extend the sexual act but also his biological age. Without the use of the Deer Exercise, it is harmful to interrupt the man's orgasm or prolong the sexual act with the usual Western methods. In these types of measures, the prostate gland remains extended for too long until the semen is carried away by the blood. This occurs because the contractions that expel the semen and relieve the prostate gland do not take place.

In a certain sense, the prostate gland can be compared to a rubber band. It must return to its original flexibility since it will otherwise become over-extended and lose its elasticity. An overly stretched, inflexible prostate gland no longer functions as it should. It can no longer contract and relax. Ultimately, it becomes weak, unable to function, and diseased; the ability to have an erection is lost and the man becomes impotent. Practicing the Deer Exercise not only extends the orgasm and the sexual act but the prostate gland is also protected and its musculature strengthened so that it can regenerate itself and the man can regain his potency, even in the case of illness.

The act of contracting the sphincter muscles exerts a light pressure—like a gentle massage—on the prostate gland since the anus acts like a little engine that drives the prostate gland. When stimulated in this manner, the prostate gland begins to excrete hormones, endorphins, and other stimulators that trigger an emotional high. When the prostate gland begins to twitch, the man even feels a small orgasm. The alternating contracting and releasing of the anal and pelvic musculature during the Deer Exercise produces this natural high, which is reminiscent of a top athletic performance—and does so without any type of doping or side effects! Using this natural method, top-ranking athletes in particular could achieve a much better and prolonged performance, be kind to their bodies, and relax their nervous systems.

THE EFFECT OF THE MALE DEER EXERCISE ON PREMATURE EJACULATION

Western orthodox medicine assumes that premature ejaculation and nocturnal emissions have psychological causes. Nocturnal emissions during sleep are therefore considered completely normal under the medical perspective. However, many extensive scientific studies in the East, as well as the West, confirm the Taoist viewpoint that premature ejaculation or nocturnal emissions indicate a weakness of the prostate gland. A healthy prostate gland can easily tolerate the tension that mounts for about 20 to 30 minutes during the sexual act. However, if the prostate gland is weakened, it cannot deal with the pent-up pressure. It slackens and excretes its contents without any warning, which means the loss of the jade stem's erection. By means of the Deer Exercise, it has been demonstrably possible to provide effective therapy for general potency disorders, especially nocturnal emissions.

Young, inexperienced men—as well as those who engage in an extreme amount of sports, are subject to severe military training, or mentally overworked—are most susceptible to premature ejaculations. Men with weak nervous systems or quickly swelling prostate glands are also endangered. One general common factor in all of these situations is a special sensitivity of the nerves and prostate gland so that even the slightest stimulation causes the prostate gland to swell and contract.

The Deer Exercise desensitizes the prostate gland, which becomes stronger and more powerful as a result. This extends the duration of the erection and feelings of desire. This exercise prevents all of the diseases of the prostate gland since every tensing of the anal and pelvic muscles massages the prostate gland. In addition, the Deer Exercise is probably the most economical healing remedy in the world: It doesn't cost anything accept daily practice, which no one sees. In the process, it rejuvenates the endocrine system, strengthens the immune defense, cleanses the lymphatic glandular system, and relieves the nervous system.

In both the man and the woman, the contractions of the PC muscle and pelvis activate the "eight extraordinary meridians," which are responsible for health and longevity.

Father energy— the yang energy of exhaling

KIEN

4 Southeast **Wind Gb 41** Gallbladder	9 South **Fire Lu 7** Heart	2 Southwest **Earth Ki 6** Spleen/Pancreas
☰☷ DAI MAI	☰☷ REN MAI	☷ YIN CHIAO MAI
3 East **Thunder TW 6** Liver	**5** Adrenal glands	7 West **Lake SI 3** Large intestine
☳ YANG WEI MAI		☰☷ DU MAI
8 Northeast **Montain CV 6** Stomach	1 North **Water Bl 62** Kidney	6 Northwest **Heaven Sp 6** Lung
☷ YIN WEI MAI	☵ YANG CHIAO MAI	☵ CHONG MAI

Mother energy— the yin energy of inhaling

KUN

74

INSTRUCTIONS FOR THE MALE DEER EXERCISE

Renewal and Stabilization of the Erection

"Even today, those skilled in the art of healing in the East place special value on preventative measures and maintaining the sexual equilibrium between the body and the mind."

SIZE AND FORM OF THE "IDEAL JADE STEM"

The most advantageous form of the penis in the aroused state is considered to be the so-called mushroom form (see illustration on page 46). This gives the woman the greatest satisfaction, especially when the glans is large and the shaft narrow. A large glans makes the jade stem particularly desirable because it thoroughly and effectively stimulates and massages the inner walls of the jade gate and the G spot. This makes the sexual act very pleasurable for the woman, and she can easily attain her full orgiastic potential as a result.

When done on a regular basis, it is possible to achieve the mushroom form as the "most desirable form of the jade stem" through the methods of penis milking, penis squeezing, and desensitization of the penis, as well as the anal-sphincter and pelvic contractions of the male Deer Exercise.

Many men who are afraid that they cannot satisfy a woman because of the size of their jade stem are ashamed when they compare it in a flaccid state with those of other men. However, their concerns are completely unfounded since many of the men who have a large jade stem in a flaccid state experience very little change in size when it is aroused. But a jade stem that is small when flaccid may expand considerably when the man is aroused. The size of the jade stem is only important for two reasons:

- Because of the psychological effect on the man who thinks that his penis is too small.

- Because of the harmony with the size of his partner's jade gate since it is very important for the jade stem and the jade gate to match.

The jade stem in the positive cycle of the five elements

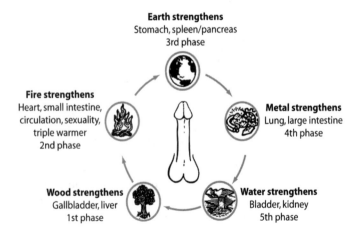

Earth strengthens
Stomach, spleen/pancreas
3rd phase

Metal strengthens
Lung, large intestine
4th phase

Water strengthens
Bladder, kidney
5th phase

Wood strengthens
Gallbladder, liver
1st phase

Fire strengthens
Heart, small intestine,
circulation, sexuality,
triple warmer
2nd phase

THE FIVE ABILITIES OF THE ERECTION

- 1st phase: Development of the thought = associated with Wood

- 2nd phase: Consideration of the thought = associated with Fire

- 3rd phase: Thought process = associated with Earth

- 4th phase: Feelings like love = associated with Metal

- 5th phase: Jealous, envy, hate, malevolence = associated with Water

Our mental abilities rest in the organs of our bodies. When any organ is disturbed in its function, the corresponding partner organ will also be afflicted as a result. This means that the related mental abilities will also suffer a negative influence. Ultimately, this will also have an effect on potency and erection. If, for example, an individual is confronted with worries and distress, this will impair the functional circulation of the lungs and large intestine. Worrying promotes diseases and functional disorders of the respiratory and digestive tracts. Diseases of the lungs are expressed through the nose and sense of smell, as illustrated by the expression that something "stinks." The taste in the mouth is acrid. People with lung disorders are often sad and careworn. Constipation is an additional consequence of interrupted energy circulation between the lungs, the large intestine, and the sexual stimulus.

THE "FIVE PHASES OF CHANGE" FOR THE ERECTION

According to the teachings of traditional Taoist medicine for human health and longevity, the jade stem symbolizes the creative or divine force; as the yang symbol, it embodies the sun as the vital force. It has "five phases of change":

1. **Friendliness:** The jade stem serves as a tool and giver of delight that not only satisfies the woman but also proves its qualities in the reproduction of humanity. It continuously gives its energy when it is needed and exhausts itself.

2. **Uprightness:** The jade stem fulfills its duty since its task is to not be fixated upon itself. On the inside, it is empty and possesses nothing

of its own: It reacts to feminine charms like a volcano and dies a "little death" after each loss of energy (orgasm). This energy loss is then passed on to the man's personality.

3. **Politeness:** It is polite and soft or hard at the proper time. At the right moment, it appears or retreats. The jade stem is neither square nor sharp. It causes no injury and displays no lack of discipline. The jade stem is also particularly discreet.

4. **Honesty:** The jade stem continues its activities until it has fulfilled its task. If it cannot fulfill its task, it admits its weakness in due time and gives up. It is completely honest and loves being together with its jade gate.

5. **Wisdom:** Nature has taught the jade stem how to satisfy a woman. As a result, it attempts everything in its power to achieve this, stimulating the "reflex zone area" and activating the endocrine system anew—without a loss of semen:

1. Pineal gland	(House of the Mind)	– Meridian-energy circulation
2. Pituitary gland	(House of Intelligence)	– Circulation, sexuality, triple warmer
3. Thyroid gland	(House of Growth)	– Heart/small intestine
4. Thymus gland	(House of the Heart)	– Lung, large intestine
5. Pancreas	(House of Transcendence)	– Stomach, spleen/pancreas
6. Adrenal glands	(House of Water)	– Liver, gallbladder
7. Sexual glands	(House of the Semen Essence)	– Kidney, bladder

NOTE: The tip of the jade stem (glans) is directly connected with the heart/circulation and the nervous system. When it is over-stimulated by something like oral sex, this can trigger circulatory collapse, heart attack, or stroke.

THE "THUMB ANALYSIS"

There are several bodily characteristics that provide information about the length and form of the jade stem. For example, it has a shape similar to that of the thumb.

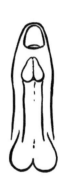

Mushroom-shaped thumb: If the thumb has a mushroom shape, the jade stem has a large, outwardly rounded glans and a small shaft. The large glans makes this form of the jade stem especially desirable since it thoroughly and effectively stimulates and massages the inner walls of the jade gate and the G spot.

Pencil-shaped thumb: The triangular or pencil shape, in which the glans is small and pointed and the shaft is wide, is the least desirable form of the jade stem. With this type of jade stem, it is considerably more difficult for a man to satisfy a woman. However, this shape of the jade stem can be changed through Taoist meridian massage, milking and squeezing, desensitizing, massage of the pubic bone, and ultimately, the contractions of the male Deer Exercise.

RENEWAL AND STRENGTHENING OF THE ERECTION THROUGH MILKING AND SQUEEZING THE JADE STEM

1ST PART: MILKING THE JADE STEM

Exercise Instructions: "Milking the Jade Stem"—renewal of the erection Whatever is exhausted will be renewed. Push the shaft of the jade stem with the left hand 72 times from the base at the testes and upward to the start of the glans as if milking it. The milking process should be done from bottom to top. This brings the blood into the glans, enlarges it, and strengthens the erection. The mushroom form can be attained in this way. In conclusion, repeat the milking process 72 times with the right hand.

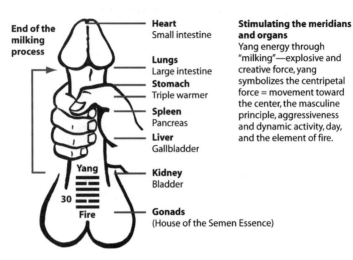

End of the milking process

Heart
Small intestine

Lungs
Large intestine

Stomach
Triple warmer

Spleen
Pancreas

Liver
Gallbladder

Yang

30
Fire

Kidney
Bladder

Gonads
(House of the Semen Essence)

Stimulating the meridians and organs
Yang energy through "milking"—explosive and creative force, yang symbolizes the centripetal force = movement toward the center, the masculine principle, aggressiveness and dynamic activity, day, and the element of fire.

2nd PART: SQUEEZING THE JADE STEM

Exercise Instructions: "Squeezing the jade stem"—intensification of the erection

Whatever is weakened will be made firm. Squeeze the shaft of the jade stem with the left hand 72 times directly below the glans until it becomes as hard as a rock. This type of squeezing will lead to increasingly stronger erections of the jade stem. In conclusion, repeat the squeezing process with the right hand 72 times.

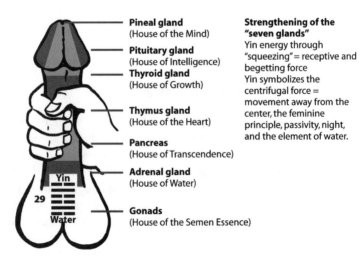

Pineal gland
(House of the Mind)

Pituitary gland
(House of Intelligence)

Thyroid gland
(House of Growth)

Thymus gland
(House of the Heart)

Pancreas
(House of Transcendence)

Adrenal gland
(House of Water)

Yin

29
Water

Gonads
(House of the Semen Essence)

Strengthening of the "seven glands"
Yin energy through "squeezing" = receptive and begetting force
Yin symbolizes the centrifugal force = movement away from the center, the feminine principle, passivity, night, and the element of water.

3rd PART:
DESENSITIZATION AND STABILIZATION OF THE MUSHROOM FORM

After the two previous massage forms of milking and squeezing have been completed, sit on a chair with spread thighs and feet firmly rooted on the ground.

Exercise Instructions:

1. Hold the jade stem firmly at the root and move it back and forth 72 times so that the glans alternates between touching the two thighs. This can be done energetically, but not to the point of pain.

   Start at 72 times with the left hand and 72 times with the right hand, moving the jade stem from the side of one thigh to the other thigh.

2. The question is certain to arise as to why the jade stem should be desensitized or made less sensitive when, to the contrary, every man is interested in becoming more sexually sensitive. Desensitization in no way reduces sexual pleasure but primarily contributes to delaying the discharge of semen as long as possible so that the orgasm is experienced more intensely than ever before.

3. When the nerve endings of the glans are less sensitive, the man can remain sexually active for a much longer period of time, which gives both partners more intense sensations and greater satisfaction.

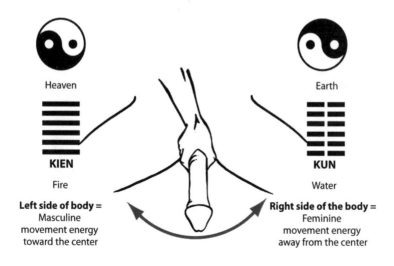

Heaven

KIEN

Fire

Left side of body =
Masculine
movement energy
toward the center

Earth

KUN

Water

Right side of the body =
Feminine
movement energy
away from the center

This form of desensitization exercise strengthens and enlarges the glans, as well as improving the form and firmness of the jade stem. The glans becomes larger, wider, and therefore attains the desired mushroom form. This contributes to making the jade stem less sensitive so that the man can remain sexually active for a longer period of time, which gives both partners greater satisfaction and lets the woman achieve a climax much more easily. The erection lasts longer, preventing a premature softening of the jade stem.

4th PART:
ALTERNATELY SQUEEZING AND
LETTING GO OF THE TESTES

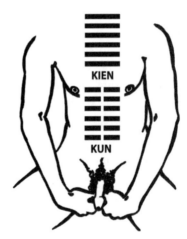

KIEN

KUN

**Activation
of the left-brain
hemisphere**

**Activation
of the right-brain
hemisphere**

Exercise Instructions:
Hold the scrotum with both hands. Gently squeeze it and then let it go again. This massage can also be done through loose underwear, such as boxers, if preferred. Repeat the alternating squeezing and letting go of the testes 49 times.

This exercise increases the secretion of the male hormone, as well as maintaining and supporting the healthy functions of the male sexual organs. In addition, it is good for the brain.

5th PART:
MASSAGE OF THE PUBIC BONE
FOR STABILIZING THE ERECTION

Massaging the pubic bone in a clockwise and counterclockwise direction activates the "lower Dantien," the sea of yin energy (CV-5 = main alarm point of the triple warmer, union of all yin meridians). The CV-6 acupuncture point, where the forces of youth are located and which is also called the "center of energy," is situated above it. Both points increase sexual desire in man and woman, leading to a renewal of the endocrine system in relation to the "medulla oblongata" GV-16 (governor vessel).

Exercise Instructions:

1. Stand with legs shoulder-distance apart, knees slightly bent, or sit on the edge of a chair so that the testes hang down freely.

2. Rub both palms together quickly and intensely, along the middle fingers, until they feel hot (circulation/sexuality).

3. Hold the testes in the right hand so that the palm of the hand completely covers them. Caution: Do not squeeze too tightly—just use gentle pressure! Feel the warming energy in your hand.

4. Place the left palm above the pubic region and make circular movements with a firm amount of pressure. First move in a counterclockwise direction for 81 times so that the pubic region gradually

Giving energy and healing

Pubic-bone massage in counterclockwise direction
The creative cycle of the five elements maintains the erection

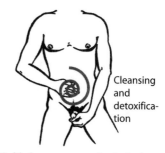

Cleansing and detoxification

Pubic-bone massage in clockwise direction
The positive cycle of the five elements activates the development of the erection

gets warm. Then vigorously shake out your hands in order to get rid of the used residual energy that can be seen in the moist palms.

5. Immediately rub your hands together quickly and intensely until they become hot. The left hand now encloses the testes and the right hand is on the region around the pubic bone. Now do a circular massage 81 times in the clockwise direction. In conclusion, vigorously shake out both hands for 15 seconds.

The greatest amount of sexual chi energy is located in the pubic-bone center and is activated from 11 p.m. to 1 a.m. It is therefore best to do this exercise during that time.

The male urinary and sexual organs

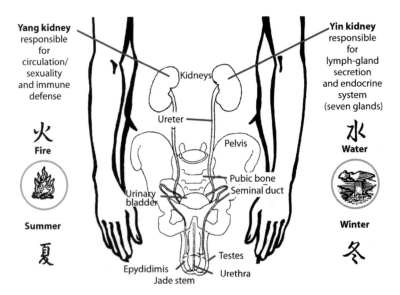

When massaging the pubic bone, concentrate on the goal of bodily movements and the increasing development of warmth since this is the only way that sexual energies unite with the body and mind. Directly beneath the area where the right and left pubic bones meet, there is an important point for sexual stimulation. There are additional stimulation points to the left and right of the pubic area. When the pubic-bone massage is used here, first in a counterclockwise and then in a clockwise direction, this activates the spleen, stomach, and kidney meridian, as well as the conception vessel. The acupuncture points Sp-12, St-29, Ki-12, and CV-12 are located about one inch horizontally from the centerline.

The circulation/sexuality meridian is stimulated through the two middle fingers, which quickly triggers sexual arousal. The bodily energy is gathered and then transmitted into the hands through the palms of the hands and up to the tips of the middle fingers. Among the effects of the pubic bone massage is an increased production of semen through the sexual hormone testosterone, rejuvenation, and a longer period of arousal, as well as an intensified erection of the jade stem and the elimination of impotence.

The massage of the pubic bone activates the vital force of the acupuncture point CV-1, which is located in this area and provides all of the other nerve centers with energy. It becomes the fire power of the wisdom energy and rises upward, penetrating all of the nerve canals, and dissolves any type of physical or psychological knot.

For this exercise area, the man must become aware of the five energetic signs. These are the five elements or five phases of change: wood, fire, earth, metal, and water. They are associated with yin and yang, the four directions, the four seasons, the five organs, intestines and openings of the body, whose energy headquarters is the pubic bone.

6th PART:
CONTRACTIONS OF THE PC MUSCLE AND PELVIC FLOOR FOR ACTIVATING SEXUAL ENERGY

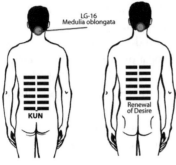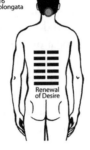

| **Inhaling through the nose**
(15 seconds) =
receptive force with
tensed anal region.
Activation of the
"seven glands"
through the PC muscle
and tensing of pelvic floor | **Holding the breath**
(10 seconds) =
creative force
with pelvic floor
drawn upward.
Distribution of the energy.
Activation of the
lymphatic glandular system
(cell renewal) | **Exhaling through the mouth**
(5 seconds) =
relaxed force with
relaxed pelvic floor.
Cleansing of the lymphatic
glandular system, relaxation
of the nervous system
and the "seven glands" |

Exercise Instructions:

1. With the middle fingers of the both hands, press into the hollow at the base of the skull and pump the acupuncture point GV-16 for a total of 49 times. This activates the energy of the right and left brain hemispheres at the entry canal of the nerves into the brain.

2. While inhaling through the nose, place the tongue on the gums and leave it there until the end of holding the breath. While exhaling through the mouth, place the tongue behind the lower row of teeth.

3. Tense the pelvic floor by quickly and vigorously drawing it upward. Simultaneously inhale deeply for 15 seconds. Hold the breath and the tension for 10 seconds, then exhale in a relaxed state for 5 seconds. As a result, the energy will be transported directly into the brain through the spinal canal and the medulla oblongata.

4. During the entire course of the exercise, close your hands around the thumbs. Keep the legs firmly rooted to the ground and the upper body and head upright. Relax the hands only after ending the tensing and relaxation of the PC muscle.

5. Repeat the course of the exercise 21 times—after getting up and before going to bed.

The Head's Reflex Zones

The contraction of PC muscles and the pelvic floor is used to activate specific segments of the body.

> *"If you feel a pain, stay still*
> *and ask yourself what it wants." (Emanuel Geibel)*

Physical complaints and pain are the consequences of bodily malfunctions and therefore serve as an important source of information about organic disorders. The English neurologist Sir Henry Head (1861-1940) researched these correlations quite precisely and developed a type of "map" of the skin reflex zones, which have been named "Head's Zones" in his memory. These are segments of the body that are connected with inner organs and are supplied by the nerve from the same segments of the spinal cord. Through the reflexes, each part influences the others so that a functional unity is created between the individual organs and meridians. These Head's Zones are stimulated by the tensing of the PC muscle in the Deer Exercise.

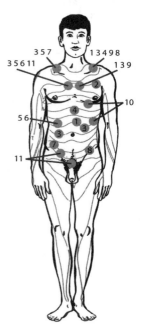

1. Heart
2. Coronary vessels/aorta
3. Lung/pleura
4. Stomach
5. Liver/gallbladder
6. Duodenum
7. Appendix
8. S-shaped large intestine
9. Pancreas
10. Spleen
11. Kidney/ureter

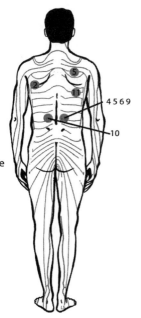

THE PC MUSCLE:
THE MYSTERIOUS SACRAL PUMP

The pubococcygeal muscle, abbreviated as the PC muscle, extends across the pelvic floor in the form of a butterfly in order to connect the anus and genitals with the ischium and legs. It runs from the pubic bone to the coccyx, supports the anus and the adjacent inner organs (bladder and kidneys), and makes sure that these do not sag (uterine prolapse, slipped disk, and prolapse of the large intestine).

The PC muscle is the main muscle of the pelvic floor. It controls the opening and closing of the urethra, spermatic canal (prostate gland), vagina, penis, and anus. The pelvic floor consists of three muscle groups: the muscle-holding cross (a fan-shaped muscle plate), the horseshoe muscle (a cross-wise muscle plate), and the anal-sphincter muscle (a cross-wise muscle cord). It is formed by the lowest, the middle, and the innermost layer of the pelvis.

The PC muscle is located about one inch beneath the surface of the skin and is largely controlled by the so-called pudendal nerve (pubic nerve), which registers the activity of the sexual organs and the anus. This nerve sends signals to the brain and back again. The nerve connection extends from the PC muscle to the pelvic nerve. A branch of the pelvic nerve connects the uterus and the bladder in the woman and the bladder and the prostate gland in the man with the lower portion of the spinal column.

If the sacral pump—which is another term for the PC muscle—is strong, then it is the greater contributor of energy: a true power plant within the human being. When this muscle is tensed, it stimulates the prostate gland in the man and the uterus in the woman. In this way, the body's own hormones and endorphins that trigger an emotional high are released. If the PC muscle is not put to adequate use through sex or specific energetic exercises on a regular basis, it will become steadily weaker and atrophy. It not only loses its holding function in the sexual area but also weakens the posture of the respective person, especially in the lower back region, which is then cut off from good circulation and the energy supply.

If someone is sexually inactive for a longer period of time, the PC muscle may first require reactivation. The Taoist Deer Exercise, the key to renewing sexual potency for both the man and the woman, is particularly effective here. After giving birth, many women also have problems with a weak PC muscle. This can result in sexual disorders, as well as depressions and constant fatigue.

However, this should not cause concern because sexual equilibrium and mental power and endurance return with the general strengthening of the PC muscle. Moreover, the PC muscle is one of the most effective sources of power for rebuilding the endocrine glandular system. It is also the "rejuvenation generator," which can be charged easily, simply, inconspicuously, and at any time with the contractions of the Taoist Deer Exercise. Through this form of exercise, the PC muscle becomes a source of energy that creates and maintains life, rejuvenating the cells of the human organism.

HOW TO RECOGNIZE THE PC MUSCLE CONTRACTIONS

There is a simple method for locating the PC muscle: Lay naked on your back with your legs spread slightly and hold a cosmetic mirror with magnification in your hand. Now observe what happens at the middle point between the anus and the genitals during the PC muscle contractions. If you are able to tense the PC muscle and this tension is strong enough, you should be able to deliberately let the perineum point CV-1 (in the area between the anus and genitals) retract and protrude when you tense and then relax the PC muscle. When doing this, be sure that your belly, buttocks, and the thigh musculature do not move along with it or get tense. If this happens involuntarily, this is a sign that you

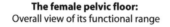

The female pelvic floor:
Overall view of its functional range

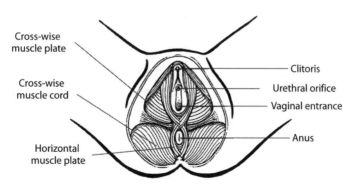

Cross-wise muscle plate

Cross-wise muscle cord

Horizontal muscle plate

Clitoris

Urethral orifice

Vaginal entrance

Anus

still cannot properly activate your PC muscle. It is important to learn to control this mysterious key for health, youthfulness, and longevity independent of all the other muscles.

The male pelvic floor:
Overall view of its functional range

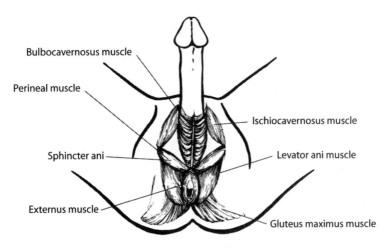

Bulbocavernosus muscle

Perineal muscle

Ischiocavernosus muscle

Sphincter ani

Levator ani muscle

Externus muscle

Gluteus maximus muscle

Probably the best-known method for testing the PC muscle is the attempt to interrupt the flow of urine in the beginning phase. It works like a valve that closes and opens the genital area. When attempting this, you can feel how the muscular area around the anal and genital area contracts. If you have an elastic and dynamic PC muscle, you can interrupt the flow of urine at any time and as often as you like.

Men feel their PC muscle when they want to forcefully squeeze out the last drop of urine. This muscle stimulates the flow of blood to the penis and promotes both the sensation of pleasure and the ability to maintain the erection, as well as stopping ejaculation. Women feel their PC muscle in particular when they actively push during the third stage of birth. Through this exercise, a woman gains the ability to more tightly enclose the man's penis with her vagina. This intensifies the erotic sensations for both of the partners.

During coitus, there is a spontaneous rhythmic contracting and relaxing of the PC muscle, comparable to a pump—which is why the term "sacral pump" is quite appropriate. This procedure is also one of the most important coordinated movements during orgasm in intervals of fractions of a second. By slowly and consciously activating the sacral pump, we can learn to intensify and control the orgiastic sensations during love play.

THE FUNCTION AND ACTIVE MECHANISM OF THE PC MUSCLE

When the PC muscle in the lower pelvic region is stimulated, the vital energy of chi begins to flow through the spinal cord to the brain and spread throughout the nervous system. The energy of the PC muscle is divided into yin and yang:

- Yin conducts the female energy up the right side of the spinal column.
- Yang conducts the male energy down the left side of the spinal column.

Both canals begin between the anus and the perineum. They are connected with every energy center along the spinal column and meet at the root of the nose.

When the spinal fluid begins to rise, we can actually feel a type of electrical current along the spinal column. The spinal cord is the starting point for every electromagnetic development within the organism. This highest energy can only develop by means of tensing and relaxing the PC muscle in connection with the Crane Breathing.

The duality in the relationships of every human being unites the masculine and feminine characteristics within itself. In our sexual relationships, we seek wholeness by selecting partners who complement us. From them, we can learn how to depict our own latent demands. After many years of togetherness, some couples look very similar and behave in almost the exact same manner. They have assumed each other's characteristics and meet each other in the center between the polar extremes.

The yang power of heaven, the creative and explosive energy, dominates in the man. This is why his jade stem is an outward penetrating form that can be maintained through meridian massage and the male Deer Exercise.

The yin power of the earth, the receptive and begetting energy, dominates in the woman. This is why the jade gate gives her an inward, receptive form, the firmness and flexibility of which can be maintained through the female Deer Exercise.

This is how the force of heaven, which circulates in a counterclockwise direction, and the force of the earth, which circulates in a clockwise direction, mutually complement each other during sexual contact and unite in the orgasm.

Die Yin-Kraft der Erde, die empfangende und gebärende Energie, dominiert in der Frau. Deshalb verleiht sie dem Jadetor eine nach innen gehende, empfängliche Gestalt, deren Festigkeit und Geschmeidigkeit mittels der weiblichen Hirschübung erhalten bleiben kann.

So ergänzen sich die Kraft des Himmels, die gegen den Uhrzeigersinn, und die Kraft der Erde, die im Uhrzeigersinn zirkuliert, während des sexuellen Kontaktes gegenseitig und vereinigen sich im Orgasmus.

THE PC MUSCLE IN THE LIGHT OF MODERN RESEARCH

The following is a brief summary of study findings in the area of chi research at the Institute for Applied Biocybernetics and Feedback Research in Vienna under the direction of Director Gerhard H. Eggetsberger.*

The Austrian research group around Eggetsberger has succeeded in developing a viable measurement system for the inner-body vital energy of chi and its flow along the spinal column. With this computer-supported system, it is now possible to make the inner energy processes visible. Occurrences that have only been described by yogis, Taoists, and mystics can now be brought "online" for the first time by this system. This will make it possible to scientifically research them for the first time. In addition, the research group has succeeded in gathering new findings with this system that leave no doubts about the possibility of modifying the brain and bringing it to a higher level of energy.

When there is an intense increase in the flow of energy in the brain, it initially reacts with over-stimulation phenomena, such as those known from the practice of Kundalini Yoga. These are manifested in ways such as feelings of dizziness, noise in the ears, or optical effects like points or flashes of light behind closed eyelids, as well as twitching of the feet and legs, a tingling sensation in the entire body, feelings of movement in the spinal column, occasional minor vision disorders, and various types of emotional fluctuations.

* The entire report (in German) can be ordered from the Institute for Applied Biocybernetics and Feedback Research, Josefstaedter Str. 72, A-1080 Vienna, Austria..

The study of these side effects showed that individual cell groups in the brain—which already react to low levels of electrical currents—are activated by the supply of more energy and are therefore stimulated. If this occurs more frequently, our brain will react with a simple but effective remedy: It isolates the over-stimulated cells. The cell groups become somewhat less sensitive so that they only become active at a higher voltage level. In this manner, some of the brain centers become desensitized. Accordingly, a human being is shielded against many stress-related disorders and fears.

However, probably the most interesting effect surfaces only when this period of desensitization—which usually lasts several weeks—has been completed. At this point, the various disruptive cell groups no longer switch on involuntarily even if there is just a minor level of brain energy. This means that the higher brain areas, which otherwise would never be put to use, can themselves activate because the brain centers that had previously always blocked them can no longer interfere. Consequently, this new measurement technique for the inner life energy shows us a way to initiate an evolution of the brain—and therefore human consciousness.

With the Taoist Deer Exercise, it is possible to modify the substance of the brain, desensitize overly nervous centers, and activate the idle higher areas of the brain. The consequences of this discovery for science cannot yet be appraised in any way. As a result, the human being could develop a higher consciousness and have abilities that have not been imagined up to now. But this process can only take place when the inner energy has been increased over a period of time, as happens through the training of the PC muscle. This procedure can now be monitored to the greatest extent with measurement techniques, which means it can also be used for specific purposes.

With the electromyogram examination (EMG) of the PC muscle, it has been demonstrated in methods of Kundalini Yoga that the pure mental concentration on one chakra produces a measurable increase in the tone of the PC muscle. Many people experience a slight, sometimes even a strong, tensing of the PC muscle when they focus intensely on the pelvic area. This indicates that the main energy rises from the pelvic area in meditation as well.

The measurements of the vital energy chi bring us new perceptions and, above all, an understanding of the inner processes that extends far beyond anything we have imagined up to now. The possibilities of a different consciousness, a "new human being," open up. These new, scientifically researched phenomena show us a possible path into the new millennium.

The information exchange between the PC muscle and the brain during the deer exercise

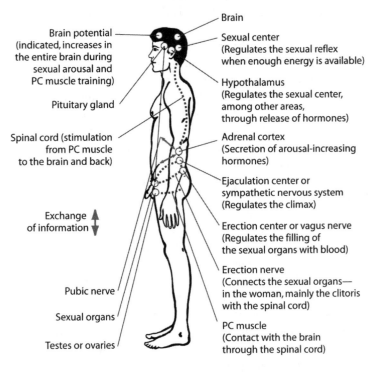

Brain potential (indicated, increases in the entire brain during sexual arousal and PC muscle training)

Pituitary gland

Spinal cord (stimulation from PC muscle to the brain and back)

Exchange of information ⬆⬇

Pubic nerve

Sexual organs

Testes or ovaries

Brain

Sexual center (Regulates the sexual reflex when enough energy is available)

Hypothalamus (Regulates the sexual center, among other areas, through release of hormones)

Adrenal cortex (Secretion of arousal-increasing hormones)

Ejaculation center or sympathetic nervous system (Regulates the climax)

Erection center or vagus nerve (Regulates the filling of the sexual organs with blood)

Erection nerve (Connects the sexual organs— in the woman, mainly the clitoris with the spinal cord)

PC muscle (Contact with the brain through the spinal cord)

In the man:
Creative and explosive force; is pressed upward and becomes emotional sexual energy through sensation and movement.

In the woman:
Receptive and begetting force; emotional force becomes physical energy; movement energy downward and to the side.

MALE IMPOTENCE

THE UNWARRANTED FEAR OF IMPOTENCE

Impotence is the inability of a man to achieve and maintain a satisfying erection. For many men, impotence is an agonizing problem that can dramatically change the course of their lives. The spasms that are triggered in this process can ultimately also damage these organs: the heart, spleen, liver, and kidneys. Potency disorders and erectile dysfunctions are usually caused by the prostate gland, which controls all of the sexual processes, including erection.

As we know, men over 45 years of age tend to have prostate complaints, according to the perspective of Western medicine. However, the ancient Chinese diagnosis and therapy procedure believes—and its experiences have proved this—that it is absolutely abnormal for the prostate gland to fail in old age. According to this viewpoint, the prostate gland only becomes diseased because of "abuse." The ancient Taoist sages basically give no other advice than for the man to relax during foreplay—the "deep, hidden valley"—and not worry about his erection. Instead, he should concentrate on erotically stimulating his partner.

Even in ancient Chinese, the potency of a man was synonymous for masculinity and was an extremely desirable quality. When a man was unable to have or keep an erection, he was just as embarrassed, ashamed, or angry about his presumed weakness as modern-day men.

Despite the help of modern science, physicians, psychologists, and psychiatrists cannot give their patients with better advice today than that their fear of impotence is unwarranted. Yet, despite all of the scientific evidence, most men refuse to believe that occasional or temporary impotence is a natural and widespread occurrence. Or they believe it but are still ashamed. Such temporary impotence is nothing worse than a cold—namely, unpleasant and disruptive, but no reason to worry!

Even a man who has just had one single experience with temporary impotency related to a kidney weakness can be subject to a deep-rooted fear of lasting impotence. During every opportunity for sexual contact, he will be dominated by the fear of whether or not he will be potent enough to become aroused and fulfill his function, as expected from a "normal" man. In oversimplified terms, we could say that in such a case, the man prevents the erection himself because of his fear. For many men who are afraid of sexual activity, the natural reaction pattern is so disturbed that they literally break out in a cold sweat at every opportunity that arises. It is sad, even tragic, that a man would react to the opportunity of loving ecstasy with panicked terror because he believes that he is helplessly at the mercy of his erectile and potency problems. Yet, this situation can be effectively battled with the ancient Chinese Deer Exercise and the massage of specific meridians (see pages 82-85) so that his potency and erection will return within a short time. However, the precondition for this happening is that is must be practiced on a regular basis.

Important note: Men should not use stimulating medication that promises them potency since this can lead to devastating health problems, as the medical-scientific reports in the daily newspapers show. For example, according to the statistics of the experts, the so-called "potency pill" Viagra has already claimed 522 casualties throughout the world. At the first WHO conference on potency disorders in Paris, participants said that this figure was only the tip of the iceberg. They assume that only one-tenth of the affected cases have actually been recognized as Viagra victims.

"Most of the Viagra patients, who died of heart failure, should never have been permitted to take this medication," says urologist Hartmut Porst of Hamburg, Germany. This specialist for the so-called dysfunction can demonstrate his years of effectively treating erectile disorders through local injection therapy.

ACUPRESSURE AND MERIDIAN MASSAGE AS A REMEDY FOR IMPOTENCE

Treatment Instructions for Impotence

A	B	C	D	E	F	G
Ki-2	Bl-15	Sp-6	CV-2	Lu-7	St-30	He-8
Ki-10	Bl-31		CV-6			
Ki-12	Bl-32					
	Bl-35					
	Bl-38					
	Bl-47					
	Bl-49					

All acupressure points—except those located at the middle of the body—must be equally treated on both sides of the body. Never put any pressure on varicose veins!

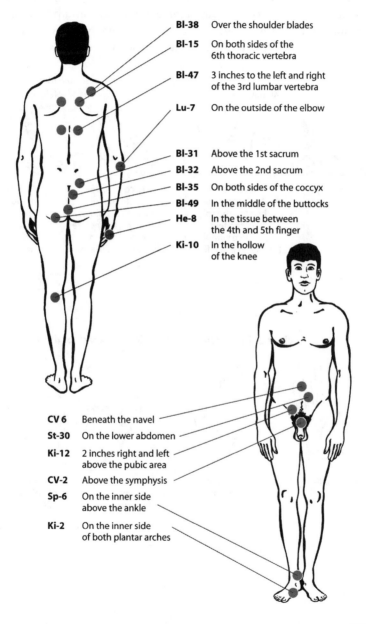

Bl-38 Over the shoulder blades

Bl-15 On both sides of the
6th thoracic vertebra

Bl-47 3 inches to the left and right
of the 3rd lumbar vertebra

Lu-7 On the outside of the elbow

Bl-31 Above the 1st sacrum

Bl-32 Above the 2nd sacrum

Bl-35 On both sides of the coccyx

Bl-49 In the middle of the buttocks

He-8 In the tissue between
the 4th and 5th finger

Ki-10 In the hollow
of the knee

CV 6 Beneath the navel

St-30 On the lower abdomen

Ki-12 2 inches right and left
above the pubic area

CV-2 Above the symphysis

Sp-6 On the inner side
above the ankle

Ki-2 On the inner side
of both plantar arches

STIMULATING THE SEXUAL GLANDS

In order to stimulate the meridians of the sexual glands, bladder, and kidneys at the points on the ankles and feet, first firmly grasp the Achilles tendon and press on it. Pain in this area means an insufficient functioning of one or more parts of the entire system. Many women and men are very sensitive in this area but do not know why this is so.

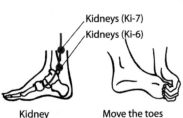

Kidneys (Ki-7)
Kidneys (Ki-6)

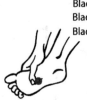

Bladder (Bl-59)
Bladder (Bl-60)
Bladder (Bl-67)

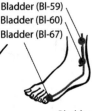

Kidney
meridian

Move the toes
back and forth,
then tap the soles
of the feet
for effective stimulation
(sinus and eye reflexes).

According to
Taoist tradition,
the kidney point is
the only acupuncture
point located
on the sole of the foot.

Bladder
meridian

Ancient Chinese acupressure points for a lack of drive

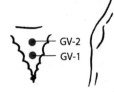

Lu-9 at side of wrist

TW-4 on upper side
of wrist

GV-1 and GV-2
on lower end
of coccyx

Li-8 at center
of hollow
of knee

GV-2
GV-1

98

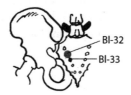

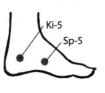

Ancient Chinese acupressure points for sterility

TW-10 just above
    the "funny bone"

BI-32 above the
    2nd sacral hole
BI-33 above the
    3rd sacral hole

Ki-5 on the inner side
Sp-5 on plantar arch
    below ankle

MERIDIAN MASSAGE FOR THE PROSTATE GLAND

This exercise increases the release of male hormones and helps maintain and promote healthy functioning of the male sexual organs. Furthermore, it is good for the brain.

When the inner foot from the heel to the ankle is massaged, this stimulates an important gland: the prostate gland. If this gland functions properly, a man will also experience good preconditions for his sexual life. In turn, the point exactly in the center of the hollow of the knee is associated with the kidneys and bladder. The correlation with sexual stimulation has not yet been precisely researched, but it is possible that the adrenal glands secrete more sexual hormones when this point is stimulated.

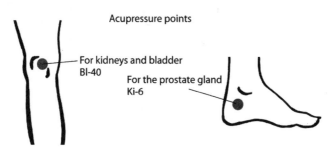

Acupressure points

For kidneys and bladder
BI-40

For the prostate gland
Ki-6

Exercise Instructions:
- Begin with the left ankle and massage it 36 times in a counterclockwise direction
- Then massage the right ankle 36 times in a clockwise direction

There should be no expectations of "miracles" happening—that feelings of desire will develop the moment these zones are pressed. Instead, the active mechanism tends to be indirect. A balanced emotional life is much more important for a functioning sexual life.

THE FEMALE DEER EXERCISE

Contractions of the PC Muscle and Pelvic Floor: The Key to Health and Longevity

"Through periods of solitude and meditation, enlightened human beings gain and maintain the inner equilibrium between yin and yang when they explore the exercise forms of the ancient Chinese diagnosis and therapy procedure."

. . . .

Note: The traditional Taoist medicine is now called Traditional Chinese Medicine (TCM)

INTRODUCTION TO THE FEMALE
DEER EXERCISE

The pelvic floor consists of muscles that are lattice-shaped and run in loops. These are attached to the bony pelvis. They form the muscular base of the abdomen and support the organs of the small pelvis like a hammock. In addition, they hold closed the direct openings of the urethra, vagina, and rectum.

When there is a corresponding demand, these muscles must relax or open widely in order to support the emptying of the bladder and rectum—or to make possible the opening and elasticity of the vagina during sexual intercourse and birth. Although the powerful carrying, supporting, and closing function slackens over time, our well-being is still dependent upon these functions. As a result, it is necessary to continue maintaining these control functions up into old age by means of contracting the sphincter muscle.

When the contractions of the pelvic floor are not strong enough to safeguard the functions of carrying, supporting, closing, and opening, this situation causes a great strain upon the human being because pathological germs can now force their way into the body unhindered. This applies to the closing of the bladder, the functioning of the sphincter of the bladder, as well as for the anus, whose ability to open and close can also be restricted by lacerations caused by giving birth and the subsequent scars. The helplessness that results lastingly shakes the sense of self-worth for many women so that they turn to medication, which usually do more harm than good.

The root of the problem is that the muscles of the pelvic floor, in comparison to other muscle groups in the genital area, are invisible and some of them lie so deep within the body that it is very difficult to perceive their tensing and relaxing. But with the contractions of the sphincter muscles in the female Deer Exercise and the related upward pull of the pelvis, the ancient sages managed to overcome the timidity about this region of the body (which is connected with sexuality, excretions, feces, and urine, as well as the related insecurities). This is based on the feeling of uncleanness that parents have passed on to their children for generations because of their false shame and have taught them as an unexamined child-rearing measure.

There is no special attention given to the pelvic floor in the biology classes of our schools or in the physiotherapeutic training given to midwives. Consequently, the "Taoist secret of rejuvenation," which cannot be replaced by any medication in the world, has been overlooked. Medical professionals, even those specialized in the fields related to the pelvic floor such as gynecology or urology, do not know much about the function of the pelvic floor and usually learn too little about the rejuvenating and healing effects of an active pelvic floor muscle and anal sphincter muscle.

People are therefore largely unaware of how important the contractions of the pelvic floor muscle and anal sphincter muscle are for women and men, as well as the various tasks and abilities that these muscles possess. Only when we understand how they work and have felt the effect of the Taoist Deer Exercise within us can we include this form of exercise in all the movements of our lives in order to achieve health and longevity.

THE PELVIC FLOOR AND ITS MUSCULAR STRUCTURE

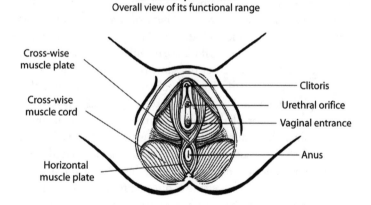

The female pelvic floor:
Overall view of its functional range

Cross-wise muscle plate

Cross-wise muscle cord

Horizontal muscle plate

Clitoris

Urethral orifice

Vaginal entrance

Anus

The pelvic floor consists of three layers of muscles that are on top of each other:

- The cross-wise muscle plate
- The cross-wise muscle cord
- The horizontal muscle plate

103

The respective muscle fibers of these three layers alternate as they run from front to back, from right to left, and again from front to back in the form of the number eight so that a lattice-shaped structure is created.

The individual layers have different tasks. As a result, by using the Taoist rejuvenation exercise we can clearly and tangibly perceive how the muscle layers conduct the newly gained chi energy through the body. With the pelvic floor contractions, we experience how the individual muscle layers work and we can therefore use them in a more specific and effective manner. The beginning insecurity disappears the longer and more intensively we become acquainted with our pelvic floor and contractions of the anal sphincter muscle in their entirety.

The task of these muscles is to narrow the side of the bony pelvic outlet when pressure is exerted in a downward direction from the abdominal cavity. All of the long muscle fibers contract toward the center when they are tensed. As they do this, they move the bony skeleton just as, for example, the bicep muscle in the upper arm can draw up the lower arm. In a similar manner, the fibers of the muscle plate tighten on both sides of the bony parts of the pelvis that run from the bridge of the pubic bone to the ischial tuberosities and draw them together. When the ischial tuberosities are drawn together firmly and held in this position, we feel a tension in the middle layer of the pelvic floor. As opposed to the lowest layer of the pelvic floor, we inevitably feel that many other muscles are also being tensed at the same time since the muscle plate supports them in their work. The joint effort of the buttock muscles, as well as the abdominal and back musculature, can be clearly felt.

In this middle layer of the pelvis, many women have an indirect weak point since their muscle tissue is not as solid because of pregnancies. The muscle tissue also does not develop the same strength to protect their pelvic floor as in men. This means that a heavy physical activity through which massive pressure is directed from the abdominal region into the pelvic floor has an adverse effect on women: The pressure is transferred to the uterus and can endanger to later births or cause a prolapse of the uterus.

Explanation of Pressure in the Abdominal Region
Whenever the abdominal area is put under pressure (this strain should also be heeded during sports), our body sends a reflex-like impulse to the pelvic floor. If this situation is compounded by the wrong type of breathing, such as thoracic (chest) breathing, the main pressure point

shifts to the bladder. This can result in frequent urination during the day. The female Deer Exercise, with its simple methods, therefore offers a possibility for any women to balance this weak point and maintain a flexible but firm pelvic floor area.

The deeper-lying, cross-wise muscle plate consists of muscle fibers that run from the right inner side of the bony pelvis diagonally to the left inner side. It begins somewhat above the superficial, crosswise muscle cord and lie very close to the pubic bone so that this muscle plate covers three-fourths of the pelvic outlet. The backmost and longest muscle fibers also run closely together with the muscle crossing between the vagina (or testes) and anus: only the anus itself is free. The muscle plate is integrated from both sides into a layer of firm connective tissue, which has the medical name of *musculus transversus pevinaei profundus.*

The portion of muscle tissue in this muscle plate is different for men and women. Men have almost twice as much muscle tissue here as women. In addition, this muscle plate is weakened in women by the vagina, which is situated cross-wise in relation to the muscle fibers. Nature planned this so that babies can more easily push aside this resistance with their heads during the birth process. If only because of these reasons, the additional pelvic training offered by the Taoist Deer Exercise is extremely advisable.

In the back muscle pair, one muscle is anchored to the right and one to the left of the inner side of the sacrum. Both of these are stretched flatly. These muscles also unite when they leave the small pelvis next to the sacrum. Furthermore, they are attached directly beneath the joint on the upper thigh bone (femur). In medical terminology, these muscles are the right and left *musculus piriformis.* Both pairs of muscles help in the sideward movement of the pelvis, as well as tilting back and forth; they always work in connection with the inner main muscle. This is a muscle that appears to have a fan shape and practically closes off the entire movement space of the small pelvis in an upward direction. The muscle fibers come from the same bone groove to which the lateral muscle pair is anchored. They begin at about the height of the thigh joint. Here, on the inner side, is where they are attached as they come from both sides and almost merge into each other. These muscle fibers also concentrate in the direction of the back so that the muscle can be compared to an opened fan.

The powerful extensor of the back (sacrospinalis muscle), which runs toward the back, is attached on the lower end of the sacrum. It runs toward the back in a slight downward direction so that all of the organs lie above it. The bladder in particular and, indirectly, the uterus rest on it. Some of its muscle fibers, which come laterally from the pubic bone, loop around the rectum above the anal sphincter and run back to the pubic bone again in the shape of a horseshoe. They support and hold the rectum at an angle that is important for the activity of the anal sphincter.

The muscle fibers that run in the middle surround the vagina and rectum. One portion of these muscle fibers runs down the front of the inner side of the pubic bone and doesn't leave until the point where it forms the holding-cross muscle of the lowest layer of the pelvic floor. Of all the animals that have a tail with vertebrae, the deer in particular knows how to masterfully use this tail to stabilize its potency. In contrast to all of the other animals, its muscle fibers of this innermost pelvic-floor muscle extend along the tail vertebrae to the end of the tail. The coccyx of the human being is just a remnant of the tail apophysis and is located at the end of the sacrum, the so-called sacral pump that directs the transport of energy on to the brain. The Taoist Deer Exercise stimulates the sensitive nerves located in the buttocks and activates the sexual energy to the medulla oblongata (GV-16).

Just as the position of the tail is an important element of body language for all animals, the same also applies to the human being since all movements from the innermost pelvic-floor muscle supply the organism with valuable energy. If our innermost pelvic-floor muscle is tensed, our body will stand deeply rooted, as the Taoist sages say. A soft, relaxed innermost pelvic-floor muscle gives the body a feeling of letting go everywhere.

The medical term for this fan-shaped tail muscle is *musculus levator ani*. Levator means "raising" or "raising the anus." At this point, we should note the special meaning of its supportive function for the lower rectum. While animals that move on all four legs do not overstrain the innermost pelvic floor, human beings—because of their upright posture and rearward angled musculature -have considerable problems since this pelvic-floor muscle is overstretched in the course of time. Whenever we bend down, we are especially endangered by the intensified pressure on the intervertebral disks, which also considerably restricts the lifting function. Women should generally not lift heavy objects from the floor in a bent posture or move furniture since this would lead to a displacement of the innermost pelvic-floor muscle. Slipped disks, sciatica, intense back complaints, or uterine prolapse can be the later consecutive symptoms as a result.

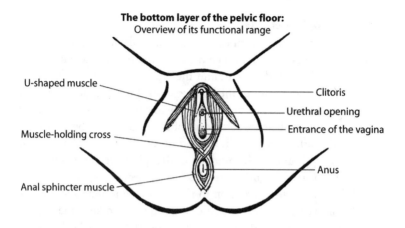

The bottom layer of the pelvic floor:
Overview of its functional range

U-shaped muscle

Muscle-holding cross

Anal sphincter muscle

Clitoris
Urethral opening
Entrance of the vagina

Anus

The Bottom Layer of the Pelvic Floor
The bottom layer of the pelvic floor runs beneath the surface of the skin and consists of three muscle groups:

- The muscle-holding cross
- The horseshoe muscle
- The anal sphincter muscle

1. The Muscle-Holding Cross
The muscle-holding cross consists of two muscle cords that run from the bottom inner edge of the pubic bone to the back and are attached to the end of the sacrum. The muscle cords cross between the vagina and the anus. In the process, the muscle cords do not just pass each other; instead, the fibers mix so that a solid crossing point is created. In the front V of the cross are the clitoris, urethral opening, and vagina. In the back V area is the anus. Behind the anus, both muscle cords close in order to anchor themselves on the sacrum. If we look at this muscle cord from the bottom to the top, it looks like the number 8. The medical term for this muscle-holding cross is *musculus pubococcygeus*, which is shortened to the PC muscle. The

107

muscle-holding cross gives both of the other muscles of the bottom pelvic-floor layer, the horseshoe muscle and the anal sphincter muscle, stability and supports them in their activities.

2. The Horseshoe Muscle

The horseshoe muscle runs, as they name already implies, in the form of a horseshoe. It also comes from the bottom lateral edge of the pubic bone and runs around the vagina and back to the pubic bone next to the cords of the holding cross. Between the vagina and the anus, the horseshoe muscle mixes with the muscle-holding cross and its muscle fibers are soft. Some of them run to the bottom vaginal walls, others to the clitoris, and others in turn to the urethral opening and support the function of the sphincter urethral muscle. If we must firmly/tightly tense this muscle because of a full bladder, this impulse is also passed on to the horseshoe muscle and curtails the ability to contract. In addition, it also helps to keep the vaginal entrance slightly closed. During sexual arousal, the muscle fibers have slight erectile properties. This increases the ability to feel and lets the vaginal entrance become softer and looser while the vagina itself becomes tighter and firmer. The medical term for the horseshoe muscle is *musculus bulbospongiosus.*

3. The Anal Sphincter

The anal sphincter muscle consists of a bundle of orbicular muscles that lie just beneath the surface of the skin and mix laterally with the muscle fibers of the muscle-holding cross: Its task is to suffocate pathological germs and close the rectum. The medical term for the anal sphincter is *musculus sphincter ani.*

The horseshoe muscle is directly connected with the muscle-holding cross through its muscle fibers, which creates a joined muscle layer with muscles that cannot be used individually. If we tense the horseshoe muscle, this pulls the cross point between the vagina and the anus somewhat forward since this is where the muscle fibers, muscle-holding cross-, and horseshoe muscle mix. At the same time, the anal sphincter is also tensed and slightly drawn forward because of its connection with the muscle-holding cross. Consequently, the chi energy is transported upward through the body to the brain. Inversely, we also feel how the horseshoe muscle is tensed when we contract the anal sphincter muscle.

The bottom layer of the pelvic floor has one more special characteristic through which we can perceive it. It can be tensed by itself, without any other muscle of the body. Even the abdominal muscles are completely relaxed when we do this. We can alternately tense and relax this bottom pelvic-floor layer and make sure that no other muscles are moving in the body. In keeping with this, with enough practice we can slowly hold the muscles with more tension and for a longer period of time. When concentrating on the horseshoe muscle, women feel the vibration of the labia majora (large pudendal lips) while men perceive a pulsation in the penis.

The Middle Layer of the Pelvic Floor
The middle layer of the pelvic floor lies above the bottom muscle layer, which has just been described in detail, and is deeper inside the body. Its muscle fibers run from right to left. They consist of two muscles:

- A superficial cross-wise muscle cord
- A deeper-lying muscle plate that also runs cross-wise

The superficial muscle is weak and narrow. It runs from the inner side of the ischial tuberosity into the muscle-crossing point of the bottom layer of the pelvic floor and back out to the other ischial tuberosity. It only has a stabilizing function. Its medical name is *musculus transversus superficialis*.

The Innermost Layer of the Pelvic Floor
This muscle layer is the innermost layer of the entire pelvic-floor complex and consists of:

- The horseshoe muscle (U muscle)
- The muscle-holding cross
- The anal sphincter muscle
- The cross-wise muscle plate
- The PC muscle cord

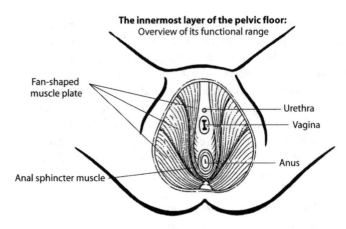

The innermost layer of the pelvic floor:
Overview of its functional range

Fan-shaped
muscle plate

Urethra

Vagina

Anus

Anal sphincter muscle

The muscle pairs of the innermost pelvic-floor layer come from the inner side of the small pelvis and run from there through the bone recesses to the outside. They are attached at the upper end of the thigh bone (femur). The bony floor consists of the large and small pelvis. The large pelvis is the name for the openly projecting ala of the ilium, which is attached to the sacrum. The small pelvic is the bony circle beneath the ala of the ilium, which are rounded toward the front and meet at the pubic bone. At the back, the small pelvis is closed by the sacrum. The muscles for the thigh joint are located at the outer sides on the bony pelvis. It forms a circle, and the inner side of the transition from the large to the small pelvis has a distinct, somewhat protruding groove. The muscle pair that is located to the side of the innermost pelvic-floor layer, one muscle to the right and one to the left, is attached to this groove. The muscle fibers concentrate toward the rear, where they leave the small pelvis through the bony recesses in a flat form and run to the thigh bones, where they are attached. The medical term for this muscle pair is *musculus obturator internus*.

By tensing and relaxing the PC muscle, we can clearly feel the circulation of chi from the sacrum upward to the nerve-entry canal into the brain (medulla oblongata): No other muscle group has such an extensive and rejuvenating influence on our body. However, the decisive impulse for all movements always comes from the position of the pelvis and its state of tension. The pelvic floor—its tensing and relaxing, its actions and reactions, which have a great significance for the areas of sexuality and rejuvenation—basically mirror our sense of self-worth to the outside world, as well as to the inside.

THE EFFECT OF THE FEMALE DEER EXERCISE ON THE ORGANISM

The Tao of sexuality shows women a reliable way for controlling their menstruation and therefore also their fertility. When the female Deer Exercise—the breast massage as well as the tensing and relaxing of the anal sphincter muscle and lifting the pelvic floor in connection with the Crane Breathing—is done on a regular basis for a longer period of time, the monthly bleeding will stop. This can have an extremely positive effect on the female organism.

Every month, the mucous membrane of the uterus grows and thickens, forming additional tissue in order to receive a fertilized egg, if necessary. If the egg is fertilized by a sperm of the male semen, it comes to rest on the thickened, nutrient-rich wall of the uterus, penetrates it, and lives from it. The fetus is nourished by the mother's blood and grows into a complete baby. However, if fertilization does not take place, no egg will implant in the uterus. The thick, blood-rich tissue is no longer required and therefore shed. In this manner, a great deal of blood and nutrients are lost every month.

If the organism is not overridden with toxins, menstruation will cease after a relatively short time as a result of the female Deer Exercise. If such toxins are in the body, this process will take considerably longer since the effects of the Deer Exercise are initially aimed at detoxifying the body. However, many women are afraid to interrupt the menstrual cycle because they consider it unnatural or even dangerous to no longer menstruate before the change of life. However, this concern is unnecessary because interrupting menstruation is nothing unusual; for example, it also occurs temporarily during pregnancy or while breastfeeding.

When menstruation is interrupted, pregnancy will normally not occur. However, as soon as the woman ceases to do the breast massage as part of the Deer Exercise, her menstrual cycle will also return. Interrupting the menstrual cycle is therefore not permanent but temporary and has an extremely healing effect on the female organism. This increases the prospects of an even healthier pregnancy later on.

In addition, the Deer Exercise also eliminates frequently occurring menstrual complaints such as an irregular cycle, mood fluctuations, hormonal blocks, water accumulation, cramps, and excessively heavy bleeding. Weak bleeding indicates blocks and toxins in the body. Chi kung breathing and movement exercises also help against premenstrual complaints such as a feeling of tension and soreness in the breast that can turn into downright pain. However, if the period suddenly stops, and this event has not been influenced by the Deer Exercise, the cause is a disorder of the sexual glands and/or weakness of the kidneys.

In addition, the breast massage—as part of the female Deer Exercise—stimulates the production of the hormone estrogen in a very natural way and helps distribute it to the sexual organs. The fact that estrogen is produced by the body itself is very important for the hormonal process in the female organism. As a result, the body itself knows best how much of the hormones it needs and at what time. The natural increase of hormone production boosts the woman's sexual readiness and ability, contributing to her rejuvenation. However, this does not lengthen the phase of fertility. Menopause comes when the corresponding biological age has been attained, but the typical menopausal complaints as accompanying symptoms are distinctly mitigated.

When a woman is pregnant and menstruation stops, the body absorbs the additional amount of blood and gives it to the growing fetus. Blood and nutrients that are normally lost through monthly bleeding are now primarily used by the sexual glands to nourish the fetus. The sexual glands are virtual engines of rejuvenation. They produce hormones—the fire that helps the cells and tissue remain young.

When there is an insufficient functioning of the sexual glands, the cells and tissue cannot regenerate properly and the mental and physical performance diminishes. If the expectant mother is mentally and physically tired, depressed, and listless, additional problems and diseases will develop that will ultimately also be transferred to the fetus. The process of aging begins and already weakens the baby as it grows in the uterus. We are all adequately familiar with the consequences of this for the mother and child. These include: miscarriages and handicapped children, as well as mothers with suicidal tendencies because of a lack sense of self-worth. With the Deer Exercise, all of these problems can be prevented from the start or even eliminated once they have already developed.

The system of the female sexual organs consists of the vagina, the ovaries, the uterus, and the breasts. There is a close correlation between these organs and the processes of menstruation, pregnancy, birth, and breastfeeding. After conception and during pregnancy, menstruation stops and the blood that would have been lost benefits the fetus or newborn child. When the mother breastfeeds her newborn after birth, menstruation does not immediately return automatically since the blood is sent to the breasts and contributes to the production of milk there. Menstruation only resumes when the child is weaned or the woman prematurely stops breastfeeding.

The process that prevents menstruation during breastfeeding is the same as in the breast massage practiced as part of the female Deer Exercise. The female organism reacts to the breast massage as if a baby was sucking at the breast. Instead of letting the blood flow to the uterus, the body sends it to the breasts where many small blood vessels, nerves, milk glands, and lymphatic vessels are connected with each other. As a result of breastfeeding or the breast massage, the breasts are stimulated. This influences all of the other sexual organs as well. Through the breast massage, the production of sexual hormones is stimulated even where no sexual intercourse takes place.

The Deer Exercise —the contractions of the PC muscle—is also particularly valuable for the vagina. It becomes tighter, firmer, and more flexible as a result. A woman who has given birth to children can therefore profit greatly from the Deer Exercise. Every birth strains the vagina; it is stretched and loosened, whereby the partner loses quite a bit of the sensation. The Deer Exercise has the effect that the man's desire for a tightening vagina increases and the sexual act is once again attractive for both of the participants. With the Deer Exercise, every woman can return herself to an almost "virginal state" because it strengthens and tautens the "palace of life," as well as harmonizing the loss of vital energy.

"SENDING BACK THE BLOOD" AS A FOUNTAIN OF YOUTH

By practicing the Deer Exercise, the woman triggers a rejuvenation mechanism that permits her to stop aging. In this sense, the simple movement sequence of the female Deer Exercise fulfills the ancient search for the fountain of youth, the inexhaustible source of youthfulness. The Taoist healing procedure of stopping the "red snow" (menstruation) is also called "Sending Back the Blood." As a result, the entire female organism is strengthened and tautened—particularly the system of the sexual organs.

For thousands of years, the female Deer Exercise has been one of the most effective methods of birth control and family planning (and absolutely without side effects), as well as being employed for preserving youthfulness. There are official records that women were praised for their intelligence, beauty, and youthful appearance even after several births. They became famous in Chinese history because they used the technique of "Sending Back the Blood."

Through the female Deer Exercise, all types of congestion and constipation can also be eliminated. The blood and energy channels are freed of deposits so that a natural cleansing process is initiated in the body, clearing away the existing blockages. With this series of exercises, it is not only possible to avoid future problems but also to achieve a rejuvenation of the entire organism.

The biological aging process stops when you begin with the Deer Exercise. This means that the sooner you stop your menstruation, the younger you will look and remain. This recommendation also applies to the man, who achieves this goal through the technique of the male Deer Exercise and prevention of ejaculation by inhaling into the abdomen.

Many of my chi kung students and patients have used the stimulating Deer Exercise for birth control, as well as preparation for pregnancy. They have been surprised by the effectiveness of this method. At the same time, all of these individuals were able to manage without the administration of hormones or other pharmaceutical remedies, mechanical contraceptives, or surgical operations.

In order to benefit from the Deer Exercise, you must completely concentrate on your goal. It isn't enough to just practice it occasionally. If you want to achieve a long-term increase in your state of well-being and a rejuvenation of the body and the mind, it is important to practice it daily—just as you are accustomed to eating and drinking every day.

The amount of time required for attaining the state of "Sending Back the Blood" and completely stopping menstruation is different for every woman. The first phase of this process is the breast massage of the Deer Exercise; the second phase is the contraction of the anus, vagina, and perineum and drawing the pelvic floor upward. Most women can achieve this within four weeks, but it can sometimes—despite intensive practice—also take an entire year.

THE DEER EXERCISE AND THE FEMALE BREAST

The breast plays an important role in the life of the woman—above all, in sexuality and for breastfeeding. However, her feeling of self-worth is often also related to the form of her breasts and how they are treated.

In the Tao of sexuality, the breasts are a component of the reproductive system and are just as important as the vagina, ovaries, and uterus. Through the nerve paths and hormones, from foreplay to sexual intercourse to pregnancy and nourishment of the baby, the breasts are closely related to the other female sexual organs.

The female Deer Exercise is based on this relationship. When the hands circle the breasts from the outside to the inside during the breast massage, this has the effect of toning them and is regarded as stimulation. One result of this exercise is that very small breasts expand in size. When the hands circle from the inside to the outside during the breast massage, this has a sedative effect and is called dispersion. Large and slack breasts become smaller and firmer as a result. In addition, the Deer Exercise prevents the formation of nodes in the breasts and has a healing effect.

The inner structure of the breast is very complex. Many little blood vessels, nerves, milk glands, and lymphatic vessels are interwoven with each other. Improper handling of the breasts can easily damage them. Every injury to the breast tissue can lead to contusions and congestion of fluids, which in turn can become nodes and tumors, and possibly even cancer. Through the Deer Exercise, the blood and energy channels are freed of deposits such as nodes and cysts, which prevents breast cancer. In addition to self-examination and medical check-ups on a regular basis, the preventive measures of the female Deer Exercise are the best weapons against breast cancer.

EXERCISE INSTRUCTIONS FOR THE FEMALE DEER EXERCISE

1ST PART OF THE FEMALE DEER EXERCISE: BREAST MASSAGE—DISPERSION (PREVENTION)

1. Sit in a way that allows the heel of your right foot to press against the opening of the vagina in order to exert an even, firm pressure on the clitoris. If it is difficult for you to bring your foot into this position, then place a hard, round object (such as a tennis ball) on the opening of the vagina. This stimulation of the genitals may feel pleasant to you and release your sexual energy.
2. Intensely rub the palms of your hands against each other so that both of the middle fingers touch each other. This creates heat in the hands because the bodily energy then flows into the palms and the fingers (the meridians of circulation/sexuality and the triple warmer run through the middle finger).
3. Place your hands on your breasts in a way that allows you to feel how the warmth from the palms radiates into the skin below them.
4. Now slowly circle the hands from the inside to the outside for a total of 72 times with the left hand turning clockwise and the right hand counterclockwise. Avoid touching the nipples during the massage since they are extremely sensitive and can easily be over-stimulated.
5. Continue with the 2nd portion of the breast massage, the stimulation.

Breast massage, 1st part: Dispersion (prevention)
When the hands circle from the inside to the outside, this has the effect of sedation and is called dispersion. It prevents the formation of nodes in the breasts, prevents breast cancer, and has a healing effect. Menstruation will continue as before. The massaging circles are done from the inside to the outside during dispersion with its calming effects. Repeat this breast massage 72 times with both palms, but do not touch the nipples in the process.

Start the breast massage at the solar plexus

Receptive and birth-giving force

KUN

2ND PART OF THE FEMALE DEER EXERCISE:
BREAST MASSAGE—STIMULATION (REHABILITATION)

1. Continue to sit in a way that allows the heel of your left foot to press against the opening of the vagina. An even, firm pressure must also be exerted on the clitoris for this portion of the exercise. The resulting stimulation of the genitals is not only pleasant but also releases your sexual energy.

2. Intensely rub the palms of your hands against each other so that both of the middle fingers touch each other. This creates heat in the hands because the bodily energy then flows into the palms and the fingers (the meridians of circulation/sexuality and the triple warmer run through the middle finger).

3. Place your hands on your breasts in a way that allows you to feel how the warmth from the palms radiates into the skin below them.

4. Now slowly circle the hands from the outside to the inside for a total of 72 times with the left hand turning counterclockwise and the right hand clockwise. Also avoid touching the nipples during this part of the massage.

Breast massage, 2nd part: Stimulation (rehabilitation)
When the hands circle from the outside to the inside, this has the effect of sedation and is called dispersion. It prevents the formation of nodes in the breasts, prevents breast cancer, and has a healing effect. Menstruation will continue as before. The **Start the breast massage at the sternum** massaging circles are done from the inside to the outside during dispersion with its calming effects. Repeat this breast massage 72 times with both palms, but do not touch the nipples in the process.

Creative and explosive force

KIEN

Do the 1ˢᵗ and 2ⁿᵈ part of the female Deer Exercise in the early morning and late evening on a regular basis. If you want to interrupt your menstruation, then you must do the breast massage 360 times a day. Once menstruation has actually been interrupted, it is enough to just do 72 circular hand motions every day as a breast massage so that menstruation does not begin again. Every woman will best know when she should interrupt or resume her menstruation. The bleeding will automatically return when you no longer do the Deer Exercise, meaning the breast massage.

3ᴿᴰ PART OF THE FEMALE DEER EXERCISE: ABDOMINAL MASSAGE FOR STIMULATING THE PRODUCTION OF FEMALE HORMONES

Circular Pressing of St-29—Guilai

Using your thumbs, massage the acupuncture point St-29, which is located beneath your navel to the right and left of the midline of the abdomen. Apply moderate pressure and do 49 small circular movements.

This exercise increases the natural production of the body's own hormones, raises the level of estrogen, promotes the healthy functioning of the female reproductive organs, and has beneficial effects on brain activity.

Please note: Do not attempt to visualize how your sexual energy rises along your spinal column since the interaction of body and mind is very important for a harmonious and powerful functioning of the vital energy chi. The most significant part of this exercise is directing the chi energy to the pineal gland.

 The exercise stimulates the production of the female hormone estrogen and causes it to be distributed to the vagina, uterus, the breasts, and the ovaries.

4ᵀᴴ PART OF THE FEMALE DEER EXERCISE: CONTRACTION OF THE PC MUSCLE AND THE PELVIC FLOOR

How to Close the Door of Energy

In the 4th part of the female Deer Exercise, the PC muscle—which was called the "love muscle" by the Taoist sages—plays the most important role. It is connected with the labia (lips of the vulva) of the jade door and the other parts of the female genitals.

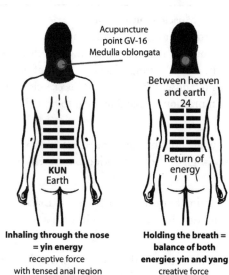

Inhaling through the nose = yin energy	**Holding the breath = balance of both energies yin and yang**	**Exhaling through the mouth = yang energy**
receptive force with tensed anal region activation of the "seven glands" through the PC muscle and tensing of pelvic floor	creative force with drawn-up pelvic floor, increased oxygen to the cells	creative and relaxed force with relaxed pelvic floor, cleansing of the lymphatic gland system, relaxation of the nervous system

Exercise instructions:

1. With the middle fingers of both hands, press into the indentation at the base of the skull and pump the acupuncture point GV-16 (nerve-entry canal into the brain = medulla oblongata) 36 times. This will activate the energy of the right and left brain hemispheres.

2. Tense the PC muscle quickly and powerfully by drawing it upward and inhale deeply for 7 seconds while doing so. Hold the breath and the tension for 7 seconds and then exhale in a relaxed state for another 7 seconds. This will transport the energy through the vertebral canal and the medulla oblongata directly into the brain.

3. Close your hands around your thumbs during the entire course of the exercise. Keep your feet firmly rooted to the ground, with an upright upper body and head. Release the hands only after completing the tensing and relaxing of the PC muscle.

4. Contract the PC muscle, close the outer and inner vessel, open and expand it. Repeat this for a total of 7 x 7 = 49 times until the doors of bliss have opened. This is the secret of the female Deer Exercise.

Additional Exercise for the PC-Muscle Contraction

1. Tense the muscles of the jade door, anus, and perineum with a drawn-up pelvic floor for 10 seconds, as if you wanted to close all three openings. While doing this, press the tongue against the roof of the mouth and inhale through the nose. When you do this exercise correctly, you will have the impression of sucking air into your intestines and the jade door.

2. Maintain the contraction while holding your breath for 10 seconds. This will provide the "seven glands" of the endocrine system with energy.

3. Relax and release the contraction of the entire pelvic floor. Exhale for 10 seconds through your mouth. Immediately begin with a new exercise cycle.

4. Repeat the anal-sphincter contractions with drawn-up pelvic floor at least 21 times and increase this to 49 times. The number of 7 x 7 = 49 repetitions contains the complete exchange of spent energies from the "seven glands" of the endocrine system.

> To check the strength of your PC muscle contraction, you can place a finger in the vagina during the exercise phase and feel the contraction there.

> Additional points of stimulation are the sensitive labia (lips of the vulva), which should be massaged and stimulated during the Deer Exercise. Try to determine whether massaging clockwise or counterclockwise increases your sexual sensations.

> In addition to your heel, a chi kung ball—jade is the best material—or a tennis ball has almost the same stimulating

effect. During love play with your partner, you can naturally achieve a much higher degree of stimulation since you can express your individual wishes.

During the beginning stage, the contractions may be difficult. However, with consistent practice you will come to appreciate the additional stimulation and gradually increase the number of repetitions from 21 to 49.

DEPRESSION

Every one of us probably has a bad day now and then. We feel despondent and torment ourselves with negative thoughts, without having any particular reason to do so. We encounter our fellow human beings with mistrust, even though they haven't given us any reason to do so. We lack willpower and actually don't feel like doing anything.

Perhaps you are now thinking: well, there are days like this and there's nothing we can do about it. And besides, it's not that tragic because the next day the world looks friendly again. However, doctors see this in a different light: They speak of psychological disorders and the beginning of depression. The statistics claim that every third person occasionally suffers from depressive moods—and not only older and isolated people are affected, as in earlier times, but also increasingly more young people who can't or don't want to withstand the pressure of everyday life.

Unfortunately, the doctors are right. Depression has become a widespread disease in our age. This is also reflected in the rising use of antidepressives, which can cause addiction over a longer period of time similar to that of alcohol, nicotine, or illegal drugs. In China, psychoactive drugs are not prescribed, except for the few serious cases in which medication is the only way to help the patient. However, most cases of depression can be helped with acupressure alone, as claimed by the Chinese saying: The correct pressure of the hands and fingers allows the source of life to flow.

1st Step:

Lay down for a moment, relax all of your muscles, and close your eyes. There is also a point that you can treat with acupressure for these types of incidents: the crease of skin between the nose and the upper lip. The Chinese term for this acupuncture point is shui-gu.

Place your middle finger in this crease of skin and firmly press the skin against the teeth for a total of 36 times. This is usually accompanied by a somewhat unpleasant feeling, but continue applying pressure anyway. You will soon discover that the accompanying symptoms will stop.

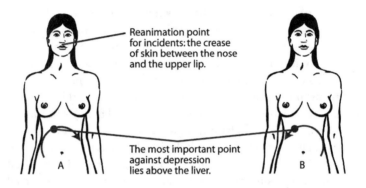

Reanimation point for incidents: the crease of skin between the nose and the upper lip.

The most important point against depression lies above the liver.

A

B

2nd Step:

The most important point against depression and for a good mood is located above the liver, in the area of the right upper abdomen. Treat this point in the morning, right after you wake up and are still in bed. To do this, place your hand flat on the right upper abdomen and press on it briefly and firmly for 36 times. Conclude by respectively massaging this point 36 times clockwise and counterclockwise.

When applying acupressure at this point, some people feel a dull to sharp pain. This is almost always a sign of a liver disorder, which has possibly remained unrecognized up to now. Visit your physician as soon as possible if you feel a tenderness caused by pressure and have your liver examined thoroughly. However, you can still continue doing the acupressure to improve your mood. There are even reports from China about how liver disorders discovered in this manner have been healed through acupressure.

122

3rd Step:

In this position, the shoulder blades can be easily felt on the back. Above all, the inner edges of the shoulder blades are important. Place both hands on them and press these points 36 times in a row. The pressure should only be of medium intensity. This

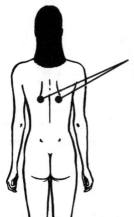

Most people are not flexible enough to reach these points on the back. Another person can also do this acupressure treatment.

acupressure treatment should be done twice daily—after getting up and before going to bed.

4th Step:

The next points through which we can fight depression are located next to the nails of the two middle fingers. You can automatically find these points when you tap your thumb against the middle finger. This acupressure should also be done first thing in the morning after you wake up and can be repeated twice daily. Use two large clothespins and place them on the fingertips at both sides of the middle finger. Slowly remove the clothespins after 5 minutes. Exhale slowly if you feel pain left by the clothespins.

The psyche can also be influenced with acupressure on both of the middle fingers. This also influences the circulation/sexuality, allergies, and blood vessels.

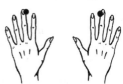

5th Step:

Now treat the wrists with acupressure—exactly at the point where you can feel your pulse. The easiest way to do this is to use the thumb of the opposite hand. Simply wrap your hand around the opposite wrist. Don't press too hard because acupressure on this point has a very strong effect. It stimulates the circulation and can even accelerate the heartbeat..

123

The point on the wrist has a very strong effect on the circulation. First treat the left hand 18 times and then the right hand 18 times.

People with a weak heart should therefore be especially careful and not apply acupuncture at this point if they experience heart palpitations as a result.

6th Step:

In conclusion, treat some of the points on the inner side of the arms. First use acupressure to treat the entire crease of the elbow that forms when the arms are bent slightly at the elbows.

It is best to begin with the left arm. After pressing it 18 times, change over to the right arm.

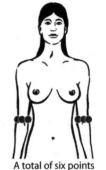

A total of six points in the crease of the elbows have a supportive effect.

7th Step:

Since depressions are frequently also caused by an insufficient activation of the PC muscle, the concluding step is the training of the PC muscle. Repeat this for a total of 49 times (see page 119).

Please note: Anyone who treats herself with acupressure—just like acupuncture—should know that minor incidents might occur. You may begin to sweat, have feelings of dizziness, flickering in front of your eyes, or nausea. This may sound dangerous, but it is completely harmless. After all, it is only a sign that the body is responding to the acupressure and a readjustment to the harmonization of the organism has begun.

GYNECOLOGICAL PROBLEMS

MENSTRUAL DISORDERS

Many women suffer from irregular menstruation—which the Chinese call yue fing by tiao—even though they are completely healthy in every other way. Yet, they are still very concerned when their periods do not start on time. This was also the case for Erika S. She was 28 years old, married, and did not want to have any more children since she already had three. When the irregularities in her menstruation occurred, she naturally believed that she was pregnant again, which caused considerable agitation in her family.

She went to a nearby physician with this problem, who said she had a glandular disorder and her thyroid gland had to be treated. However, her basal metabolism was completely normal. When the medication for the thyroid gland proved to be ineffective, the physician recommended a course of treatment with male hormones. Afterward, she received female hormones in the form of estrogen shots, and finally, a combination of estrogen and progesterone. But the problem continued and her condition worsened.

Since this had developed into a family problem in the meantime, Ms. S. asked me for my advice. We discussed how she—in contrast to other women who suffered from menstrual disorders as a result of concealed infections, glandular disorders, or organic ailments—was appar-

Chinese acupressure points for irregular menstruation

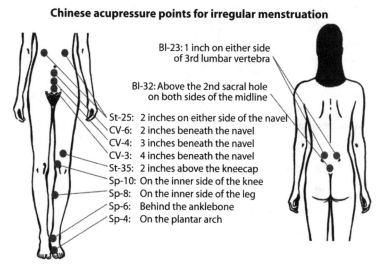

Bl-23: 1 inch on either side of 3rd lumbar vertebra

Bl-32: Above the 2nd sacral hole on both sides of the midline

St-25: 2 inches on either side of the navel
CV-6: 2 inches beneath the navel
CV-4: 3 inches beneath the navel
CV-3: 4 inches beneath the navel
St-35: 2 inches above the kneecap
Sp-10: On the inner side of the knee
Sp-8: On the inner side of the leg
Sp-6: Behind the anklebone
Sp-4: On the plantar arch

ently as fit as a fiddle. I suggested the following treatment, and her 28-day cycle was once again intact within three months.

Treatment Instructions for Irregular Menstruation

A	B	C	D
Sp-4	CV-3	St-25	Bl-23
Sp-6	CV-4	St-33	Bl-32
Sp-8			
Sp-10			

DYSMENORRHEA (PAINFUL MENSTRUATION)

Painful menstrual periods or dysmenorrhea can have many causes. Juliane, a teenager, had pain that began with cramps in the lower abdomen. Shortly before the start of her period, the pain radiated as far as her back and into her thighs. She had suffered from this condition since the start of her periods at the age of 14 years. A medical examination revealed nothing except the fact that she was no longer a virgin but there was no evidence of an organic disorder. I told her parents that dysmenorrhea usually disappears at latest when a girl has her first child.

In the meantime, for the treatment of this painful menstrual problem, I suggested an approach called tong fing by the Chinese. After this treatment, the pain did not return.

Treatment Instructions for Dysmenorrhea

A	B	C	D	E	F	G
He-5	St-24	Li-8	CV-4	Bl-23	Sp-9	GV-12
St-25		Li-13	CV-6	Bl-31	Sp-10	
St-44		Li-14		Bl-17	Sp-12	
				Bl-62		

Supplemental Measures

1. Physical Therapy:

- Massage all the muscles of the lower back
- Apply packs to the lumbar and sacral area, as well as a hot-water bottle on the lower abdomen
- Warm foot bath

Chinese acupressure points for dysmenorrhea

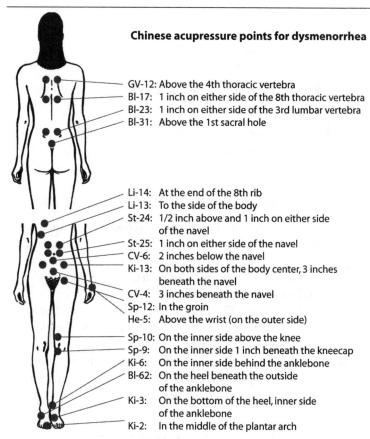

GV-12: Above the 4th thoracic vertebra
Bl-17: 1 inch on either side of the 8th thoracic vertebra
Bl-23: 1 inch on either side of the 3rd lumbar vertebra
Bl-31: Above the 1st sacral hole

Li-14: At the end of the 8th rib
Li-13: To the side of the body
St-24: 1/2 inch above and 1 inch on either side of the navel
St-25: 1 inch on either side of the navel
CV-6: 2 inches below the navel
Ki-13: On both sides of the body center, 3 inches beneath the navel
CV-4: 3 inches beneath the navel
Sp-12: In the groin
He-5: Above the wrist (on the outer side)

Sp-10: On the inner side above the knee
Sp-9: On the inner side 1 inch beneath the kneecap
Ki-6: On the inner side behind the anklebone
Bl-62: On the heel beneath the outside of the anklebone
Ki-3: On the bottom of the heel, inner side of the anklebone
Ki-2: In the middle of the plantar arch

2. Diet

🌞 Nourishing food with extra vitamin E

3. Exercises

🌞 Daily walks between periods

🌞 Rest in bed during periods

4. Avoid:

🌞 Hypothermia

🌞 Sexual excesses

🌞 Belts and pants that are too tight, skimpy skirts

🌞 Exhaustion and nervous tension

5. Important Points:

If acupressure does not bring relief, then you are either treating the wrong acupuncture points or

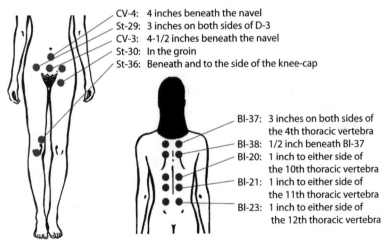 The ovaries are affected if the pain occurs even before the period starts.

There could be a disorder of the uterus if the pain begins with the period.

AMENORRHEA (ABSENCE OF MENSTRUATION)

Amenorrhea is the term for the complete absence of menstrual bleeding. In most of the related cases, the bladder meridian is damaged. In Western medicine, the absence of menstruation before menopause is ascribed to a hormonal deficiency. An underdeveloped uterus, ovarian failure, and disorders of the thyroid gland are considered the triggering factors for this condition. The pituitary gland and the adrenals may also play a role here. Malnutrition, organic diseases, obesity, and diabetes are also considered possible causes.

Western medicine usually uses "pellet" therapy, administering various hormones in the hopes that one of them will be effective. However, Chinese acupuncture takes a more specific approach

Chinese acupressure points for amenorrhea

CV-4:   4 inches beneath the navel
St-29: 3 inches on both sides of D-3
CV-3:   4-1/2 inches beneath the navel
St-30: In the groin
St-36: Beneath and to the side of the knee-cap

Bl-37: 3 inches on both sides of the 4th thoracic vertebra
Bl-38: 1/2 inch beneath Bl-37
Bl-20: 1 inch to either side of the 10th thoracic vertebra
Bl-21: 1 inch to either side of the 11th thoracic vertebra
Bl-23: 1 inch to either side of the 12th thoracic vertebra

Treatment Instructions for Amenorrhea

A	B	C	D
Bl-20	CV-3	Sp-6	St-29
Bl-21	CV-4		St-30
Bl-23			St-36
Bl-37			
Bl-38			

Supplementary Measures

1.   **Physical Therapy:**

 Massage lower back to relax all the muscles. They should be completely relaxed. This also influences all of the Chinese meridians that are related to the pelvic area.

 Daily warm packs in the lower back, lumbar and sacral area.

 Warm vaginal douches at a temperature of 90° F for 5 minutes

2. Contra-indications:

 Do not overwork

 Avoid cold and wet conditions

 Don't let your condition get you down. Eat well, get enough sleep, and take walks.

LEUCORRHEA (THE WHITES)

Leucorrhea, dai xai in Chinese, is also called the "white flow" and refers to the non-bloody discharge from the vagina. This condition is extremely bothersome for a woman and is normally caused by a vaginal or cervical infection. Many factors can reduce these organs' powers of resistance so that fungus, bacteria, or protozoa may penetrate them.

A patient called Karin M., said that she has been suffering from discharge since her childhood. Her underwear had been soiled as far back as she could remember and her vagina was swollen red and sticky. When she married, she infected her husband. This is why she came to see me. After all the laboratory tests and examinations had resulted in negative findings, we began with the Chinese therapy. The following acupuncture points helped cure the affliction:

129

Chinese acupressure points for leucorrhea

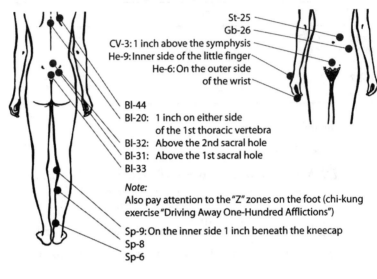

St-25
Gb-26
CV-3: 1 inch above the symphysis
He-9: Inner side of the little finger
He-6: On the outer side
of the wrist

Bl-44
Bl-20: 1 inch on either side
of the 1st thoracic vertebra
Bl-32: Above the 2nd sacral hole
Bl-31: Above the 1st sacral hole
Bl-33

Note:
Also pay attention to the "Z" zones on the foot (chi-kung
exercise "Driving Away One-Hundred Afflictions")

Sp-9: On the inner side 1 inch beneath the kneecap
Sp-8
Sp-6

Treatment Instructions for Leucorrhea

A	B	C	D	E	F	G
Bl-20	Gb-26	St-25	CV-3	Sp-6	He-6	All
Bl-23				Sp-8	He-9	"Z Zones"
Bl-27				Sp-9		on the
Bl-31						foot
Bl-32						
Bl-33						
Bl-44						

Supplementary Measures

1. Physical Therapy:

- Cold packs for 30 minutes daily from the middle of the back to the end of the spinal column

- Massage to relax all of the back muscles

- Much rest

- Only shower briefly for cleansing purposes

2. Contra-indications:

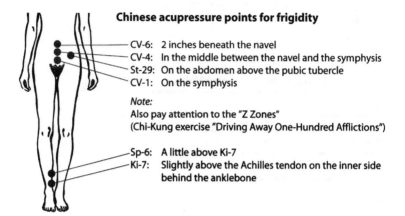

🟢 Don't overexert yourself

🟢 Don't get excited about every little thing

FRIGIDITY

Chinese acupressure points for frigidity

CV-6: 2 inches beneath the navel
CV-4: In the middle between the navel and the symphysis
St-29: On the abdomen above the pubic tubercle
CV-1: On the symphysis

Note:
Also pay attention to the "Z Zones"
(Chi-Kung exercise "Driving Away One-Hundred Afflictions")

Sp-6: A little above Ki-7
Ki-7: Slightly above the Achilles tendon on the inner side behind the anklebone

Treatment Instructions for Frigidity

A	B	C	D	E
Ki-7	St-29	St-1 St-6	CV-4	Sp-6

PRURITUS VULVAE
(ITCHING OF THE OUTER PUDENDA)

Pruritus vulvae is a tormenting itching of the entrance to the vagina. This bothersome affliction is called yin yang in Chinese. The cause for it is often as difficult to discover as the necessary treatment.

Melanie M. had suffered for months from this stubborn itching, and it became so severe that she almost couldn't stand it anymore. When she called me, she was crying. She said that the itching was so intense that she couldn't even hold back urine anymore and had to change her underwear six times a day. Since she had already visited all of the physicians in the city and tried everything recommended to her, I suggested that we use acupressure. The following treatment was effective:

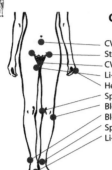

Chinese acupressure points for pruritus vulvae

CV-3: 4 inches beneath the navel
St-30: 3 inches on both sides of the symphysis
CV-1: On the symphysis
Li-11: At the top of the thigh
He-8: On the tissue between the 4th and 5th finger
Sp-10: On the inner side of the knee joint
Bl-54: Beneath the hollow of the knee
Bl-60: On the outer side behind the anklebone
Sp-6: On the inner side behind the anklebone
Li-2: On the tissue between the 1st and 2nd toe

Treatment Instructions for Pruritus Vulvae

A	B	C	D	E	F	G
Sp-6	Li-2	Bl-54	CV-1	St-30	GV-1	He-8
Sp-10	Li-11	Bl-60	CV-3			

Supplementary Measures

1. Physical Therapy

Ice pack above the sacrum for one hour every day

Massage and relax all of the muscles in the lower back three times a week.

2. Pay attention to hygiene.

CYSTITIS (INFLAMMATION OF THE BLADDER)

Cystitis is an inflammation of the urinary bladder that is caused by bacteria or toxic metabolic products, medication, food, or a direct injury. An inflammation of the bladder can occur in an acute or chronic form. In the acute form, urination may be painful and there may be a continual desire to urinate with a constant, involuntary leakage of urine. In the chronic form, urinating is also frequently accompanied by a burning sensation and pain. Pus can often be found in the urine as well.

A policewoman with this affliction came to see me. She asked many questions, but would not listen to my answers. I explained to her how infections can reach the bladder through the urethra: They can descend into the bladder through the ureter from the kidneys or neighboring organs; that there are many different causes, none of which are very simple and that the pain may precede, accompany, or follow urination in the case of cystitis.

The woman explained that urination always ends for her with a series of painful cramps, that she sometimes feels a constant pain deep within her pelvis, and that this pain sometimes radiates upward into her abdomen and sometimes downward into her thighs. In addition to pus, she also found blood in her urine. She said that the bleeding occurred at the end of urination. A medical examination and additional tests did not find anything.

When I asked her about her lifestyle, it turned out that she was learning karate. She remembered that she had once been hit "deep in the belly." Here is the acupressure program that I gave her:

Chinese acupressure points for cystitis

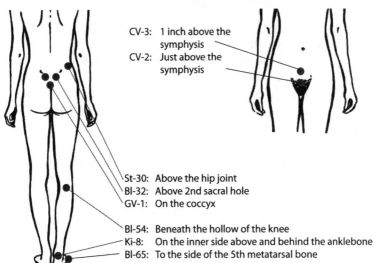

CV-3: 1 inch above the symphysis
CV-2: Just above the symphysis

St-30: Above the hip joint
Bl-32: Above 2nd sacral hole
GV-1: On the coccyx

Bl-54: Beneath the hollow of the knee
Ki-8: On the inner side above and behind the anklebone
Bl-65: To the side of the 5th metatarsal bone

Treatment Instructions for Cystitis

A	B	C	D	E	F	G
CV-2	Bl-32	GV-1	Ki-8	St-30		
CV-3	Bl-54					
	Bl-65					

Supplementary Measures

1. Physical Therapy:

 Rest in bed with hips elevated

 Cold packs on the lumbar and sacral area. If, in connection with acupressure, this does not bring relief, then use an ice-water enema followed by hot packs on the bladder.

2. Diet:

 Light meals only (soups)

 Drink plenty of water. Peppermint tea is also excellent as a therapy measure.

MENOPAUSAL COMPLAINTS

Menopause—called yin lian in Chinese—is the time in the life of a woman when her ability to conceive ceases. Even though the change of life is a normal consequence of aging, this is not expressed in the same way for all women. Some women hardly notice the related change, while others go through hell and also let the people around them suffer as well. Then there are those who remain sexually active up into ripe old age and can even give birth to children, to everyone's astonishment.

Normally, the ovaries stop producing viable eggs somewhere between the 45th and 50th year of life. Menstruation becomes irregular at this time. All types of complaints occur because of the hormonal imbalance, which is caused by instability of the autonomic nervous system. When the loss of ovarian functioning occurs slowly, a woman may not notice any of the symptoms caused menopause. But when these functions stop suddenly, the symptoms of menopause are intense and troublesome: hot flashes, shivering, increased irritability, unfounded rage, crying fits, depression, forgetfulness, fatigue, dizziness, headaches, tingling in the limbs, joint pain, backaches, sweating, heart palpitations, urinary irregularity, abdominal complaints—a multitude of complaints that torment a woman because the ductless glands (thyroid, adrenal, pituitary, and ovaries) are functioning insufficiently.

The autonomic nervous system that controls these glands is beneficially influenced by acupuncture and acupressure. So these are appropriate methods for treating these complaints, which give so many women such unpleasant moments in their lives.

Case History

Johanna K. had remained single and dedicated herself to taking care of her mother and handicapped sister. Time and again, she suffered from irregular menstruation, hot flashes and chills, dizziness, tingling in the limbs, heart palpitations, and a frequent urge to urinate. She had it all—a true string of complaints caused by aging, many signs and symptoms that needed to be thoroughly examined by a physician because the same complaints are all too frequently based on organic and/or physical ailments.

After a thorough examination, I told her that I was not absolutely sure about the diagnosis. Since she had already endured a massive treatment with estrogen, which only brought her temporary relief, I thought it was best to try acupressure on her. We applied the acupressure and also treated the reflex zones on her feet. One week later, she came back to see me. I was astonished. The small, slightly bent woman who I had met one week before was totally transformed. She stood upright, her shoulders were straight, and she proudly stretched out her chest. She beamed. I couldn't believe my eyes, but it actually was her. She reported that she now slept soundly every night, which hadn't happened for months. She also no longer suffered from hot flashes and chills.

"I feel like I've started to live again," she said. The acupressure had apparently changed the course of her life because she met the man of her dreams six months later and married him after a year.

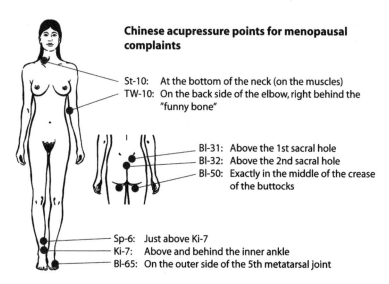

Chinese acupressure points for menopausal complaints

St-10: At the bottom of the neck (on the muscles)
TW-10: On the back side of the elbow, right behind the "funny bone"

Bl-31: Above the 1st sacral hole
Bl-32: Above the 2nd sacral hole
Bl-50: Exactly in the middle of the crease of the buttocks

Sp-6: Just above Ki-7
Ki-7: Above and behind the inner ankle
Bl-65: On the outer side of the 5th metatarsal joint

135

Treatment Instructions for Menopausal Complaints

A	B	C	D	E	F
Sp-6	Bl-31 Bl-32 Bl-50 Bl-65	St-10	Ki-7	TW-10	"Z Zones" (for ovaries, pituitary gland, and thyroid gland) on the foot

TAO CHI KUNG:
TRADITIONAL CHINESE MEDICINE
FOR HEALTH AND LONGEVITY

Chi Kung Health Exercises for Increasing
Sexual Performance, Based on Thousands of Years
of Taoist Tradition

The "Yellow Emperor" Fu Shi
Founder of Traditional Taoist Medicine

INTRODUCTION TO THE SHEN-SHOU TEXT

The Oldest Chi Kung Text
on the Ancient Chinese Diagnosis and
Therapy Procedure of Taoist Medicine

At an archeological site in China, the oldest document to date on the therapy forms of Taoist chi kung was recently discovered: a rectangular jade stone with twelve side surfaces on which an inscription has been scratched. . According to the opinion of the archeologists, this jade stone comes from the "first half of the epoch of the Fighting Kingdom" (475-221 B.C.) and can be dated back to the year 380 B.C., which means that the jade stone is 2,300 years old. The original is now in the municipal museum Tientsin.

However, the inscription, which is called the "Shen-Shou Text," may even be much older. It may therefore be possible that the jade stone is older than 3000 years and originated in the Spring and Autumn Period (770-476 B.C.) In any case, this is the oldest known text about physical chi kung therapy anywhere in the world, not only in China.

There is a very clear relationship between this ancient text and the numerous schools and theories of the chi kung exercises, which can look back on more than 8,000 years of living Taoist tradition. Even a turtle shell with eight trigrams on its back that was found on the boundary between China and Russia, which archeologists and other scientists estimate to be between 3,000 and 5,000 years old, does not shed any doubt on the dating of this Taoist cultural asset.

The text on the twelve side surfaces of the original jade stone has three characters in seal-script on each side. However, since nine of the characters appear doubled, this makes a total of 45 characters (45 = 9 cycles with 5 respective phases of change). These describe how to achieve a high goal by means of the Taoist chi kung exercises for prevention, diagnosis, therapy, and rehabilitation.

The poet, scholar, and statesman Kuo Mojo (1892-1978) recorded and explained the dialectic development of the ancient characters in a text version. The verbatim translation by the sinologist Helmut Wilhelm is based on this version:

This is how to do Taoist chi kung breathing:
Hold the breath and it will be gathered.
When it has been gathered, it will expand.
Once it has expanded, it will move downward.
Once it goes downward, it will be still.
Once it is still, it will be strengthened.
Once it is strengthened, it will sprout.
Once it has sprouted, it will grow.
Once it grows, it will be drawn back upward.
Once it has been drawn back upward, it will reach the crown of the head
At the crown of the head it pushes against it and the heavenly force throbs upward.
At the lowest point, the breath pushes against the bottom and the earthly force throbs downward.
Whoever follows this breathing rhythm will live eternally.
Whoever acts in opposition to this breathing rhythm will die.

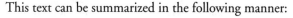

This text can be summarized in the following manner:

- During chi kung breathing—which can be done while standing, laying down, or sitting—the chi in the body goes through one complete cycle.

- During the exercise of the chi kung, we deeply inhale "pure chi" (ching chi = "pure energy") through the nose. In this way, much more chi = tsung chi (energy) can gather at the center of the chest in the shan = chung (thymus gland) point.

- When enough tsung chi has gathered here, then it can extend downward into the body and descend to the center, the lower Dantien.

- Once it has arrived here, the breath and chi is held very lightly; in this way, some of the chi is kept in the lower Dantien.

- This makes it possible for the life essence (ching chi) to gather and concentrate on its own. During this transformation process, impure chi (chou chi) is also created, which is then sent back to the lungs and gradually leaves the body again.

- At the same time, the remaining life essence flows to the "gate of life," the ming-men point on the spinal column across from the lower Dantien, so that an energy reserve for all parts of the body can gather here.

As soon as the impure chi is exhaled, the life essence shows a corresponding blossoming and activity in the organism. Because the spiritual energy (shen chi) of the human being is decisively dependent on an adequate supply of life essence, it can rise alone to the crown of the head (bai-hui), while the impure chi is discharged and the life essence enriched.

This explanation of the first "nine sentences of the inscription" describes how the chi passes through the body during respiration in one complete energy cycle, the so-called major energy cycle. The text is based on the medical theory of Huang Ti Nei Ching.

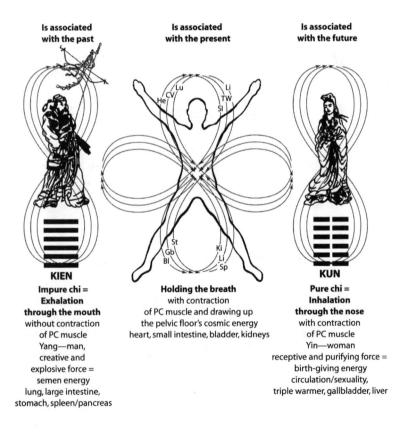

Is associated with the past	**Is associated with the present**	**Is associated with the future**
KIEN		**KUN**
Impure chi =	**Holding the breath**	**Pure chi =**
Exhalation	with contraction	**Inhalation**
through the mouth	of PC muscle and drawing up	**through the nose**
without contraction	the pelvic floor's cosmic energy	with contraction
of PC muscle	heart, small intestine, bladder, kidneys	of PC muscle
Yang—man,		Yin—woman
creative and		receptive and purifying force =
explosive force =		birth-giving energy
semen energy		circulation/sexuality,
lung, large intestine,		triple warmer, gallbladder, liver
stomach, spleen/pancreas		

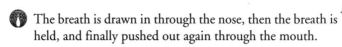 The breath is drawn in through the nose, then the breath is held, and finally pushed out again through the mouth.

The chi energy of the earth turns in a clockwise direction from right to left and is called late-term birth energy.

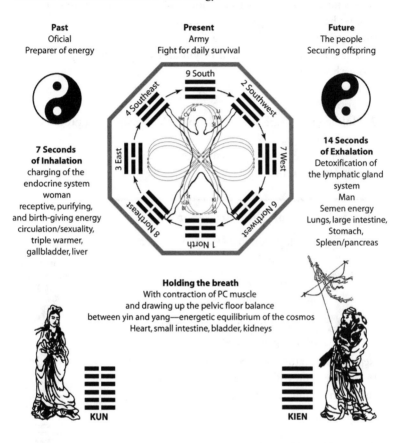

Past
Oficial
Preparer of energy

Present
Army
Fight for daily survival

Future
The people
Securing offspring

7 Seconds of Inhalation
charging of the endocrine system
woman
receptive, purifying, and birth-giving energy
circulation/sexuality, triple warmer, gallbladder, liver

14 Seconds of Exhalation
Detoxification of the lymphatic gland system
Man
Semen energy
Lungs, large intestine, Stomach, Spleen/pancreas

Holding the breath
With contraction of PC muscle
and drawing up the pelvic floor balance
between yin and yang—energetic equilibrium of the cosmos
Heart, small intestine, bladder, kidneys

KUN

KIEN

The Taoist secret of cosmic breathing:
- Inhale through the nose for 7 seconds with contraction of PC muscle.
- Hold breath for 21 seconds while continuing contraction of PC muscle.
- Exhale through the mouth for 14 seconds while relaxing PC muscle.

Repeat this exercise 9 times in a row. This is the Taoist secret of cosmic breathing.

RELAXING AND ENERGY-INCREASING BREATHING EXERCISES

The human source of energy is an "ion-generator" that produces both positive and negative ions. Maintaining our inner harmony and peace is dependent upon a balanced amount of ion production since disharmonies have a very negative effect on us. We can influence this process through yin and yang breathing.

The control and regulation of yin and yang energy depends upon proper breathing:

1. Deep or long inhalation through the nose creates yang energy (activation).

2 Holding the breath balances both of these energy and promotes the renewal of cells.

3. Powerful or extended exhalation through the mouth creates yin energy (relaxation).

How to Breathe for Quick Relaxation (Yin Energy):

 Inhale through the nose for 5 seconds (activation).

 Hold the breath for 10 seconds (balancing of energies).

 Exhale through the mouth for 15 seconds (spent energy).

Repeat this breathing procedure for a total of 9 times. In this way, you will be able to behave in a positive and calm manner in even the most difficult situation.

Mother energy = yin energy of inhaling and holding the breath (earth)

The energy source of our breath consists of

KUN

Yin energy: deep, long exhalation = deep, quiet, calming, and receptive. The parasympathetic nervous system stimulates the yin energy, which produces negative ions and nerve impulses. The result is lowering of the blood pressure, slowing down the breath and heart rate, and decreasing the libido.

An excess of yin energy, the "breathing of the scholars," leads to an increased need for sleep, depression, sadness, weakness, diminished drive, and lack of exercise.

How to Breathe for Quick Activation (Yang Energy):

 Inhale through the nose for 15 seconds (creates energy)..

 Hold the breath for 10 seconds (balancing of energies).

 Exhale through the mouth for 5 seconds (spent energy).

Repeat this breathing procedure for a total of 9 times. This will quickly make new energy available to you in critical situations.

Father energy =
yang energy
of exhalation and
relaxation
(heaven)

KIEN

The energy source of our breathing consists of

Yang energy: deep, long inhalation = Positive, stimulating, motivating, and receptive. The sympathetic nervous system activates the yang energy. It increases the breath and heart rate, the blood pressure, sexuality, and produces positive ions.

An excess of yang energy, the "breathing of the warriors," creates high blood pressure, stress situations, and increased states of tension, as well as intense unrest.

Powerful, extended inhalation increases the desire for or focuses on orgasm while deep, prolonged exhalation reduces the desire or delays the orgasm.

The Yin and Yang Breathing Points on the Meridians

The yin breathing of the scholars

▼

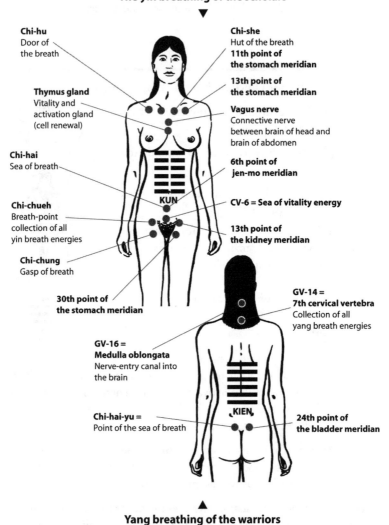

Chi-hu
Door of
the breath

Thymus gland
Vitality and
activation gland
(cell renewal)

Chi-hai
Sea of breath

Chi-chueh
Breath-point
collection of all
yin breath energies

Chi-chung
Gasp of breath

**30th point of
the stomach meridian**

Chi-she
Hut of the breath
**11th point of
the stomach meridian**

**13th point of
the stomach meridian**

Vagus nerve
Connective nerve
between brain of head and
brain of abdomen

**6th point of
jen-mo meridian**

CV-6 = Sea of vitality energy

**13th point of
the kidney meridian**

KUN

KIEN

**GV-14 =
7th cervical vertebra**
Collection of all
yang breath energies

**GV-16 =
Medulla oblongata**
Nerve-entry canal into
the brain

Chi-hai-yu =
Point of the sea of breath

**24th point of
the bladder meridian**

▲
Yang breathing of the warriors

The yin and yang breath points on the acupuncture meridians serve to detoxify the lungs, liver, kidneys, nerves, and system of lymphatic glands. They are stimulated by the yin and yang breathing described above. The Chinese-Taoist terms indicate the relationships with the activity of breathing.

144

THE TECHNIQUE OF TAOIST CHI KUNG BREATHING

In an ancient Taoist medical text, this breathing technique was described as follows:

 Inhale once through the nose:

After inhaling pure chi through the nose, direct it to the lower Dantien (one hand's width beneath the navel) with the help of the eyes and saliva and hold this pure inhaled energy somewhat firmly here.

 By now slightly tensing the PC muscle and drawing up the pelvic floor, use the power of visualization to let the chi rise through the governor meridian along the back from the coccyx (lower door) through the middle door and through the jade pillow (upper door = back of the head) to nao-kung, the Palace of the Brain. Hold your breath while doing this.

 Now exhale through your mouth.

If you practice this in the early morning every day between 5 and 7 a.m. and in the late evening between 11 p.m. and 1 a.m. for 30 minutes at a time, your life force (ching shen) will become strong and flourishing, making it impossible for the "one-hundred afflictions" to develop.

This is nothing other than the cosmic energy cycle—the "immortal breath" (Deer, Crane, and Turtle), as it is mastered today by only a few chi kung masters. On the whole, the "five characters" on the ancient jade stone mentioned above represent the technique of breathing:
1. Inhaling
2. Holding the breath and allowing it to collect
3. Extending the breath and allowing it to move downward
4. Being calm
5. Slowly exhaling again.

The five special characteristics of Taoist chi kung breathing:
1. hsi = inhaling: inhale through the nose and hold the breath; place the tongue on the gums.
2. tso = tensing: tense the PC muscle (pelvic floor) and draw it upward.
3. pi = closing: close the eyes and turn them upward.
4. ti = laying on: lay the tip of your tongue on the front gums.
5. shu = exhaling: place the tongue behind the lower row of teeth.

Exact Details of Exercise:

1. After you inhale through the nose, the chi runs through the conception vessel and then flows over the tensed pelvic floor to the coccyx (lower door). "Driven by the power of the imagination," it slowly rises to the middle door and gradually accelerates.

2. When you close your eyes and turn them upward, continuing to inhale through your nose and not breathe deeply. The chi will then penetrate the jade pillow (upper door). Turn your eyes to the front again.

3. The chi now circles through the kun (skull cap) and flows down over the Magpie Bridge (tongue). Now swallow your saliva several times, always in small portions, so that the chi can enter the Purple Palace (the heart) and return to the Sea of Chi (the chi-hai point) at the center in the lower Dantien (one hand's width beneath the navel).

4. Briefly hold your breath there.

5. Then exhale through your mouth and the lower Dantien.

6. When finished, repeat the breathing cycle 8 more times.

POSTURE DURING TAOIST CHI KUNG BREATHING

Why was the oldest known chi kung inscription scratched in the sides of a jade stone that looks like a square column of jade? According to the ancient Taoist perspective, this symbolizes that it is always best to do the chi kung therapy for both prevention and rehabilitation while standing.

When performing the chi kung exercises in a standing position, the human being should look like a heavenly column and stand like a tree, which is also called the "standing brother to the human being," according to the jade inscription. The position is stretched upright, with the chi dropped to the center (lower Dantien). The head should not hang downward since the House of Growth (thyroid gland), pituitary gland, and pineal gland would otherwise be blocked. Both legs should be deeply rooted as if they had grown nine yards deep into the earth, like the deep roots of a large tree. This position of standing between heaven and earth, like columns of jade that support the heavens, leads to rejuvenation and rebirth, according to another section of the jade inscription.

This is the only way for the person practicing chi kung to follow the law of heaven, human being, and earth. This starting position also promotes the circulation of the inner chi so that even the smallest inner source of the body can be provided with chi energy.

With its unusually original and artistic inspiration, the symbol of the "square column of jade" proves how important knowledge—in this case, about sexual energies—can be passed on to future generations in an encoded form. The character chung (threshing) also appears in both of the above sentences of the jade inscription. This may also be the ancient Chinese way of writing chuang (post or pole), which in Chinese means chan chuan (standing pole): standing like a pole, standing in the rider's seat. This is a special reference to the effectiveness of the traditional chi kung therapy of standing at shoulder's width.

Let's take a closer look at the two last sentences of the Taoist inscription:

🔘 Whoever follows this breathing rhythm will live eternally.

🔘 Whoever acts in opposition to this breathing rhythm will die.

The following analogies can be used to explain these statements:
1. Heaven is in harmony with the human being, the human being is oriented toward the sky and its eight directions (feng shui).
2. When we consider the concurrent and contrary movements of heaven and earth, we recognize the decline and flourishing of the human being in his environment when he lets his movements (vibrations) take their own free course.
3. The human being has one-hundred afflictions and these diseases have one-hundred symptoms; in turn, these are created from yin and yang, the movement of heaven and earth.
4. The five storage organs of the liver, spleen, lungs, kidneys, and heart/circulation/sexuality are associated with the yin energy.
5. The six hollow organs of the small intestine, gallbladder, stomach, large intestine, bladder, and triple warmer are associated with the yang energy.
6. If the human being follows the natural movement of heaven and earth, he will grow and thrive (wood) in the emotional/mental and physical sense.
7. If the human being resists the natural cycle of heaven and earth, he will be burned like wood by the fire of energy.

8. Only when both forces harmonize with each other can they each live eternally because "water carries wood" and "wood nourishes the fire," etc.

The yin and yang of heaven and earth and the cycle of the five phases of change nourish the human being. When we practice chi kung, we can go beyond the law of yin and yang, striving for the secret forces of heaven and earth, and joyfully adapt to the cycle of the five phases of change: wood, fire, earth, metal, and water.

The following explanation is given in the essay on the cycle of cold and heat:

Whoever follows the natural cycle of change related to cold and heat will live a long life. Whoever does not follow the natural change of cold and heat will die. All of these recommendations completely agree with the two closing sentences of the jade inscription, which explain the forces of heaven (yang) and earth (yin). Moreover, this continually refers to one of the two directions of movement of the chi energy circulation, which is created through the yin and yang breathing.

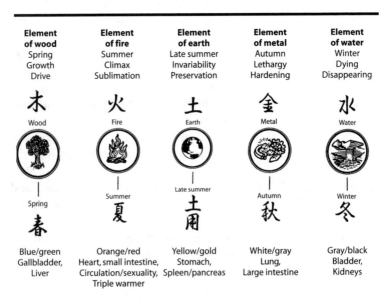

The five phases of change and their characteristics

When the chi flows properly and unimpeded (shun), then the ching, which is the semen essence (masculine energy) thrives, as well as the shen, the spiritual energy (feminine energy). This means that the life force of the human being is in full bloom.

However, when chi flows in the contrary direction, the essence of the ching becomes exhausted and there is also a lack of spiritual energy. These are signs of decline and death.

The jade inscription explains how beneficial chi kung exercises are for charging the electromagnetic energy of ching, chi, and shen—the three Taoist treasures of health, strength, vitality, endurance, and longevity. At the same time, the ancient Chinese inscription emphasizes that we should always follow Mother Nature when doing the chi kung exercises. We should adapt to the circumstances like the incessant change of yin and yang, heaven and earth, sun and moon and take the cyclic phases of change into consideration during nature's seasons.

THE THREE CONSTANTLY PRESENT TREASURES OF LIFE AND ACTION

There are three wonderful energies, born "of the Tao," the ceaseless growth of nature, which penetrate the unlimited and all-encompassing cosmos:

1. The ching essence
2. The chi life energy
3. The shen spiritual energy

All three of these are the life-giving force with which the Tao nourishes the universe. They cause the creation of being at the center of the boundless nothingness, as well as the "ascent and fall of the myriads," which form the realm of manifestations.

In their subtle cosmic or original "form," these three life-giving, energetic forces are pure and holy, the true source of light and life. They bring forth this creative force in wonderful variations. Only an enlightened sage can appreciate their immaculate perfection. Like everything else, the human being is equipped with a basic supply of these three wonderful treasures—ching, chi, and shen. They have their seat in the sacrum, the command headquarters for all physical and mental movements. Because of the effects of uncontrolled lifestyles, they are in a coarse form in human beings and require refinement by means of the Taoist chi kung exercises in order to restore their original purity. We can also understand the meaning of "secret Taoist alchemy" as a result of this explanation. Although the goal is identical with what the Buddhists call the achievement of enlightenment, the path there is distinctly Taoist.

While these energies of ching, chi, and shen are too subtle to easily be noticed in their pure cosmic and invisible form—except in the changes that they cause—they are present in the human body to a considerable degree. If they are nourished, maintained and strengthened, increased and transformed, they support the achievement of those immense physical and spiritual riches that initiates strive for during an entire lifetime.

The Taoist chi kung system of ching, chi, and shen is the archetype and source of all chi kung systems and the ancient Chinese method of diagnosis and therapy. These exercise forms for the seven glands, which kindle and sustain the fire of life, are the actual core of Taoism's spiritual efforts and the practices and rites of chi kung. As a result, the Taoist chi kung exercises:

- Refine and transform the ching, chi, and shen in order to achieve and increase health, strength, vitality and longevity on all three levels.

- Increase and purify the natural treasures of the mind and body.

This secret process of "constantly occurring rejuvenation" has been misunderstood as something completely different by the uninitiated. In ancient times, this resulted in the widespread opinion that Taoist masters were nothing other than alchemists who strove to achieve immortality—similar to the attempt of transforming base metals into gold.

BODY-MIND-SOUL:
THE THREE-DIMENSIONAL HUMAN BEING

The ancient Taoist sages supported the viewpoint that:

- The seat of the heavenly force (tien chi) is in the head
- The seat of the kidney force is in the sacrum
- The seat of the earth force (ti chi) is in the feet

The Taoist system of chi energy and the cyclic recurrent movements of nature

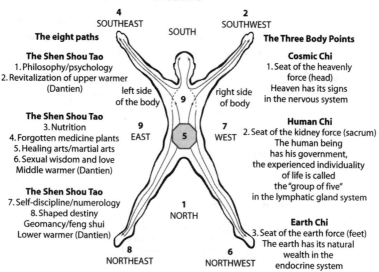

The eight paths

The Shen Shou Tao
1. Philosophy/psychology
2. Revitalization of upper warmer (Dantien)

The Shen Shou Tao
3. Nutrition
4. Forgotten medicine plants
5. Healing arts/martial arts
6. Sexual wisdom and love Middle warmer (Dantien)

The Shen Shou Tao
7. Self-discipline/numerology
8. Shaped destiny Geomancy/feng shui Lower warmer (Dantien)

The Three Body Points

Cosmic Chi
1. Seat of the heavenly force (head) Heaven has its signs in the nervous system

Human Chi
2. Seat of the kidney force (sacrum) The human being has his government, the experienced individuality of life is called the "group of five" in the lymphatic gland system

Earth Chi
3. Seat of the earth force (feet) The earth has its natural wealth in the endocrine system

Diagram labels: 4 SOUTHEAST, 2 SOUTHWEST, SOUTH, left side of the body, right side of body, 9, 9 EAST, 5, 7 WEST, 1 NORTH, 8 NORTHEAST, 6 NORTHWEST

This Taoist teaching also differentiates between the three levels of life. According to the energy components, they are classified as follows:

- **Human being** = a vegetative and sensitive (animalistic) and rational soul; living chi, feeling chi, and thinking chi.

- **Animal** = a vegetative and animalistic soul; living and feeling chi.

- **Plant** = a vegetative soul; living chi.

- **Non-living substances** = possess only material chi.

THE INNER MERIDIANS

The approximately 3,000 year-old book on the Chinese healing arts entitled "The Inner Meridians" describes how needle-stones, acupressure, and chi kung are suitable for healing health disorders. The following basic rules should be followed in using these methods:

- Stimulation of the organs should be done in a counterclockwise direction = spiral-shaped circles from the outside to the inside; associated with yang.

- Calming of the organs should be done in a clockwise direction = spiral-shaped circles from the inside to the outside; associated with yin.

Position of the meridians on the extremities

The circulation of life energy occurs in three cycles
1st cycle: lung-large intestine-stomach-spleen/pancreas
2nd cycle: heart-small intestine-bladder-kidneys
3rd cycle: circulation/sexuality-triple warmer-gallbladder-liver

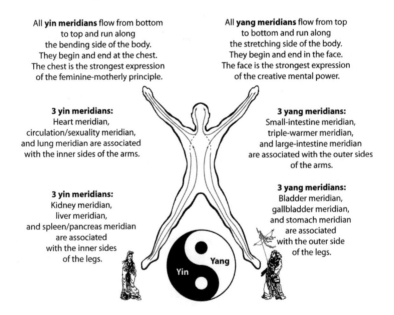

All **yin meridians** flow from bottom to top and run along the bending side of the body. They begin and end at the chest. The chest is the strongest expression of the feminine-motherly principle.

All **yang meridians** flow from top to bottom and run along the stretching side of the body. They begin and end in the face. The face is the strongest expression of the creative mental power.

3 yin meridians:
Heart meridian, circulation/sexuality meridian, and lung meridian are associated with the inner sides of the arms.

3 yang meridians:
Small-intestine meridian, triple-warmer meridian, and large-intestine meridian are associated with the outer sides of the arms.

3 yin meridians:
Kidney meridian, liver meridian, and spleen/pancreas meridian are associated with the inner sides of the legs.

3 yang meridians:
Bladder meridian, gallbladder meridian, and stomach meridian are associated with the outer side of the legs.

152

INTRODUCTION TO THE EIGHT TAOIST
CHI KUNG EXERCISES

The Preface has already referred to the general growing need for suitable therapy and treatments that lastingly increase energy and performance, as well as counteract the development and advancement of health disorders. The value of health, longevity and well-being is playing an increasingly larger role in our society. Consequently, the ancient Chinese wisdom of healing has also become more interesting in the eyes of Western medicine, even though the latter has achieved great progress in the treatment of acute diseases. On the other hand, conventional medicine does not always offer satisfactory treatment possibilities for the growing number of chronic illnesses and functional symptoms. In addition, it is also necessary to offer "preventive medicine" such as that of the ancient Chinese diagnosis and therapy procedure.

This holistically oriented Taoist Medicine is a complementary path that can work together with Western conventional medicine. Its healing procedures are used in a manner that is complementary to conventional medicine and not in competition with it. This makes it possible to help people requiring "rehabilitation" to restore their physical powers in a natural manner. Through these medical-gymnastic methods, the self-healing powers of the respective person are newly activated and holistic healing is initiated from within.

The eight Taoist chi kung exercises are movement and breathing exercises from the ancient Chinese culture of immortality, which had remained largely unknown in the Western world until 1986. These medical-gymnastic activities correspond with the holistic self-healing system of Taoist Medicine. They help us experience our bodies, feel the flow of our energy and bodily fluids, as well as recognize our own capacity. These eight ancient chi kung exercises with their more than 8,000-year history of Taoist wise sayings related to the healing arts and martial arts are the source of Traditional Chinese Medicine (TCM) and its wisdom of life.

Because of the various forms of movement, the newly acquired chi energy or life force can be strengthened with the result of:

- Healing health disorders

- Strengthening the body

- Improving the immune defense

153

- Delaying the aging process
- Prolonging life
- Rejuvenating the organism.

This has corresponding positive effects on the figure and appearance. In addition, chi kung also stimulates latent abilities and develops the self-healing powers of the organism. It leads the body to more strength and vitality, as well as a higher level of performance and better health.

According to statements by Eastern and Western medical professionals, therapeutic chi kung gymnastics are especially effective in the postoperative treatment of ambulatory surgery, orthopedics, and muscular rehabilitation of the entire locomotor system. This Taoist therapy procedure has been shown to achieve a very substantial therapeutic effect of holistic healing and causes no side effects whatsoever.

Wei Zhenren, Immortal of Taoist Medicine
Wei Zhenren, also called Cizang, was a public official during the governing period of Jing-long (707-710) within the Tang Dynasty and responsible for the emperor's meals. He was also an expert in the Taoist art of healing. In the book Xu Shen Xian Zhuan (Continuation of the Biographies of Gods and Immortals), author Shen Fen writes about a Wei Zhenren, who was also called Gudao or Guizang and came from India. In the 25th year of the governing period of Kaiyuan (737), Wei Zhenren came to Chang'an, the capital of the Tang Dynasty, where he provided medical treatment for patients without charge. Others report that Wei Zhenren was also called Shanjun and came from the city of Jingzhao (with the current name of Xian). He is said to have been a Taoist and vegetarian who frequently had a black dog named Malong (horse-dragon) with him. Later generations revered him as an immortal of medicine, and the three traditions of Whei Zhenren flowed together within him. The illustration shows the immortal holding a squash in his left hand and rolling a pill between the fingers of his right hand. Malong is reclining in front of the table.

GENERAL DESCRIPTION OF THE EIGHT TAOIST CHI KUNG EXERCISES

1. Each of the energy exercises should be done according to the number of repetitions stated here. In order to stabilize the success of the exercise, you should not change the number of times it is done because this figure has been determined according to the endocrine cycle of the seven glands.

2. During the course of the exercises and after the exercises, you will feel an influx of energy—a genuine surge of chi energy. The result may sometimes be too much energy, which can lead to nausea when the energy canals of the body are detoxified.

3. Begin each exercise with a long movement rhythm and don't let yourself be distracted by other speed patterns. A calm and slow flow of the movements will guarantee the greatest possible experience of success and the best effects.

4. Always remember that every form of movement begins with inhaling through the nose and ends with exhaling through the mouth. Every movement is a type of number meditation, whereby the repetitions are always counted. So concentrate on every phase of the movement during the course of the exercise. Meditation is the key for achieving the optimal results with these energy exercises. Combine them with the following breathing technique:

    Inhalation = means calm; supply of energy and awakening of the holistic powers of self-healing; energy in a counterclockwise direction.

    Holding the breath = letting the right thing happen; permeation, renewal of cells, and transformation: energy remains in the nervous, lymphatic gland, and endocrine system.

    Exhalation = means relaxation; purification and detoxification of the "seven glands," the nerves, and the lymphatic gland system; energy in a clockwise direction.

5. After completion of the exercise series, you will have an unbelievable amount of sexual energy if you have done the exercises correctly. You will feel just as if you wanted to start making love and felt strongly

stimulated. Through the closing exercise of "Driving Away One-Hundred Afflictions," you will solidify these newly acquired energies so that they can flow through the body. Now they can reactivate afflicted meridians, organs, glands, muscles, etc.

6. As a daily diet, the ancient Taoist chi kung masters recommended the following recipes:

> Mix honey with ghee (clarified butter = melted butter without the foam on top) in equal parts. Take one teaspoon of this mixture every day on an empty stomach in order to supply your inner organs with strength and energy and let your skin glow.

> Mix 1/4 quart of red wine, 2 egg yolks, 1 banana, and 2 tablespoons of honey, hazelnuts, and peeled almonds for two minutes in the blender and drink on Tuesdays and Thursdays before going to bed.

7. Solar substances are the basis of many rejuvenation systems since the sun's energy gives us strength. Modern technology has discovered that one of the foods containing chlorophyll with the most intensive rejuvenating effects is one to two glasses of coach-grass juice every day. The chi kung masters have observed the following effects of this remedy within a six-month period: the hair turned black again, chronic states of pain disappeared, and energy and vitality increased to an astonishing degree. The healing of wounds also took place at a much quicker rate and regenerative diseases were reversed. We recommend that you drink this extremely effective tonic as part of your rejuvenation program.

8. If possible, the exercises should be done in the early morning between 5 and 7 a.m. or in the evening between 11 p.m. and 1 a.m. Avoid sex from 9 p.m. to 11 p.m. since this is the time in which the triple warmer (circulation/sexuality, nervous and lymphatic gland system) is most intensely strained. You can naturally also practice the exercise series in the early morning and late evening, but only advanced students should engage in this intensive stimulation.

9. Never take a cold shower or bath after performing these energy exercises. Water that is too cold will cool the inside of your body and once again close the meridians that have opened. The exercise has

very little effect in this situation. The recommended minimum time to wait before doing this is 45 minutes. The same cautionary measures apply to hot showers and baths, or saunas, since you would just unnecessarily heat up your organism. The result of this would be the intensification of inner adhesions and ulcerations of the vessels and in the connective tissues, resulting in unnecessary strain on the heart and circulation. Also avoid all cold drinks after completing the chi kung gymnastics.

Please observe:

• Never exercise with a full stomach and do not drink during the exercises.

• Lukewarm drinks are generally recommended after the exercises—no coffee or coke. The ideal beverages are apple juice mixed with sparkling water, red wine mixed with sparkling water, or a glass of champagne. Please don't drink white wine, beer, or schnapps!

• Drink teas without added aromas or fruit juice mixed with warm water (1/3 juice and 2/3 warm water). The following herbal mixture is highly recommended: 1 tablespoon each of St. John's wort, white hawthorn, balm mint, and mallow blossoms. Let this tea mixture brew for ten minutes after boiling slightly and drink without any sweetener (exceptions: condensed agave or beekeeper honey).

Important Notes:

1. The length of the exercises and number of repetitions for all Taoist chi kung exercises depends on the age, sex, and constitution of the person performing them.

2. We strongly emphasize that the Taoist chi kung exercises are not intended to replace a physician, medication, or course of treatment. Instead, they are to be understood as therapeutic accompanying measures coordinated with the physician's applications. Chi kung exercises promote the general healing process and serve both prevention and rehabilitation.

3. Exercise only under the direction of an experienced master, chi kung teacher, or therapist who can properly teach you the Taoist chi kung exercises.

THE OPENING EXERCISE:
"FANNING THE FIRE IN THE STOVE"

STRETCHING THE SPINAL COLUMN AND THE TRUNK, ACTIVATING THE PELVIS AND THE BLOOD CIRCULATION, HARMONIZING THE SEXUAL ENERGY

Before the ancient Taoist sages began with their exercises, they first warmed up their bodies, set their blood in motion, and prepared all of their organs for the energy exercises.

For this exercise sequence, 81 repetitions are prescribed.

1. Turn in a counter-clockwise direction and exhale through the mouth. Look at your left heel.

2. Return to the starting position, look up, and slowly inhale through the nose until the abdomen curves forward.

3. Turn in a clockwise direction and exhale through the mouth. Look at your right heel.

When turning to the left and right, keep both legs firmly rooted to the ground. Bend the knees slightly, but don't let them move during the course of the exercise.

Exercise Sequence:
1. Point feet slightly inward at shoulder's width. Keep them firmly rooted to the ground and relax knees.
2. Let your body weight rest on the outer edge of the feet with your toes slightly curled.

3. Like the tips of the toes, the slightly bent knees are pointing somewhat inward, which promotes better circulation of the chi. At the same time, the cervical spine, thoracic spine, and lumbar spine, as well as the sacrum and coccyx, are relieved through this posture.
4. Relax the PC muscle during inhalation and tense it during exhalation; stretch the legs.
5. Starting from the hips, turn your upper body from the waist up in a swinging motion from left to right until you see the opposite heel. This pushes the pelvis to one side; the trunk remains upright and does not bend forward or backward.
6. Do the exercises in a gentle and rhythmic manner.

Note: As a warm-up exercise, "Fanning the Fire in the Stove" requires five minutes of your time. You can also do it outside of the established practice periods at any other time of day as an independent exercise if your body feels cramped or tired in order to relax and re-stimulate the circulation of blood and energy.

1ST IN-BETWEEN EXERCISE:
THE MERIDIAN SHAKING EXERCISE FOR THE HANDS

Relaxation Exercise for the Inner Organs and Meridians

"Controlling the Fire in the Stove"

This relaxation exercise should be done after each energy exercise. True relaxation is the state of greatest possible strength since it is natural, healthy, and powerful. However, most people do not know how to genuinely relax.

This exercise, which will be explained and shown here, is truly relaxing and very simple to do. Since this type of relaxation is stable, you can easily check it by pressing on your shoulder or stretching out your arm in this state: It won't let itself be moved or bent. This is the state of greatest possible strength.

When the string of a bow is constantly tensed, it will fail at the point when it is really needed. The human being is just as incapable of developing strength when it is necessary because his muscles are constantly tensed. As a result, people frequently have difficulty in relaxing at work or at home with the family, at seminars or courses, as well as at sporting events, etc.

1. Concentrate on the lower Dantien (one hand's width beneath the navel). Point the feet inward and root them to the ground.

2. Intensely shake the hands for 15 seconds until you can feel the vibrations in your toes (keep your arms stretched and just shake your wrists).

3. Stretch hands in a downward direction and let the spent energy flow off of them (can be felt is tingling in the fingertips). Repeat this shaking one more time for 15 seconds.

Effect

The Meridian Shaking Exercise for the Hands and Arms serves to relax the yin and the yang. This is a Taoist form of meridian relaxation for the central and autonomic nervous system, the endocrine system, and the lymphatic gland system.

2ND IN-BETWEEN EXERCISE: STRETCHING THE ENTIRE BODY

"The Golden Dragon Stretches Well to Distribute the Newly Acquired Chi Energy in the Body."

Stretching the entire body is a very important concluding exercise for the distribution of the newly acquired chi energy in the organism. It should be done after each energy exercise of the medical chi kung system. The proper position for it is with your head facing north and your feet pointing south.

1. In a supine position, inhale through your nose for 5 seconds. Point the tips of your toes toward the sky and raise both arms backward in a large arc. Keep your fingers stretched while you do this. Tense the PC muscle. Inhalation = rest and receiving new energy for the organism.

2. Hold your breath for 10 seconds. Completely stretch legs and fingers. Link the thumbs with each other. Overstretch the tips of the toes. Continue to hold the PC muscle tensed. Holding the breath = balancing of yin and yang energies.

3. Both arms return to the starting position in a large arc. Exhale through the mouth for 15 seconds. Relax the PC muscle while you do this. Exhalation = relaxation and detoxification of the organism.

Repeat this exercise sequence 3 times in a row.

Effect

The Taoist chi kung exercise "The Golden Dragon Stretches Well..."

 Opens the three meridian energy cycles and distributes the newly acquired energy through the

1. Lungs/large intestine, stomach/spleen/pancreas
2. Heart, small intestine, bladder and kidneys
3. Circulation/sexuality, triple warmer, gallbladder and liver

 Activates the endocrine system, lymphatic gland system, and nervous system and relaxes the organism through the stretching effect.

 Breathing instructions can be found under Yin and Yang Breathing (see page 142 f).

GENERAL EXPLANATIONS OF THE OPENING TECHNIQUE

Because of its particularly comprehensive positive effects on the entire spinal column, the lymphatic gland system, and the nervous system, as well as the endocrine system, this exercise has a special position within the eight chi kung diagnosis and therapy procedures of Taoist Medicine. Incidentally, Dr. Nakamura, M.D. from Japan, who is a professor of clinical medicine and physiology and trained in Western medicine, as well as a renowned respiratory specialist and writer of numerous medical books, calls this Taoist Opening Exercise (which is supposedly more than 6,000 years old), the best prevention and rehabilitation measure for the entire organism.

"Fanning the Fire in the Stove" means activating the meridians of the triple warmer so that the three levels of the body can once again be united. This means the three waterways that connect the three parts of the triple warmer with each other.

 Upper warmer = upper Dantien = head area including the throat.

 Middle warmer = middle Dantien = chest area down to the navel

 Lower warmer = lower Dantien = one hand's width beneath the navel.

EXPLANATION OF THE BREATHING TECHNIQUE
FOR THE OPENING EXERCISE

Turn the upper body in a counterclockwise direction on its own axis until you can see the left heel and exhale through your mouth. When you have exhaled completely and reached the maximum degree of twist, inhale through your nose again while you bring your body back to the starting position. Be sure to precisely synchronize your breathing and the movement of the rest of your body. When you have finished inhaling, your body should reach the frontal position again.

Turn the upper body in a clockwise direction on its own axis until you can see the right heel and exhale slowly through your mouth. When you have turned far enough to see your heel again, stop the movement and breathing for a brief pause. Then return your body to the front starting position and slowly inhale through the nose again.

With each exhalation, relax the PC muscle (turning to the back) and tense it during each inhalation.

POSITIVE EFFECTS

During the first turns, you may possibly hear a cracking or crunching sound in your spinal column or neck. This shows that your vertebrae are returning to the proper position since they are frequently displaced from their position during the course of the day. This particularly applies to people who must work continuously in one sitting or standing position.

In addition, these turns stretch and relax the spinal column, which in turn frees the nerves that have been jammed there as a result of muscle tension or lack of exercise. These nerves can cause considerable pain. Important energy channels that run along the spinal column are reopened, which promotes the free flow of the chi energy between the roots of the sacral region and the "blossom of the brain" (pituitary gland).

The energy exercise "Fanning the Fire in the Stove" is one of the most important preventive measures against the feared "morning heart attack and stroke."

This exercise strengthens the hips, lumbar region, and upper body. It is effective against false posture of the spinal column, as well as stiffness of the hips and sacrum. It also promotes the healing of neurasthenia and other types of nerve failure.

It strengthens the nerves, the central, peripheral, and autonomic vegetative nervous system, the lymphatic gland system, and the seven glands (endocrine system, triple warmer meridian).

In addition, it activates the liver, the eyes, and the gallbladder, as well as supporting weight loss in particular since it counteracts stagnation in the digestive tract.

It corrects the false position of the hips, the pelvis, the knees, and the ankle joints. It is highly recommended for degenerative injuries to the spinal column and serious neuritis, as well as slipped disks and disk lacerations.

Furthermore, it stretches the Achilles tendon, stabilizes the equilibrium, and prevents rotary vertigo.

This exercise should be done several times a day as a preventive measure since **an ounce of prevention is worth a pound of cure!**

EFFECTS ON THE CENTRAL NERVOUS SYSTEM

The "medulla-oblongata button," which corresponds with the meridian point GV-16, is considered a source of energy. In the case of exhaustion, the powers of resistance can be strengthened by pressing on the medulla-oblongata button at the back of the head (see ill.).

Medulla oblongata (part of the central nervous system) and its acupressure point

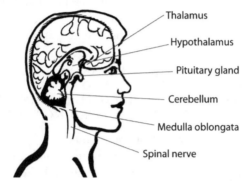

Thalamus

Hypothalamus

Pituitary gland

Cerebellum

Medulla oblongata

Spinal nerve

The Chinese meridian GV-16 is directly next to the medulla

These nerves are actually stimulated by the Opening Exercise:

All nerves in the throat area that lead from the brain to the extremities are stretched, stimulated, and charged with energy through this exercise. The back of the neck is the main traffic road for all of the nerves that lead to and from the brain through the central nervous system. When we succeed in mastering this complex of nerves, we can also control all of our bodily functions. It is possible for a person to lose an arm and still remain alive, but we are unable to live without a head. Consequently, we must comprehend how important it is to train the neck region; it increases the circulation downward and carries off deposits that would otherwise impair the functioning of the nerves, tissue, arteries, and veins.

The Opening Exercise stretches the entire spinal column, supplies the neck with energy, strengthens the shoulder musculature, and eliminates fatigue, stiffness, and pain in the neck and shoulder muscles. Furthermore, it has a stimulating and strengthening effect on the thyroid gland and the parathyroid glands. As a result, it improves the overall metabolism. People who do the Opening Exercise every day feel younger and radiate an inner beauty based primarily on the harmonious functioning of the inner energy systems.

The best times to exercise are in the early morning after you get up and immediately before going to bed at night. You can also do the exercise whenever your neck, shoulders, and the upper and lower parts of your back feel tense or hard—of if you have problems with lumbago, sciatica, and disks.

HOW THE SPINAL COLUMN AND ITS CONNECTIONS TO THE TISSUE, GLANDS, AND ORGANS, AS WELL AS THE IMPORTANT ACUPUNCTURE POINTS, CAN BE INFLUENCED BY THE OPENING EXERCISE.

Number code of the meridian classifications:

Each conductive pathway is associated with a number from 1 to 7 (cervical vertebrae), 1 to 12 thoracic vertebrae), and 1 to 5 (lumbar vertebrae). There are 24 vertebrae and 12 functional systems because:

• 2 vertebrae each have a pathological or therapeutic relationship to the respective functional systems.

• The position of the vertebrae provides indications of whether the therapy should be started on the right or left side.

On the basis of the pain that occurs between the spinal processes of the vertebrae, a practitioner can see which functional process is disturbed. Please note the separating line between the 5th and the 6th thoracic vertebrae (see arrow).

Above all, the exercise activates the acupressure points (from bottom to top):

GV-3 Yao Yangguan	= 4th lumbar vertebra
GV-4 Mingmen	= 2nd lumbar vertebra
GV-8 Jinsuo	= 10th to 11th thoracic vertebrae
GV-9 Zhiyang	= 8th thoracic vertebra
GV-10 Lingtai	= 7th thoracic vertebra
GV-12 Shenzu	= 4th thoracic vertebra
GV-13 Taodao	= 2nd thoracic vertebra
GV-14 Dazhui	= 7th cervical vertebra
GV-16 Medulla Oblongata	= 1st cervical vertebra

Important Acupuncture Points

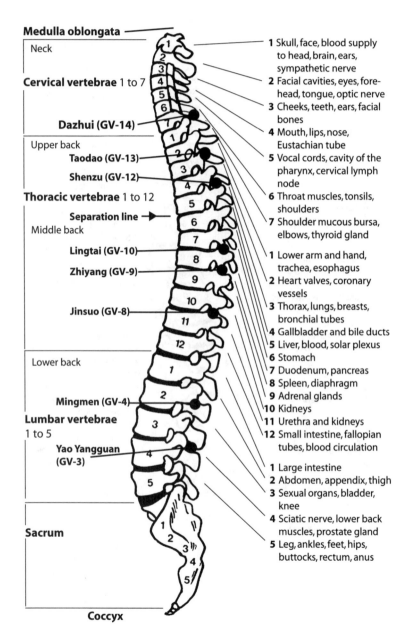

Medulla oblongata

Neck

Cervical vertebrae 1 to 7

Dazhui (GV-14)

Upper back

Taodao (GV-13)

Shenzu (GV-12)

Thoracic vertebrae 1 to 12

Separation line →

Middle back

Lingtai (GV-10)

Zhiyang (GV-9)

Jinsuo (GV-8)

Lower back

Mingmen (GV-4)

Lumbar vertebrae
1 to 5

**Yao Yangguan
(GV-3)**

Sacrum

Coccyx

1 Skull, face, blood supply to head, brain, ears, sympathetic nerve
2 Facial cavities, eyes, forehead, tongue, optic nerve
3 Cheeks, teeth, ears, facial bones
4 Mouth, lips, nose, Eustachian tube
5 Vocal cords, cavity of the pharynx, cervical lymph node
6 Throat muscles, tonsils, shoulders
7 Shoulder mucous bursa, elbows, thyroid gland

1 Lower arm and hand, trachea, esophagus
2 Heart valves, coronary vessels
3 Thorax, lungs, breasts, bronchial tubes
4 Gallbladder and bile ducts
5 Liver, blood, solar plexus
6 Stomach
7 Duodenum, pancreas
8 Spleen, diaphragm
9 Adrenal glands
10 Kidneys
11 Urethra and kidneys
12 Small intestine, fallopian tubes, blood circulation

1 Large intestine
2 Abdomen, appendix, thigh
3 Sexual organs, bladder, knee
4 Sciatic nerve, lower back muscles, prostate gland
5 Leg, ankles, feet, hips, buttocks, rectum, anus

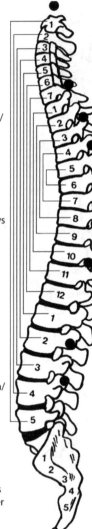

1st cervical vertebra = small intestine
2nd cervical vertebra = circulation
3rd cervical vertebra = triple warmer
4th cervical vertebra = spleen/pancreas
5th cervical vertebra = stomach
6th cervical vertebra = lungs
7th cervical vertebra = large intestine

1st thoracic vertebra = kidneys
2nd thoracic vertebra = bladder
3rd thoracic vertebra = liver
4th thoracic vertebra = gallbladder
5th thoracic vertebra = heart
6th thoracic vertebra = small intestine
7th thoracic vertebra = circulation
8th thoracic vertebra = triple warmer
9th thoracic vertebra = spleen/pancreas
10th thoracic vertebra = stomach
11th thoracic vertebra = lungs
12th thoracic vertebra = large intestine

1st lumbar vertebra = kidneys
2nd lumbar vertebra = bladder
3rd lumbar vertebra = liver
4th lumbar vertebra = gallbladder
5th lumbar vertebra = heart

1 Skull, face, blood supply to head, brain, ears, sympathetic nerve
2 Facial cavities, eyes, forehead, tongue, optic nerve
3 Cheeks, teeth, ears, facial bones
4 Mouth, lips, nose, Eustachian tube
5 Vocal cords, cavity of the pharynx, cervical lymph node
6 Throat muscles, tonsils, shoulders
7 Shoulder mucous bursa, elbows, thyroid gland

1 Lower arm and hand, trachea, esophagus
2 Heart valves, coronary vessels
3 Thorax, lungs, breasts, bronchial tubes
4 Gallbladder and bile ducts
5 Liver, blood, solar plexus
6 Stomach
7 Duodenum, pancreas
8 Spleen, diaphragm
9 Adrenal glands
10 Kidneys
11 Urethra and kidneys
12 Small intestine, fallopian tubes, blood circulation

1 Large intestine
2 Abdomen, appendix, thigh
3 Sexual organs, bladder, knee
4 Sciatic nerve, lower back muscles, prostate gland
5 Leg, ankles, feet, hips, buttocks, rectum, anus

The following table provides an overview of the complaints that can be influenced through the Opening Exercise from the corresponding parts of the spinal column:

Cervical spine	Effects
C 1 Skull, face, blood supply to head, brain, ears, sympathetic nervous system	Headaches, nervousness, insomnia, high blood pressure
C 2 Facial sinuses, eyes, forehead, tongue, optic nerve	Deafness, earache, blindness, complaints of the facial sinuses
C 3 Cheeks, teeth, ears, facial bones	Acne, eczema, neuralgia, neuritis
C 4 Mouth, lips, nose, Eustachian tube	Allergies (hay fever), polyps, catarrh
C 5 Vocal chords, cavity of the pharynx, throat glands	Laryngitis, hoarseness, sore throat
C 6 Throat muscles, tonsils, shoulders	Tonsillitis, croup, stiff neck, pain in the arms
C 7 Shoulder mucous bursa	Colds, goiter, mucous bursa

Thoracic spine	Effects
Th 1 Lower arm and hand, windpipe, esophagus	Asthma, cough, pain in lower arm and hand
Th 2 Heart valves, coronary vessels	Heart complaints, chest complaints
Th 3 Thorax, lungs, breasts, bronchial tubes	Pleurisy, pneumonia
Th 4 Gallbladder and bile ducts	Bronchitis, flu, bilary colic, shingles, jaundice
Th 5 Liver, blood, solar plexus	Liver complaints, lower blood pressure, anemia, arthritis
Th 6 Stomach	Stomach complaints, constipation, digestive disorders
Th 7 Duodenum, pancreas	Stomach complaints, constipation, digestive disorders
Th 8 Spleen, diaphragm	Gastric ulcer, diabetes, gastritis
Th 9 Adrenal glands	Hiccups, stomach complaints
Th10 Kidneys	Allergies (skin rashes, etc.)
Th11 Urethra and kidneys	Arteriosclerosis, kidney complaints, tiredness
Th12 Small intestine, fallopian tubes, blood circulation	Acne, furuncle, eczema, autointoxication, rheumatism, flatulence, infertility

Lumbar Spine	Effects
L 1 Large intestine	Colitis, constipation, diarrhea, rupture
L 2 Abdomen, appendix, thigh	Cramps, hyperacidity, appendix, varicose veins
L 3 Sexual organs, bladder, knees	Bladder complaints, knee complaints
L 4 Sciatic nerve, back muscles, prostate gland	Lumbago, sciatica, painful or frequent urge to urinate
L 5 Leg, ankle, foot, hips, buttocks, rectum, anus	Sudden swelling of legs and feet, insufficient circulation
Sacrum	Deformity of the spine, sacral-iliac complaints
Coccyx	Hemorrhoids, itching, complaints when sitting

The Lumbar Spine, Sacrum, Coccyx, and Their Correlations

Vertebra	Probable cause	New thought pattern
L 1	A cry for love and the need to be alone. Insecurity.	I am certain that the universe and all of life loves and supports me.
L 2	Being stuck in the pain of childhood. Not seeing any way out.	I grow beyond the limitations of my parents and live for myself. It's my turn now.
L 3	Sexual abuse. Feelings of guilt, self-hatred.	I let go of the past. I like myself and my beautiful sexuality. I am secure. I am loved.
L 4	Rejection of sexuality. Financial insecurity. Fear related to career. Feelings of powerlessness.	I love the person who I am. I stand on the solid foundation of my own strength. I am certain on all levels.
L 5	Insecurity. Difficulty in communication. Anger. Inability to accept desire.	I desire to enjoy life. I want joy and pleasure—and I accept it.
Sacrum	Loss of power. Old, stuck anger.	I am the power and the authority in my life. I let go of the past and take advantage of the good within myself.
Coccyx	Losing the inner equilibrium. Clinging. Self-reproach. Being stuck in old pain.	I bring my life back into balance through my self-love. I live in the here and now and love myself just as I am.

The Thoracic Spine and Its Correlations

Vertebra	Probable cause	New thought pattern
Th 1	Fear of life. Has much to master. Can't deal with it. Closes off to life.	I accept my life and receive it with ease. All good things are now mine.
Th 2	Fear, pain, hurt. Doesn't want to feel. Closes his or her heart.	My heart forgives and lets go. It's good to love myself. Inner peace is my goal
Th 3	Inner chaos, deep old wounds. Unable to communicate.	I forgive everyone. I forgive myself. I build myself up.
Th 4	Embitterment. Need to prove other people's errors. Judgment.	I give myself the gift of forgiveness and we are both free.
Th 5	Rejects the processing of emotions. Pent-up feelings, rage.	I let life flow through me. I am willing to live. Everything is good.
Th 6	Angry at life. Suppressed negative emotions. Fear of the future. Constant worry.	I trust that life will develop in a positive way for me. It's good to love myself.
Th 7	Collects pain. Refuses pleasure.	I willingly let go. I let sweetness into my life.
Th 8	Possessed by failure. Refusing to accept the good within oneself.	I am open and receptive to everything good. The universe loves me and supports me.
Th 9	Feels let down by life. Accuses others. Feels like a victim.	I take advantage of my own power. I lovingly create my own reality.
Th 10	Refusal to accept responsibility. Prefers to be the victim. "This is all your fault."	I open myself to joy and love, which I generously give and amply receive.
Th 11	Weak self-image. Fear of relationships.	I see myself as beautiful, loveable, and popular. I am proud to be me.
Th 12	Denying oneself the right to live. Insecure and afraid of love. Unable to digest.	I am deciding to let the joy of life circulate in my body. I am willing to build myself up.

The Cervical Spine and Its Correlations

Vertebra	Probable cause	New thought pattern
C 1	Fear, confusion, runs away from life. Doesn't feel like he or she is good enough. "What would the neighbors say?" An inner dialog that doesn't want to stop.	I am in my center, calm and balanced. The universe agrees with me. I trust my higher self. Everything is good.
C 2	Rejection of wisdom. Refusal to know or understand. Indecisiveness, resentment, and reproach. Imbalanced relationship to life. Denial of one's own spirituality.	I am one with the universe and all of life. It's good for me to know and to grow.
C 3	Accepts other people's accusations. Feelings of guilt, martyr. Indecisiveness. Belittles oneself. Swallows more than can be digested.	I am only responsible for myself, and I am happy about myself. I can deal with everything that I create.
C 4	Feelings of guilt. Suppressed anger, embitterment. Pent-up feelings, uncried tears.	I am clear in my communication with life. I am free to enjoy life right now.
C 5	Fear of being made to look stupid. Fear of humiliation. Fear of expressing oneself. Rejects the good within himself or herself. Very stressed.	My communication is clear. I accept the good within myself. I let go of all expectations. I am loved and am safe.
C 6	Burdens. Very stressed. Tries to change others. Resistance. Lack of flexibility	I lovingly let other people learn their own lessons. I am full of love as I take care of myself. I go through life with ease.
C 7	Confusion, anger. Feels helpless. Can't express oneself.	I have the right to be myself. I forgive the past. I know who I am. I touch others with love.

1ST ENERGY EXERCISE:
THE ABDOMINAL MERIDIAN MASSAGE

"THE ENERGY CENTER OF THE GOLDEN DRAGON"

1st massage direction: start on the solar plexus—5 x 36 times counterclockwise

2nd massage direction: start on the navel—5 x 36 times clockwise

For this exercise sequence, 5 x 36 circular massage movements are prescribed: first in a counterclockwise and then in a clockwise direction.

Exercise Sequence:

1. Stand with your feet shoulder's distance apart and the toes pointing inward. Rub both palms firmly together until they are hot and then place the left hand on the navel. Begin massaging in a counterclockwise direction above this area on the solar plexus from the outer left to the inner right. Keep rubbing in increasingly smaller circles until you stop at the navel in the shape of a point: 5 circles with 36 repetitions = 180 massage motions.

2. Begin massaging the relaxed abdominal wall with the right hand in small and increasingly larger circles in a clockwise direction—from the right to the left—until you reach the costal arch (ribs) above and the pubic bone below with your circular massage: 5 circles with 36 repetitions = 180 massage motions.

Effects:

- You build up a reservoir of heat energy in your solar plexus, which is responsible for the detoxification and purification of the body, as well as boosting your sexual energy.
- In a physiological manner, you promote the massage of the intestinal contents and relieve stomachaches.
- You stimulate the bowel function and normalize the water absorption in the intestines, especially in cases of constipation or diarrhea, reduce the circumference of the abdomen, and reduce overweight—but only if the massage is done every day.
- You considerably improve an existing edema formation in the abdominal region with its resulting pain and dispel flatulence and bad breath.
- You improve the functioning of your heart because there will gradually be less strain on the heart; the blood vessels are strengthened and blood pressure becomes normalized; the shoulder musculature becomes more relaxed.
- In the evening, the abdominal massage has a sleep-promoting effect since it causes stronger circulation of the abdominal region, relieving the strain on the head and brain; the head becomes less constricted and you can enjoy refreshing sleep.

THE QUICK ABDOMINAL MERIDIAN MASSAGE

This abdominal meridian massage is the quick version for counteracting obesity and constipation. Above all, this exercise is suitable in cases of chronic disorders of the inner organs. It also relieves congestion in

1. Concentrate on the sensation of warmth that penetrates the massaged tissue.

2. This heat energy lets the extra fat burn and is the key to success.

3. This exercise sequence should be done in the early morning while standing and while laying down in the late evening.

The meridians are stimulated in this order:
1. Bladder, 2. Kidneys, 3. Small intestine, 4. Spleen, 5. Pericardium, 6. Heart, 7. Lungs, 8. Stomach, 9. Liver, 10. Triple warmer, 11. Gallbladder, 12. Large intestine

the meridians, as well as disturbed peristalsis, and is especially well suited against obesity and a general sluggishness of the metabolism. In addition, it activates the sexual energy and increases the libido.

For this exercise sequence, rub up and down in 2 x 72 quick and powerful motions.

Exercise Sequence:

1. First rub both palms together firmly and then place them on the right and left sides beneath the costal arch (see direction of arrow).

2. Now quickly rub in a semi-circular motion along the sides from above to below on both sides of the abdomen; be sure that both hands meet each other at the height of the pubic bone (sexual stimulation point) below.

3. One up-and-down motion is considered an exercise unit. Feel how the warmth of the friction penetrates your abdominal area.

Effects:

• The quick version of the abdominal massage is more stimulating, gives the lower abdomen more energy, strengthens the sexual center, and has an effect on the pituitary gland (distribution of hormones).

• It is suitable for impaired sexuality, a distended belly, and constipation.

• It is very effective for chronic disorders of the inner organs and a disturbed peristalsis.

• This exercise is especially well suited for the successful treatment of all forms of obesity in the abdominal area.

• It has a harmonizing effect on the blood pressure and relieves pressure on the thyroid gland and eyes.

Please note: When the exercise sequences of any of the three abdominal meridian massages are done, this may result in vomiting, fatigue, and dizzy spells. This may occur at the beginning of the exercise series because blockages in the organs and meridians are dissolved. The increased supply of new chi energy, which revitalizes the entire body, is the trigger for such symptoms of queasiness. Even after doing these exercises for a longer period of time, individual symptoms may still occur.

After each energy exercise, do the Meridian Shaking Exercise for the Hands (see page 159) and the Stretching the Entire Body exercise to distribute the newly acquired chi energy (see page 160).

Effects of the Abdominal Meridian Massages

1. Inner organs—massage in a counterclockwise direction, starting at the upper costal arch and ending at the navel. Supply of energy and strengthening of the entire abdominal area.

Meridian circulation in a counterclockwise direction:
1. Bladder
2. Kidneys
3. Small intestine
4. Spleen/pancreas
5. Circulation/sexuality
6. Heart
7. Lungs
8. Stomach
9. Liver
10. Triple warmer
11. Gallbladder
12. Large intestine

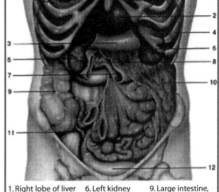

1. Right lobe of liver	6. Left kidney	9. Large intestine,
2. Left lobe of liver	7. Large intestine,	ascending colon
3. Stomach	transverse colon	10. Peritoneum
4. Spleen	8. Pancreas	11. Appendix
5. Right kidney		12. Urinary bladder

2. Inner organs—massage in a clockwise direction, starting at the navel and ending at the upper costal arch. Detoxification and purification of the entire abdominal area.

Meridian circulation in a clockwise direction:
1. Circulation/sexuality
2. Spleen/pancreas
3. Kidneys
4. Bladder
5. Small intestine
6. Large intestine
7. Lungs
8. Liver
9. Gallbladder
10. Heart
11. Stomach
12. Triple warmer

1. Diaphragm	6. Renal artery	11. Testicular
2. Pleura	7. Right kidney	artery and vein
3. Abdominal aorta	8. Left kidney	12. Intestinal vessels
with intestinal vessels	9. Vena cava	13. Ureter
4. Adrenal gland	10. Portal vein	14. Rectum
5. Renal vein		15. Urinary bladder

The "Miracle Meridian" Jen-Mo

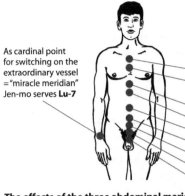

As cardinal point for switching on the extraordinary vessel ="miracle meridian" Jen-mo serves **Lu-7**

Special acupuncture points that are activated by the abdominal massage:

Vagus nerve
Respir. Alarm point of the TW meridian and Alarm point of the CV meridian CV-17
Alarm point of the heart meridian CV-14
Alarm point of the TW meridian CV-12
Alarm point of the TW meridian CV-7
Main alarm point of the TW meridian CV-5
Alarm point of the small-intestine meridian CV-4
Alarm point of the bladder meridian CV-3
CV-1 (perineum point)

The effects of the three abdominal meridian massages on the conception vessel jen-mo:

CV-3	= Alarm point of the bladder meridian	–pubic-bone massage
CV-4	= Alarm point of the small-intestine meridian	–pubic-bone massage
CV-5	= Main alarm point of the TW meridian	–pubic-bone massage
CV-7	= Sex. alarm point of the TW meridian	–strengthens nervous system
CV-12	= Digest. alarm point of TW meridian	–strengthens lymphatic glandular system
CV-14	= Alarm point of heart meridian	–strengthens endocrine system
CV-17	= Respir. alarm point of TW meridian and alarm point of KS meridian	
KG 17	= respir. Alarmpunkt des 3 E-Meridians und Alarmpunkt des KS-Meridians	

After each energy exercise, do the Meridian Shaking Exercise for the Hands (see page 159) and the Stretching the Entire Body exercise to distribute the newly acquired chi energy (see page 160).

Jen-mo (pronounced "yen-mo") is the name of the conception vessel. The meridian point Lu-7, which is activated by all three abdominal massages, is the cardinal point for switching on this extraordinary vessel or "miracle meridian" jen-mo.

REFLEX ZONES AND ABDOMINAL MERIDIAN MASSAGE

No other exercise system activates such ideal reflexes on the twelve main meridians and eight extraordinary meridians like the medical diagnosis and therapy procedure of Taoist Medicine.

 Skin reflex—occurs through skin contact

 Connective tissue reflex—occurs through contact with deeper layers

- Conditioned reflex—is trained through repetition

- Unconditioned reflex—is congenital, inherited

- Criss-cross reflex—the stimulation of one side of the body produces a reaction on the other side of the body

- Postural reflex—tonic reflex that stimulates the muscle contractions required to maintain the body equilibrium

- Antagonistic reflexes—reflexes that are simultaneously triggered at various points and can trigger contrary effects

- Connected reflexes—reflexes that—like the previous type—are simultaneously triggered at various points but intensify each other

- Autonomous reflexes—instead of running through the central nervous system, the afferent (supplying) impulses are brought to the ganglia (nerve nodes) in front of the spinal column. From here, the efferent (leading away) neurons conduct the impulses to the corresponding organs, muscles, or glandular zones. No criss-cross effect is created in this process. The autonomous reflexes are very versatile, and science has very inadequately recognized their function up to now. These autonomous reflexes are primarily used in the reflex-zone massage.

2ND ENERGY EXERCISE: "RETURN TO SPRINGTIME"

Strengthening Exercise for Activating the Vital Energy for the Kidneys, Adrenal Glands, and Bladder

This millennia-old rejuvenation exercise from the eight chi kung exercises of Taoist Medicine serves to make the meridians permeable so that they draw off the detrimental and harmful chi and expand the new sexual energy. This sexual energy is one-fourth of our overall vital energy.

For this exercise, shake only from the hollow of the knees. Keep your arms and shoulders just as relaxed as your wrists. This exercise is only done properly if you have the feeling when you shake that all of the muscles and organs, including the teeth, are shaking along with it.

The meridian shaking exercise

Important note:
Women should not do this exercise during pregnancy or in the menstruation phase. Exceptions to this are women who suffer from suppressed or sparse menstruation. After operations in the abdominal area, ask your physician when you can begin with this exercise again.

The feet are firmly rooted to the ground. Toes point inward and the eyes look into the distance.

This exercise sequence should be done for 15 minutes by men and for 10 minutes by women.

Sequence for the Meridian Shaking Exercise:
1. Stand upright. Place both feet at shoulder's distance apart on the ground with the toes pointing inward. Let your arms hang relaxed at the side of your body.

2. Relax your muscles and look straight ahead. Smile and imagine the feeling of youth and freshness. Let go of any disruptive thoughts and stay in a harmonious mood.

3. Consciously relax all of your muscles once again. Then begin a bouncing up-and-down movement from the hollows of your knees. Let its waves encompass your entire body.

4. During this bouncing exercise sequence, keep the soles of your feet firmly on the ground and absorb the exercise rhythm of the body in a springy manner. The wave-shaped bouncing comes only from the knee joints; keep your shoulders relaxed and don't pull them up.

5. In no case should you try to "command" your breathing during this exercise. It will follow this exercise rhythm completely on its own.

2. Exercise Sequence:

1. After the Meridian Shaking Exercise, place your feet shoulder's width apart and keep the body upright. Shift your weight to the soles of your feet, slightly bend the knees, and relax the body. Let your arms hang down relaxed at your side. Let your mouth have a slight smile and keep the center between your eyebrows relaxed.

2. Now alternately turn your shoulder joints in order to release muscle tension in the head and shoulders. This will allow the previously created new streams of energy to flow freely from the shoulders up to the neck and from there on to the brain.

3. The right and left shoulder each alternately circle 18 times in the order of forward, upward, and backward. The shoulders must always turn in a complete circle.

4. Repeat the 2nd exercise sequence 18 times in the reverse direction as well.

5. Use your entire body to move both shoulders in this circular motion, which in turn will set the arms in motion. When you raise the shoulders, your heels will also lift slightly (the right heel with the right shoulder and the left heel with the left shoulder). The constant turning motion of the upper body squeezes the inner organs so that the spent oxygen can be expelled and fresh oxygen can be absorbed.

After each energy exercise, do the Meridian Shaking Exercise for the Hands (see page 159) and the Stretching the Entire Body Exercise (see page 160) to distribute the newly acquired chi energy.

Effects:

- The Meridian Shaking Exercise is considered a special kidney exercise for strengthening the immune defense in connection with the thymus gland. There's a good reason for its name of "Return to Springtime." In addition to the "Exercise of the Solar Plexus," it is one of the focal points of the Taoist diagnosis and therapy procedure.
- After people have practiced this exercise for a certain amount of time, it has a tremendously rejuvenating effect. This applies especially to older people since the skin metabolism is most conspicuously affected. The improvement of the complexion is obvious. Pimples and rough, dry spots disappear from the face. The skin looks rosy and shows better circulation.
- In addition, this exercise prevents the formation of wrinkles and even mitigates deep wrinkles already present in the facial area. It lets tear sacs and dark rings beneath the eyes disappear.
- Furthermore, it fights overweight. Deposits of fat in the abdominal, hip, and pelvic area are effectively broken down. However, this only occurs when the exercise is done twice a day.
- Through the shaking exercise, all of the inner adhesions and ulcerations of the connective tissue are dissolved. Above all, this cleansing of the connective tissue is wonderfully refreshing for the body, irrespective of the person's age and sex.
- The circulation of the body is stimulated; new energy and vitality can once again flow unimpeded to the organism. The immune system and the kidneys are lastingly detoxified and strengthened.
- Functional disorders, such as shoulder complaints, are improved. The same applies to states of tension in the abdominal area. Although this should not be practiced during the menstruation phase, the exercise reduces the pain that can develop during menstruation.
- Moreover, the Meridian Shaking Exercise improves the overall health condition, stimulates the sexual function, and supports weight reduction.
- The waste substances are gradually excreted through the eliminatory organs, primarily the skin, during the course of the exercise. During this cleansing process, it is therefore important to drink large amounts of warm water (should be boiled at least 15 minutes beforehand).

Additional notes:

- During the turning movements of the 2nd exercise sequence, it is not necessary to breathe consciously. The squeezing that takes place through the turning movement of the upper body will result in spontaneous breathing.
- Beginners shouldn't exert themselves too much during this exercise. However, the shoulders must always move in a complete circle.
- Once you have mastered this exercise and your body has adapted to it, you can use more strength and make larger circles with your shoulders.

Effects of the meridian shaking exercise on the reflex zones of the front and back side of the body

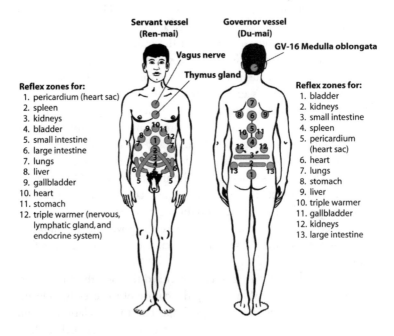

Servant vessel (Ren-mai)

Governor vessel (Du-mai)

Vagus nerve

Thymus gland

GV-16 Medulla oblongata

Reflex zones for:
1. pericardium (heart sac)
2. spleen
3. kidneys
4. bladder
5. small intestine
6. large intestine
7. lungs
8. liver
9. gallbladder
10. heart
11. stomach
12. triple warmer (nervous, lymphatic gland, and endocrine system)

Reflex zones for:
1. bladder
2. kidneys
3. small intestine
4. spleen
5. pericardium (heart sac)
6. heart
7. lungs
8. stomach
9. liver
10. triple warmer
11. gallbladder
12. kidneys
13. large intestine

3RD ENERGY EXERCISE:
"THE PALACE OF THE DRAGON"

Strengthening Exercise for Restoring the Vital Energy and Sexual Performance

In the ancient Taoist writings, this three-part exercise serves the development and transformation of the sexual vital energy by awakening the serpent force. These are three variations of the pelvic thrust, which are also called the sacral pump since its activation primarily strengthens the kidney functioning. In particular, the sacral pump is said to maintain all sexual activities up into ripe old age.

1ST PART:
"THE PALACE OF THE YELLOW JADE DRAGON"

1. Inhaling
Gently push the pelvis backward and inhale deeply through the nose without letting the upper body fall forward.

2. Exhaling
Powerfully thrust the pelvis forward and quickly exhale through the mouth without allowing your back to become hollow.

For this exercise sequence, 81 repetitions are prescribed.

Exercise Instructions for Part 1:

1. Stand with your legs at shoulder's width with your toes pointing inward and your feet deeply rooted as if they were glued to the ground. Place your hands on your hips with the thumbs at the back, which additionally activates the gallbladder and bladder meridian.
2. When thrusting the pelvis forward, exhale abruptly and spontaneously. Tense the PC muscle at the same time.
3. When inhaling through the nose, gently draw your pelvis backward so that the pelvis forms a slight arc toward the back. Relax your PC muscle and begin again with the technique of thrusting the pelvis forward.

2ND PART:
"THE PALACE OF THE RED FIRE DRAGON"

1. Inhaling	2. Exhaling	3. Inhaling

Turn in a counter-clockwise direction	Pelvic thrust in semi-circle forward without allowing your back to become hollow	Turn in a clockwise direction.

For this exercise sequence, 81 repetitions are prescribed.

Exercise Instructions for Part 2:

1. Place your feet next to each other at shoulder's width with the toes turned slightly inward. Maintain a straight back and slightly bend the knees.
2. Relax your shoulders and legs.

3. Move your pelvis in a semi-circle to the right and end this motion with a strong thrusting movement of the pelvic forward without allowing your back to become hollow. Exhale abruptly together with the thrust. Do this exercise with the same number of repetitions to the left as well.

Additional Notes:
- Your head and shoulders should not follow the movement of the pelvis. Imagine that your head is attached to a string coming down from the sky.
- The feet also should not imitate the circular movements of the pelvis; instead, keep them firmly rooted to the ground (as if they were glued to it). During the exercise, frequently concentrate on being rooted to the ground and keep your hands resting on your hips.
- In order to improve the turning motions of the hips, imagine that the turning point is located about one hand's width beneath the navel. Let the pelvis circle in one direction before you do the opposite turn.

Effects:
The exercise of the circling pelvis contributes to:
- Improving the flexibility of the pelvis and the lumbar region.
- Activating the energy circulation between the legs and the lower body making it possible to remedy sexual disorders.
- Helping against circulatory complaints, varicose veins, and cold feet, as well as sciatic-neuralgic complaints and pain in the lumbar region. Also especially effective in counteracting constipation.

3ʳᴰ PART:
"THE PALACE OF THE GREEN JADE DRAGON"

1. Inhaling—
Powerfully
thrust pelvis
forward and
inhale deeply
through the
nose without
allowing your
back to
become
hollow.

2. Exhaling—
Gently push
back the pelvis
without
allowing the
upper body to
fall forward.
Exhale gently
through the
mouth as you
do this.

For this exercise sequence, 81 repetitions are prescribed.

Exercise Instructions for Part 3:

1. After completing the 1ˢᵗ and 2ⁿᵈ energy cycle, do the 3ʳᵈ part of the exercise: inhale through the nose while thrusting your pelvis forward and simultaneously tensing your PC muscle—exactly the opposite of what you did in Part 1 of this exercise step.

2. When gliding back to the starting position, exhale through your mouth and relax the PC muscle while you do so.

3. The number of repetitions is based on the previous number of repetitions and should not be less or more.

4. This 3ʳᵈ form of the exercise is much more difficult than the 1ˢᵗ variation since you must first inhale when thrusting the pelvis forward here in order to activate the life force and sexual energy.

After each energy exercise, relax by doing the Meridian Shaking Exercise for the Hands (see page 159) and distribute the newly acquired chi energy with the Stretching the Entire Body Exercise (see page 160).

Additional Notes for All Three Variations of the Pelvic Thrust

• During the entire sequence of the exercise, touch your tongue to your upper gums while inhaling through the nose. Place your tongue behind the bottom row of teeth while exhaling.

- Swallow your saliva and do not spit it out.
- During the entire length of the exercise, focus on the balls of your feet (kidney meridian K1 = "Bubbling Source.")

Effects:

When he becomes sexually active, the man unconsciously (although information about this has been banned from almost all of the writings on sex education) does the technique of the pelvic thrust forward—but more in the "American style," meaning for one or two minutes at most. However, an extended sexual act demands more endurance. For this reason, the three variations of the pelvic thrust should be practiced every day in order to relieve stiffness and inflexibility of the entire pelvic region and activate the PC muscle.

Through the three forms of pelvic thrusting, the previously lower level of energy is refined into higher performance energy. We can feel the rising chi energy—which is also called "serpent force"—from the sacrum upward through the lumbar, thoracic, and cervical vertebrae to the crown point of the head (bai-hui). The bodily energy increases until all seven glands have reached their complete capacity. In this manner, every gland of the endocrine system serves as a generator and transformer of the bodily energy—the mysterious source of all human energies.

4ᵀᴴ ENERGY EXERCISE: "THE PRAYING MANTIS"

Energy Exercise for Activating the Seven Glands, the Lymphatic Glands, and the Nervous System

The Taoist chi kung exercise "The Praying Mantis" is probably one of the energy exercises that is most difficult to do since we people in the West must first stretch our tensed leg muscles and make them flexible. In Asia, we can see many people every day not only meditating and working in the "close squat" but also even talking to each other or playing cards in this position that is extremely uncomfortable for Westerners. This endurance in the close squat, which can last several hours, continually fascinates the Western observer.

According to the perspective of the ancient Chinese preventive health measures, this form of exercise is seen as the especially effective "heart protection." In addition, all of the organs and meridians are massaged and it helps especially against constipation and diarrhea.

Inhale through the nose—
Arch the abdomen forward.

Hold breath for 5 seconds.

Exhale through the mouth—
Deeply draw in the abdomen.

In this position, concentrate solely on the tensing of the PC muscle while inhaling and the relaxing of the PC muscle while exhaling.

This exercise should be done 2x daily.

After ending the exercise, slowly rise up out of the squat. If you feel dizzy, intensely shake out your hands and then breathe calmly into your abdomen.

For this exercise sequence, 5 minutes are prescribed.

Exercise Sequence:
1. Go into the squat from the position with your feet at shoulder's width apart—a wider position is also permitted for the beginner. While doing this, press your elbows between your knees and fold your hands into the prayer position.
2. Keep your feet flat on the ground and don't raise the heels.
3. While inhaling, press the knees apart with your elbows; when exhaling, release the pressure of the elbows and relax.
4. During each inhalation, tense the PC muscle; place your tongue on the gums. When exhaling through the mouth, relax the PC muscle once again; place your tongue behind the lower row of teeth while doing this.
5. Each time you push your elbows against the knees and simultaneously tense your PC muscle, the chi of the sexual glands is conducted upward to the head and provides the brain with the life-maintaining spinal fluid.

After each energy exercise, relax by doing the Meridian Shaking Exercise for the Hands (see page 159) and distribute the newly acquired chi energy through the Stretching the Entire Body Exercise (see page 160).

Effects:

- The squatting position stretches the calf and thigh musculature and promotes equilibrium.
- In addition, the squat supports defecation. In the squat position, the thighs press against the small intestine, which in turn stimulates the intestinal activity. The position of the Praying Mantis therefore accelerates the peristalsis of the intestinal contents through the digestive tract.
- This position is recommended particularly for constipation since the blocked fecal residue can only be squeezed out in this squatting position through the additional tensing of the PC muscle.
- Joint stiffness is relieved through the increased circulation in the back, pelvis, and legs.
- This position promotes increased blood circulation in the abdominal region, as well as a relaxation of the pelvis, feet, and knee joints.
- Furthermore, it strengthens the nerves of the lower half of the trunk and stimulates the meridians of bladder/kidneys, stomach/spleen/pancreas, gallbladder, and liver.
- t is also especially effective against all sexual disorders, such as impotence and premature ejaculation, as well as other problems of the lower abdomen since the sexual energy of both man and woman becomes clearly tangible in relation to tensing the PC muscle.
- It also helps against frigidity, menstrual pain, convulsive pain, or extremely strong menstrual bleeding.
- This exercise is also suited for pregnant women since it opens the pelvic region and makes birth easier.

Note: The exercise of the Praying Mantis opens the autonomic nervous system and the Third Eye (between the eyebrows at the center of the forehead).

5ᵀᴴ ENERGY EXERCISE: "THE BLACK TURLE OF THE NORTH"

Stretching Exercise for Improving Circulation and Flexibility

This exercise sequence completes an even better stretch since it is practiced at double shoulder's width in a deep squat. Do not change the exercise posture during the prescribed movement sequence.

Exercise Sequence:

1. You can stretch better when your feet are two shoulder-width's apart. Thrust the pelvis forward, inhale through your nose, and place your tongue on the upper gums. Tense the PC muscle.
2. Gently push back the pelvis. Exhale through your mouth and place your tongue behind the lower row of teeth. Relax the PC muscle.
3. After ending this exercise, slowly rise up out of the squat. If you have dizzy spells, intensely shake out your hands.

For this exercise sequence, 81 repetitions are prescribed.

Effects:
- The squatting position stretches the calf and thigh musculature and promotes a sense of equilibrium.
- It eliminates stiffness of joints in the pelvis and lower back.
- It improves circulation in the extremities, especially in the sacral area.
- It increases circulation of the toes, feet, and legs.
- It improves the blood circulation in the abdominal area and supports the relaxation of the pelvis, feet, and knee joints.

- It strengthens the nerves of the lower half of the trunk and stimulates the meridians of the bladder/kidneys, stomach/spleen/pancreas, gallbladder, and liver.
- It is also especially effective against all sexual disorders, such as impotence and premature ejaculation, as well as other problems of the lower abdomen since the sexual energy of both man and woman becomes clearly tangible in relation to tensing the PC muscle.
- It also helps against frigidity, menstrual pain, convulsive pain, or extremely strong menstrual bleeding.
- This exercise is also suited for pregnant women since it opens the pelvic region and makes birth easier.

After each energy exercise, relax by doing the Meridian Shaking Exercise for the Hands (see page 159) and distribute the newly acquired chi energy through the Stretching the Entire Body Exercise (see page 160).

6ᵀᴴ ENERGY EXERCISE: "THE ANGRY TIGER BECOMES A SLEEK CAT"

The Sacral Pump: Activating the Serpent Power

Absorption of the yang energy through the medulla oblongata **GV-14/16**	Absorption of the yin energy through the palms of the hands **(Circulation/sexuality) CV-6**

Inhale while tensing the PC muscle; hold breath for 3 seconds.	Exhale while relaxing the PC muscle; hold exhalation for 3 seconds.

For this exercise sequence, 36 repetitions are prescribed.

Exercise Sequence:

1. Get on your hands and knees. Stretch your arms and hold your back parallel to your feet so that your body forms a right angle.
2. Now begin to alternate between a hollow back and an arched cat's back.
3. Inhale through your nose, raise your head, and lean it back to your neck. Press down your lower back and waist so that they form a hollow back. Tense the PC muscle while you inhale. Then hold your breath for 3 seconds.
3. Exhale through your mouth again, tilt your head downward while looking at your chest, and draw the back upward (into an arched cat's back). While exhaling, relax the PC muscle. Also stay in the resting position for 3 seconds.

Effects:

- Because of the swing of the pelvis in this exercise form, the spinal column is bent and stretched in both directions, which relaxes the pressure on the intervertebral disks.
- The exercise of the energy pump is very beneficial for the entire spinal column, especially the area of the sacrum (also see the "Opening Exercise," on page 158 and illustration on page 168). This relaxes the separation line, which runs between the 5th and 6th thoracic vertebrae; the heart muscle, heart valves, coronary vessels, and solar plexus are also relieved.
- In addition, it strengthens the cervical, thoracic, and lumbar spine, as well as the sacrum and coccyx, and prevents the complaints already mentioned under the "Opening Exercise" (see tables on pages 169-170).
- It simultaneously stimulates the sexual glands responsible for the development and transformation of sexual energy and increases the circulation of the male and female sexual organs.
- During pregnancy, this energy exercise strengthens the uterus (the muscle cradle for the growing child), promotes deeper breathing in both mother and child, and relieves tensions in the lower back. It is especially relaxing when the contractions begin and helpful in preparation for birth.
- This energy exercise, together with the 2nd energy exercise "Return to Springtime (see page 179), has also proved to be effective against menstrual problems and pathological absence of menstruation.

192

- In addition, this position is also a form of relaxation for the inner organs. It gives the body a sense of strength, power, and security.

After each energy exercise, relax by doing the Meridian Shaking Exercise for the Hands (see page 159) and distribute the newly acquired chi energy through the Stretching the Entire Body Exercise (see page 160).

The chi kung exercise of "The Angry Tiger" is a simple but very effective therapy measure for all types of back complaints and bone diseases. Taoist Medicine believes that the activation of the acupuncture points GV-14, GV-16, Bl-39, Bl-11, as well as GV-4, is necessary for successful therapy of these disorders.

The sacral pump and its effects on the brain and its hemispheres

**Yin energy moves
in a clockwise direction**

**Yang energy moves
in a counter-clockwise direction**

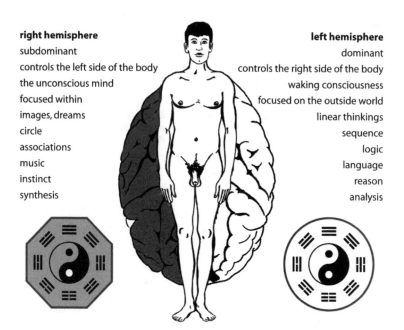

right hemisphere
subdominant
controls the left side of the body
the unconscious mind
focused within
images, dreams
circle
associations
music
instinct
synthesis

left hemisphere
dominant
controls the right side of the body
waking consciousness
focused on the outside world
linear thinkings
sequence
logic
language
reason
analysis

THE SACRAL PUMP
AS THERAPY FOR BACK COMPLAINTS AND BONE DISEASES

**Yang =
creative and
exploding force**

**GV-16
Medulla oblongata**
Energy point for nervous,
lymphatic gland,
and endocrine system

**Yin =
receptive and
birth-giving force**

**GV-14
7th cervical
vertebra as
collection of all
yang energies**

BI-11
1-1/2 inches to
both sides of the
2nd thoracic
vertebra

**Yang
palace
of life
BI-39**

**Yin
palace
of life
BI-39**

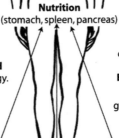

**2. Fire
Sexuality**
(heart, small intestine,
circulation, sexuality,
triple warmer)
Movement and sensation,
presses the energy upward
and functions as sexual energy.

Positive colors
red and green

Negative colors
blue and brown

**3. Earth
Nutrition**
(stomach, spleen, pancreas)

**4. Metal
Respiration**
(lungs, large intestine)
Movement energy
toward the center,
contracting, strong activity
and powers of resistance,
Energy is directed inward.

Positive colors
gold, silver, brown, and beige

**Negative colors
red and green**

**Collection of all
yin energies
GV-4**

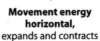

**Gate of life
and flexibility
GV-4**

**Movement energy
horizontal,**
expands and contracts

Positive colors
brown, yellow, orange, and beige

Negative colors
green

**1. Wood
Movement**
(liver, gallbladder)
**Movement, expansion,
and growth** in all 8 directions.

Positive colors
blue and green

Negative colors
gold and silver

**5. Water
Meditation**
(kidneys, bladder)
**Movement energy
downward and sideward.**

Positive colors
blue, gray, black, gold and silver

Negative colors
brown and yellow

7ᵀᴴ ENERGY EXERCISE :
"THE RED BIRD OF THE SOUTH"

Strengthening Exercise for Lower Abdomen and Sexual Organs

The first sign of aging is often expressed as sensations of cold and numbness in the legs and feet, which is a result of deteriorating circulation in the extremities. The Taoist chi kung exercise is meant to counteract stiffness of the joints and insufficient sexual energy, as well as other degenerative changes in the lower abdomen, in order to rejuvenate the organism.

1ˢᵗ part of exercise: Wrap your hands around both tips of the toes. Bounce your thighs for 5 minutes.

2ⁿᵈ part of exercise: Inhale and exhale deep into the abdomen for 36 times. Afterward, slowly sit up straight again.

For this exercise sequence, 10 minutes are prescribed.

Exercise Sequence:
1. Sit on the ground and bend your knees so that the soles of your feet meet in front of your body.
2. Firmly rub the soles of your feet against each other until they are warm and then place them so that they touch each other.
3. Wrap your hands around the tips of the toes and bend them back and forth to increase the circulation of the feet.
4. With the soles of the feet still touching, pull the heels as close to the pelvis as possible.
5. Now bounce both thighs at the same time. Keep your upper body straight during the entire exercise sequence.

6. After completing the 1st part of the exercise, bend forward as far as possible and inhale deeply into the abdomen in this position.
7. After this rate of breathing, straighten up carefully and move slowly into a supine position. Stay there for 60 seconds.

After each energy exercise, relax by doing the Meridian Shaking Exercise for the Hands (see page 159) and distribute the newly acquired chi energy through the Stretching the Entire Body Exercise (see page 160).

Effects:
• The body position during the bouncing thigh movement increases circulation in the feet, legs, abdomen, and lower abdominal organs.
• It relaxes the pelvis and stretches the lower portion of the spinal column so that the sexual energy can rise unimpeded through the medulla oblongata into the brain hemispheres.
• The feet, knees, and hips are relaxed and the nervous system of the lower half of the trunk is strengthened.
• In addition, this exercise stimulates the meridians of the kidneys, spleen, and liver, which lead up to the sexual organs along the inner sides of the legs.
• It regulates sexual disorders such as impotence, premature ejaculation, and erectile weakness.
• It also helps against menstrual complaints (cramping), extremely strong menstrual bleeding, and frigidity.
• This exercise sequence is also excellently suited for pregnant women since it opens up the pelvic area and facilitates birth.

The five magical foot points are visible as a vertex of the arch that runs through the base of the ball of the foot. This reflex has a very special significance for relaxation. It can eliminate tension and nervousness, help you achieve deeper breathing, and bring you back into a state of calm.

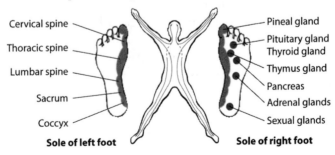

CONCLUDING EXERCISE: "DRIVING AWAY ONE-HUNDRED AFFLICTIONS"

The Pumping Yin Dragon

This exercise is ideal for harmonizing the blood pressure, as well as maintaining the energetic equilibrium of the body, stabilizing the spinal column, and activating sexual energy. It also supports strength and keen perception.

1. Slowly raise your heels. Inhale through the nose. Tense the PC muscle. Press your chin against your throat and extend your fingers.

2. Slowly lower your heels. Exhale through the mouth. Relax the PC muscle. Straighten your head and relax your fingers.

For this exercise sequence, 49 repetitions are prescribed.

Exercise Sequence:

1. Stand up straight with legs shoulder's width apart, toes pointing inward. Let your arms hang down relaxed at your side. Look straight ahead and let your mouth smile slightly. Relax the center of the eyebrows.

2. Relax your knees and let yourself sink downward slightly. When you feel the entire weight of your body on the soles of your feet, make a rising pumping motion upward and raise the heels as you do this.
3. When rising up, inhale gently through your nose. Tense the PC muscle and press the chin onto your throat. At the same time, extend all of your fingers downward with tension.
4. When gliding back down, exhale gently through your mouth once again. Relax the PC muscle. Hold the head straight, and relax your fingers again.
5. Repeat this exercise 48 times.

After each energy exercise, relax by doing the Meridian Shaking Exercise for the Hands (see page159) and distribute the newly acquired chi energy through the Stretching the Entire Body Exercise (see page 160).

THE MEANING OF THE FEET FOR THE HUMAN BODY

This exercise activates the kidney acupuncture point 1 ("Bubbling Source of Life") on the sole of the foot. The kidney meridian begins on the sole, between the two large balls of the feet, exactly at the center beneath the 3rd toe. It runs on both sides along the inner side of the leg and thigh up to the groin area. From there, it runs over the abdomen to the thorax, where it ends directly beneath the collarbone in the triangular hollow that is formed by the 1st rib, the collarbone, and the sternum.

During the exercises, you absorb chi energy from the earth through the kidney acupuncture point of the "Bubbling Source" and pump this over the legs to the thighs and up to the kidneys. Through the pumping movement, this energy source is once again cleansed and opened, distributing the energy throughout the entire body.

Please note:
When you raise the heels, stand on the balls of your feet and not on the tips of the toes in order to activate the kidney meridian.
• If the chi force cannot reach the legs and feet and flow freely through the nerve centers of the arms and legs during the chi kung exercise, the body will be like a tree with wilted leaves and branches, even if the upper body does not look slack. If this is the case, you can regain your own vitality through the path of the chi kung exercises.

- If the newly acquired chi can circulate in the feet and legs, the upper body will automatically become upright and the hip musculature can easily contract and relax. When you walk, it will feel like there is a soft blanket or cotton beneath your feet.
- Plant life is nourished through the roots that reach down deep into the earth. The ginseng root looks very much like the human body. This is why we can use this comparison to depict the meaning of the feet for the head. People who have mastered the Taoist chi kung exercises feel like their bodies are "as light as a leaf in the wind" or that they could support their bodies with just one single toe over a longer period of time when they exercise.

Controlling the sexual yang and yin energy

Upper Dantien

Brain area (central peripheral nervous system)

Middle Dantien

Kidney acupuncture point 1 (Bubbling Source)

Lower Dantien (cleanses and detoxifies the lymphatic gland system)

Sexual stored energy
The left sole controls the yang energy in the right brain hemisphere

Cervical spine (1-7)
- 🌀 pineal gland
- 🌀 pituitary gland
- 🌀 thyroid gland

Thoracic spine (1-12)
- 🌀 thymus gland
- 🌀 pancreas
- 🌀 adrenal glands

Lumbar spine (1-5)
- 🌀 sexual glands (testicles, prostate gland, breasts, ovaries, uterus) activate 1/4 of the overall life energy

Sacrum (1-5)
Coccyx (1-5)

Upper Dantien

Brain area (central peripheral nervous system)

Middle Dantien

Kidney acupuncture point 1 (Bubbling Source)

Lower Dantien (cleanses and detoxifies the lymphatic gland system)

Sexual stored energy
The right sole controls the yin energy in the left brain hemisphere

Effects:

Source "(kidney acupuncture point 1) and it reaches the kidneys through the pumping movements. Through these pumping movement, this energy source is once again cleansed and opened, distributing the energy throughout the entire body. For this reason, this exercise is also called "Driving Away One-Hundred Afflictions."

This exercise is particularly well suited for the following health problems:

- Burning, painful soles; eczema and fungus infection on the soles; weak, swollen inner malleous; shin-bone pain; calf cramps; pain in the hollow of the knee; thigh pain; varicose veins and burst small blood vessels; skin problems along the kidney meridian.

- Eczema and fungus infection in the groin and genitals; sexual problems such as infertility or uterine and prostate gland complaints; weakness of the kidneys and bladder; digestive problems in the small intestine; eliminatory problems in the large intestine; imbalances in the diaphragm and solar plexus; neuritis.

- Chest problems; tumors in the breast on the inside of the nipple; heart and circulatory problems; feeling of pressure in the chest; asthma and feelings of congestion in the lungs; throat complaints and coughing; hot, dry tongue; disorders of the thyroid gland; pain in the area of lumbar vertebrae 1-5, in the sacrum, and the coccyx.

- In addition, the muscle pump is activated (calf musculature—return of the venous blood).

- This exercise allows the body and the spinal column to vibrate and gives the previous chi kung exercises the finishing touches. The energy is distributed throughout the entire body by way of the five organs (lungs, spleen/pancreas, heart, kidneys, and liver) and the five intestinal organs (large intestine, stomach, small intestine, bladder, and gallbladder), as well as the circulation/sexuality and the triple warmer.

Effects on Muscular Tensions

- Lumbar muscle (yin energy): This muscle is part of the muscle group that bends the spinal column to the side and holds the lumbar spine upright toward the back. When there is a weakness on both sides, there is a tendency to flatten the sacral area. A one-sided weakness leads to turning the foot inward or tilting the pelvis downward. Standing or walking with the ankles turned inward strains the lumbar muscle and leads to a recurring weakness when this foot problem is not remedied.

    The consequences of this are: non-specific backache, kidney and bladder disorders. Constantly recurring foot pain can also be connected with a weakness of the lumbar muscle.

- Upper trapezoid muscle (yin energy): This muscle tilts the head and draws the shoulder blades upward. When the eyes and ears are weak, this muscle has been weakened. This exercise form also demonstrates a relaxing and healing effect in this situation as well.

- Iliac muscle (yin energy): A weakness of this muscle can indicate a problem with the muscle valve between the small intestine and the

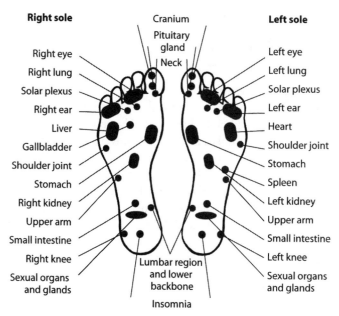

General overview of the foot reflex zones

large intestine. When the muscles are weak, far-reaching symptoms can develop as a result. These include nausea, shooting back pain, sudden feelings of thirst, dark rings beneath the eyes, and paleness.

Above all, the exercise of the "Pumping Yin Dragon" activates the acupuncture points:

GV-3 Yao Yangguan	GV-9 Zhiyang	GV-13 Taodao
GV-4 Mingmen	GV-10 Lingtai	GV-14 Dazhui
GV-8 Jinsuo	GV-12 Shenzu	GV-16 Medulla oblongata

THE FOOT REFLEX ZONES AND THE PROJECTION OF THE SPINAL COLUMN

In a natural way, the inner side of the foot depicts the curvatures of the spinal column. The spinal column, the backbone, is the central supportive structure of the body. It bears the weight of the body and is the flexible axis of the body. It consists of 34 vertebrae. These are arranged so that the spinal column shows four curvatures.

The spinal column is divided into five sections from above to below:
• 7 vertebrae (including the axis and the atlas) form the cervical spine.
• 12 vertebrae form the thoracic spine (back)
• 5 vertebrae form the lumbar spine
• 5 vertebrae form the sacrum
• 5 vertebrae form the coccyx

The vertebrae of the sacrum and coccyx are fused into one single rigid bone. The vertebrae are connected with each other through cartilage disks and are held in place by ligaments. The spinal column encloses the spinal cord, the central canal of the nervous system, which is a continuation of the brain stem.

One pair of spinal nerves belongs to each vertebra. These nerves originate in the spinal cord and influence the body on the level from which they originate. As a result, the thoracic nerves influence the chest and the lumbar nerves influence the abdomen and legs, etc. These nerves supply very specific organs, which is why there is a direct influence on the respective area of the body when they are impacted or damaged.

- The nerve connections of the vertebra go to the tissue, glands, and organs.

- The spinal column reflex runs along the inner side of both feet, whereby each foot represents one half of the spinal column.

- The cervical vertebra reflex runs from the base of the large toenail to the base of the toe (between the 1st and 2nd joint of the large toe).

- The thoracic reflex runs along the ball of the foot beneath the large toe (shoulder to waist).

- The arc from the waist to the pelvic area corresponds with the lumbar region and the heel line to the base of the heel corresponds with the sacrum/coccyx.

Projection of the spinal column on the right foot

Projection of the spinal column on the left foot

THE PROSTATE GLAND—
THE HUMAN BATTERY

"The prostate gland is a pattern of wave motions, vibrations, and cycles. Everywhere in nature and in the human realm, it has an important function since it controls the man's sexual behavior."

THE PROSTATIC MASSAGE

The Male Deer Exercise

A strong prostate gland is more capable of dealing with sexual stimulation. As a result, the erection and desire last longer. Through the Deer Exercise, prostate gland complaints can actually be prevented.

When a man sees his doctor because of a minor problem with the prostate gland, the following procedure is usually done: The doctor inserts his finger into the man's anus and massages the prostate gland, which brings relief in quite a few cases. This massage takes place automatically with the male Deer Exercise: The tension of the outer muscles has an immediate effect on the inner gland. Although premature ejaculation can be prevented through pressure on the jen-mo point in individual cases, this does not cure the problem; only the superficial symptoms of premature ejaculation can be eliminated in this way. The true cause, which is a weak prostate gland, must be treated in a different way.

In order to completely eliminate this problem, it is possible to strengthen the prostate gland by doing parts 1 and 2 of the male Deer Exercise. The prostate massage is also invaluable. In addition, a man should eat lotus and pumpkin seeds on a regular basis.

Case History:
Furthermore, the Deer Exercise is a healing remedy for the entire body since it strengthens the immune system against all types of pathogens. I once got a bad cold and lost my voice just before I was to hold a lecture in Vienna. So I did the 2nd part of the Deer Exercise (contraction of the PC muscle and pelvic floor) for an hour in my room. Afterward, my cold was gone and I could once again speak at a normal volume. My lecture went according to plan.

Note:
Contracting the sphincter muscle exercises a light pressure, like a gentle massage, on the prostate gland. The anus behaves like a little engine that drives the prostate gland. Stimulated in this manner, the prostate gland begins to excrete hormones such as endorphins, which trigger emotional high spirits. When the prostate gland begins to twitch, a man can even feel a small orgasm. The alternating contracting and letting

go of the anal muscles during the Deer Exercise creates such a natural high—without jogging or other sporting feats and without drugs or side effects.

As we know, disorders of the prostate gland do not just occur over night: Diagnosis and massages on a regular basis can prevent possible inflammations in the prostate gland. It is therefore incorrect when conventional medicine claims that diseases of the prostate gland are normal for men in their fifties. They occur more frequently at this age because most men do not know about these preventive measures.

The male Deer Exercise prevents inflammations or disorders of the prostate gland and can even make valuable healing energy available to the body in cases of disease. However, this does not happen on its own: daily practice makes perfect.

CHECKING THE PROSTATE GLAND

According to the translations of documents on the ancient Chinese diagnosis and therapy procedure of Taoist Medicine, there is another very special method of checking the prostate gland, which the man can easily do on his own. By observing his ejaculation and examining the semen, he can determine whether or to what extent his prostate gland is affected. The prostate gland is responsible for ejaculation, and every related difficulty is related to the prostate gland.

The five phases of change serve as characteristics for the exam:

1. The semen does not shoot out far enough.

2. The amount of the semen

3. Abnormal semen

4. Dripping semen

5. Impotence

The semen does not shoot out far enough
The semen does not shoot out as far as it actually should in order to ensure the goal of fertilizing the female egg. Although the prostate gland is still functioning, it is too weak. Consequently, it cannot produce the expected contractions that make it possible for the man to be sexually stimulated in the first place. So there are only a maximum of 2-3 contractions instead of the usual 6-19.

The amount of the semen

Instead of the expected amount of one full tablespoon of semen, the amount of semen is unusually small here. Everything below the amount of one tablespoon indicates:

- Digestive problems (cause thin semen)
- Weak stomach
- Weakness of spleen and pancreas
- Muscle tensions
- Or a weak erection of the penis
- Thin semen is transparent, but healthy semen is viscous

Abnormal semen

Healthy semen tastes like vitamin B (smells like yeast) and should also have a sweetish taste (pancreas).
Abnormal semen is;

- Too sweet (too much milk in the daily diet)
- Salty (indicates possible venereal disease)
- Bitter (signifies a strong concentration of toxins in the body)

When the semen and/or the woman's vagina smells like "dead fish" the morning after sexual intercourse, the man's liver and nervous system are afflicted since his liver is no longer capable of detoxifying his organism. In the same manner, his central nervous system may also be overly stressed since the liver and nerves are connected with each other.

This smell is especially conspicuous in uncircumcised men since large amounts of semen collect in the foreskin of the penis. As a result, this problem is initially recognized because of the negative response to the smell.

Dripping semen

While the normal amount of semen, which should be about one tablespoon, shoots out of the man's urethra in a high arc for a distance up to one yard (up to two yards in young men), the ejaculate only comes out of the urethra in drops when the prostate gland is afflicted. However, even at an advanced age, dripping ejaculate is not normal, Instead, it indicates the possibility of the following disorders:

- Disturbances of the adrenal glands

208

- Kidney disorders
- Bone disorders (arthritis)

At the age of 35-55 years, dripping semen is an indication of arthritis and diseases of the prostate gland.

Impotence

The term "impotence" means that a man is incapable of achieving and maintaining a satisfactory erection because of stress situations and/or physical or emotional tensions. Disease can also play a role in preventing an erection.

However, the prostate gland is responsible for the inadequate erection in most cases. When an inflamed prostate gland is ignored, the man's interest in sexuality is greatly diminished. This also affects men between the ages of 35 and 55. General statistics confirm the prejudice of Western medicine that says they must live with this condition.

But Taoist Medicine claims exactly the opposite on the topic of impotence: Even at an older age, there is no need to suffer from afflictions of the prostate gland since it only fails because of abuse and lacking massage, which is offered by the Taoist Deer, Crane, and Sphincter Exercises.

Checking the prostate gland:

During urination, try to completely interrupt the urine by contracting the anal sphincter muscle. If you cannot do this several times in a row, then practice according to the guidelines for the male Deer Exercise.

The massage of the prostate gland offers healing from within. It is a beneficial way to take care of the anal region and should be used in addition to the male Deer Exercise after cleansing the anus. Even during the Deer Exercise, you will notice that an intensive massage of the prostate gland is occurring. You can gently penetrate the anus with one finger in the direction of the navel until you feel your prostate gland. When doing this, use special rubber gloves from the first-aid kit along with the herbal St. John's wort oil for inserting the finger.

Please note: Never use any other type of lubricant since those currently on the market contain too many substances and can strain the prostate gland with long-term problems. Don't use lubricants that contain the following additives:

- Acetone
- Carbolic acid

- Lead acid
- Sodium cyclamate
- Dibutyl phthalate
- Sodium hydrogene sulfite
- Diethanolamin
- Coal tar
- Ferric oxide
- Triethanolamin
- Toluene
- P-hydroxyanisol

Since these additives have long been known as cancer-causing substances, be sure to check the ingredients of any lubricant products: These are very quickly absorbed by the large intestine, small intestine, duodenum, and stomach and can cause inflammations in the gastrointestinal tract, which as usually diagnosed as "general diseases." If this is the case, then inform your physician in due time so that he can initiate the appropriate countermeasures when there are problems in the anal region.

Also be sure that the following products do not contain any of the substances mentioned above:
- Cleansing milk, soap
- Body or hand lotions
- Facial crèmes or lotions
- Shampoos and shaving cream
- Cosmetics and tanning agents

These substances are particularly harmful for the prostate gland:
- All saturated fatty acids
- Vaseline, petroleum, cacao butter, cacao crèmes
- Coconut fat, lard, goose fat
- All animal fats in general
- Margarine, in particular, since it is heated seven times and ultimately consists of the purest saturated fatty acids (according to Professor Dr. Stephen T. Chang)

A collection of the above-mentioned cancer-causing substances in the prostate gland can lead to cancer limited to the prostate gland. Further indications that have been observed are changes in the body weight, which may possibly increase from 20 to 80 pounds in the abdominal area since saturated fatty acids can be absorbed in excessive amounts by any part of the body.

These saturated fatty acids on the skin block the natural cell fluid, change the respiratory volume, and lead to asthmatic changes in the bronchial region. An additionally recognizable signal is the premature aging of the organism and a substantial limitation of performance in all areas of life. The risk of heart attack and stroke, which prepare the explosion in the organism like a time fuse, should also be mentioned at this point.

Let's return to the topic of prostatic massage. In earlier times, this was done unintentionally by the old family doctors when they checked the functioning of the prostate gland and wanted to relieve its sensitivity and restore its functionality. In order to avoid a premature operation of the prostate gland, the male Deer Exercise should be used as a preventive measure, along with inserting the fingers to specifically massage the prostate gland. It would naturally be an ideal situation if the partner or wife were to help the man by doing this massage for him. The concern about coming in contact with germs during the prostatic massage can be avoided by using rubber gloves. Any possible negative preconceptions should be released because the preventive prostatic massage could be a lifesaver for the man since not properly caring for the prostate gland can lead to prostate cancer.

Men should frequently—at least once a week—check the condition of their prostate gland, paying attention to changes in the size and elasticity. In this way, any unnatural swelling and an enlarged, hard, or painful prostate gland can be quickly identified.

A hard or very painful prostate gland means that an illness, possibly even cancer, may exist. However, if you do the male Deer Exercise every day, you have access to both preventive measures and measures for healing any diseases that may already be present in the prostate gland through this series of exercises.

DETERMINATION AND THERAPY OF PROSTATE COMPLAINTS

Taoist Medicine has compiled a series of test methods for determining prostate complaints. If one of the following indications of prostate disease applies to you, there are a number of effective alternatives:

• Massaging the anal region with a healing ointment on a regular basis.
• Using the anal contractions to interrupt the urinary stream (5-7 times)
• Practicing the anal-sphincter contractions of the male Deer Exercise in order to prevent prostate problems or begin with rehabilitation.
• Some of the recommended Taoist chi kung therapy methods are the meridian massage and the "Driving Away One-Hundred Afflictions" and "The Crane Stands on One Leg" exercises.

Symptoms of Prostate Complaints:

1. Pain or sensitivity along the kidney meridian. Each type of sensitivity to pain in this area indicates energy congestion and insufficient circulation in the male sexual organs. These are the kidneys, adrenal glands, testicles, prostate gland, and penis.

2. Frequent urination is often caused by a kidney or bladder weakness, but it may also be caused by an enlarged prostate gland.

3. Aggravated or painful urination.

4. Pain in the perineal area during the erection.

5. Pain during ejaculation.

6. Blood in the semen.

7. The prostate gland feels hard as a rock, swollen, or too soft when it is touched. It should be somewhat egg-shaped and elastic.

8. Weak or bad-smelling ejaculate.

9. The semen is not expelled powerfully, but just comes out drop by drop. A healthy adult male should be able to shoot his semen at a distance of one yard.

10. Diminished feeling of well-being during ejaculation

11. Premature or nighttime ejaculation.

12. Impotence.

13. No ejaculation because the prostate gland is too slack.

14. Drops of urine still come out several minutes after urination.

MEDICATION AND ITS EFFECTS ON THE SEXUAL GLANDS AND ORGANS

The customary medications are chemicals that trigger a corresponding chemical reaction in the body, in accordance with their nature. In contrast to herbal remedies, which have no side effects, these medications have neither a supportive nor a strengthening influence upon the organs and meridians: They only stimulate and have side effects that have not yet been completely studied.

Such medications may bring immediate relief for every type of physical weakness: Their effects can be felt within seconds or minutes. This contrasts with the healing effects of herbs, which may only be determined after weeks or months. However, the chemical medications have the disadvantage that the patient very quickly becomes accustomed to them. Since such medications are also very easy to handle, there is a danger of the patient increasing the dosage whenever he or she feels like it. The result is that the initially prescribed therapy no longer stimulates the organs. The higher dosage causes considerable damage to the organism and only relieves the symptoms while the herbs fight against the cause of the problem.

Medications act with violence in order to force the body back into a healthy state. This excessive strain on the body blocks the bodily functions at the end of the treatment and ultimately brings them to a standstill—this also applies particularly to the sexual organs and meridians.

Whenever medication is taken over a longer period of time, the aura—the electromagnetic energy field of a human being—is disturbed and its actual mode of action is reversed. However, "chemical clubs" prescribed by a physician and taken in a careful and moderate manner over a short time span can be very helpful—just like a small amount of alcohol is relaxing but larger amounts will eventually lead to alcoholism and a weakening of the entire organism.

For example, smoking or drinking coffee on a regular basis, taking hormone tablets like the pill or hormones to correct menstrual problems and regulate menopause or migraines can destroy 10% of the liver. Smoking two or more joints of marihuana every day can destroy 15% of the liver within one month. In terms of sexual intercourse, when it occurs 3-5 times a week and the man ejaculates, this disturbs the liver function for both participants.

Any type of inhaled smoke strains the liver, just like alcohol and coffee. Because of the liver's cleansing process in which it arduously must purify the blood of toxic particles, it becomes poisoned itself. A liver that has been contaminated in this manner will never recover completely—unless it is supported by the therapeutic chi kung exercises for the liver and pancreas or by taking the leaves of the buplever bush (hare's ear) under the supervision of a chi kung master or physician.

THERAPY SUGGESTIONS FOR PROSTATE COMPLAINTS

The man's prostate gland is a structure that is part gland and part muscle. It surrounds the beginning of the urethra at the bladder opening. It is approximately the size of a chestnut. During middle age, it can enlarge and impede urination.

About 60% of all men over 40 have an enlarged prostate gland, and half of these men have no related complaints. This enlargement is sometimes attributed to tumors. But no matter what has caused this enlargement, the following complaints may accompany it: bladder infection, a distention of the bladder, retention of urine, formation of an intestinal infection, and bladder stones. These complaints can cause high blood pressure and even blood poisoning through uremia. The urge to urinate may occur without the patient being able to urinate. Sometimes this feeling is also just a false alarm. There may also sometimes be a burning sensation during urination. In the process, the bladder is often not emptied completely, and this is also one cause of the irritation.

Case History:
I remember an older gentleman by the name of Herbert K. He came to my practice from a nursing home. His blood pressure was very high and he was mentally disoriented. He said that he could no longer sleep because he constantly had to go to the toilet at night. The urine retention caused by the prostate gland was not total, but it was already accumulating in the urinary system and poisoning his blood.

We treated the acupressure points on the ankles, as well as the other points described in the treatment instructions. I gave him a copy of these instructions so that he could treat himself. Soon afterward, he called me and said that he was very happy. His self-poisoning (auto-intoxication) had apparently been relieved. The nightly trips to the toilet had stopped.

Treatment Instructions for Prostate Complaints

A	B	C	D	E	F	G
Sp-6	CV-1	Ki-5	Li-9	GV-1	Bl-31	Prostata
Sp-15	CV-4	Ki-7		Bl-32		"Z Zones"
	CV-6	Ki-27		Bl-65		on the feet
	CV-7					

Prostate acupuncture points for therapy

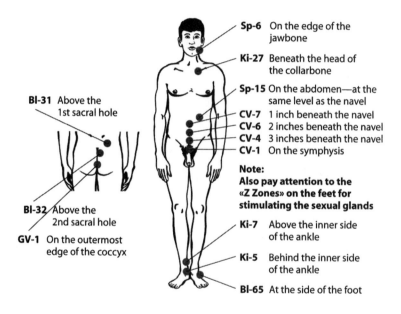

Bl-31 Above the 1st sacral hole

Bl-32 Above the 2nd sacral hole

GV-1 On the outermost edge of the coccyx

Sp-6 On the edge of the jawbone

Ki-27 Beneath the head of the collarbone

Sp-15 On the abdomen—at the same level as the navel

CV-7 1 inch beneath the navel

CV-6 2 inches beneath the navel

CV-4 3 inches beneath the navel

CV-1 On the symphysis

Note:
Also pay attention to the «Z Zones» on the feet for stimulating the sexual glands

Ki-7 Above the inner side of the ankle

Ki-5 Behind the inner side of the ankle

Bl-65 At the side of the foot

215

THE RHYTHM THEORY
The Healing Retention of the Semen Energy

"In this state, we once again harmonize with the powers of nature, which support all of our justified needs and help us in the realization of our dreams and desires."

Many people in the West worry about too little sex. The Chinese, on the other hand, worry about the opposite—too much sex. Since the man's ejaculation and the woman's orgasm (even if the latter is to a lesser degree) weaken the kidney energy (jing), too much sex is considered a possible source of illness in Chinese Medicine. The men are actually the ones in the East who take the effects of too much sex very seriously. Many men with injured kidney chi complain about tiredness after sex. The kidney chi of a woman can also be weakened by too many births within a short period of time.

Using the rhythm theory, a man can determine how frequently he should ejaculate. However, it is important to remember one thing: Taoism is concerned with retaining as much energy as possible and losing as little energy as possible. It is best to not ejaculate at all. Only men who believe that this approach is not possible for them should use the rhythm theory.

The rhythm theory is suitable only for men with a "normal" sexual life. Anyone who follows the philosophy of the Tao and wants to consciously increase his energy, as well as make his body healthier and younger, must find his own individual rhythm. For this purpose, it is possible to ejaculate once and then live in complete abstinence for a number of days—which means not even thinking about sex. If you do this experiment, it is best to avoid your partner as much as you can. But explain what you are doing in advance in order to avoid misunderstandings.

After several days, your sexual desire will probably increase slightly. Pay as little attention to this as possible and avoid every type of sexual stimulation if your desire increases with time. When you have finally reached the point that your longing can no longer be ignored, then you know that you have found your rhythm. The number of days that have passed since your last ejaculation correspond with your individual rhythm. Now you know the interval of time in which you can ejaculate without harming yourself.

When you have found your rhythm, you can also determine your biological age. Use this rhythm formula for this purpose: If you cycle lasts 4 days, then you are 20 years old from the biological perspective $(4 : 0.2 = 20)$, no matter how many years you have lived. If your rhythm is 16 days, your biological age corresponds with 80 years $(16 : 0.2 = 80)$. This also applies even if you are actually just 40 years old.

Everything in the universe has its rhythm and its cycles, including human beings. Women have their menstrual flow and men also have their cycle, even though it may be less apparent. According to the ancient Taoist writings, there are specific times during which it is not harmful for men to ejaculate. The time intervals in between serve to regain the lost energy and nutrients. The respective individual rhythm for a man can be determined with the following formula:

Age x 0.2 = frequency of ejaculation in days.

If, for example, a man is 30 years old, his cycle changes in the rhythm of 6 days $(30 \times 0.2 = 6)$. This means: he can—assuming that he is healthy—

ejaculate every 6 days without harming himself. Accordingly, one cycle lasts 4 days for a 20-year-old man and 10 days for a 50-year-old man, etc. Despite following this cycle, vital energy will still be lost through the ejaculation; however, it will be restored if he follows his rhythm. Then he can maintain his equilibrium; yet, immoderate and uncontrolled sex with frequent ejaculations will very quickly exhaust a man's energy reserves. If he behaves in this manner, he will wear himself out and draw near to death. On the other hand, if a man maintains his rhythm in accordance with the above formula, he can control his ejaculations, regulate his losses, and balance his "account" time and again in this manner. Although he may not grow richer as a result, he will also not become poorer.

Between the ejaculations, a man can and should perform the sexual act as often as possible. However, he must be able to restrain himself and experience the "higher orgasm" until he once again reaches the point where an ejaculation will not harm him.

In an advice book of the Sui Dynasty (581-618 A.D.), Master Tsu Hse, one of the founders of Taoist Medicine, gives the following recommendations for the male's frequency of ejaculation since there are also recommendations related to age for the minimum of ejaculations:
• 20 years = every 4 days
• 40 years = every 16 days
• 60 years = every 30 days

Age in Years	Good Condition	Average Condition	Poor Condition
15 – 20	1 x daily	Every 3 days	Every 5 days
20 – 30	Every 2 days	Every 5 days	Every 7 days
30 – 40	Every 3 days	Every 6 days	Every 9 days
40 – 50	Every 4 days	Every 8 days	Every 12 days
50 – 60	Every 5 days	Every 10 days	Every 15 days
60 – 70	Every 10 days	Every 20 days	Every 30 days
70 – 80	Every 20 days	Every 30 days	Every 50 days
80 – 90	Every 40 days	Every 80 days	No more ejaculations

Although this classic shows the importance of the topic, it is hardly discussed in modern-day China. This fact also corresponds with the relative disinterest of modern males in their emotions as a possible cause of disease.

Information on the most effective sexual therapy for the man and woman in relation to the healing effects of holding back during the sexual act

The Taoist methods of holding back makes it possible for the man and woman to not only achieve an "unlimited higher orgasm"; but just like the "Nine-Times-Ten Sequence," it also has a healing effect on the endocrine system of both partners and their reflex zones in relation to the penis and vagina during the sexual act.

The following effects of holding back the semen energy in the man were reported by one of the founders of the ancient Chinese diagnosis and therapy procedure of Taoist Medicine, Master Tsu Hse, a prehistoric sage who is said to have discovered the "five phases of change of the vital energy of chi": exercise, breathing, nutrition, sexuality, and meditation.

- **Wood** = the chi of the tiger.
- **Fire** = the blood and bodily fluids of the dragon or the snake.
- **Earth** = the human being between heaven and earth, symbol of the bear.
- **Metal** = the 12 main pathways, meridians energy cycle, symbol of the crane.
- **Water** = the 8 special pathways or miracle meridians, symbol of the ape.

The more frequently a man holds back during the sexual act with the woman, the more intensely his semen essence will in turn give him endurance, strength, and security, as well as health and longevity.

A reminder: During the man's customary orgasm, the prostate gland (when it is stimulated 100%) will empty itself through a series of contractions and hurl out about 200 to 500 million semen cells from the "Man's Energy Palace" (one hand's width beneath the navel). This is equivalent to an energy loss of almost six weeks' time and considerably restricts the man's health and longevity.

This is why the technique of holding back the vital semen energy should be practiced every day together with the male Deer Exercise. This stimulation should guide a man to hold back during lovemaking since the more he holds back, the more vital energy and nutrients will be developed within his body. This creates reserves for health and longevity—not only in the sexual area.

The assumption that holding back can have healing effects on the body is based upon the scientifically proven fact that male semen has a very high nutritional value. Just like the blood, the semen is part of the "receptive force" (yin) and is the feminine passive energy of the body and the universe. Semen and blood are the essence of the vital energy. The male semen is made of an unchangeable and insuperable substance that cannot even be burned. When the semen force penetrates the organism, it restores the vital force of the inner organs and replaces the weakened body cells.

THE TECHNIQUE OF EXTRACTION

Ejaculation—the coming and going of the semen—is a feeling of utmost stimulation and a very special pleasure for every man. A man who prefers the feeling of well-being caused by the emission of semen will find a directly applicable method in the technique of the healing retention of semen in which no semen energy is lost and sexual elation is undiminished. This Taoist technique is called the extraction technique.

In this form of its application, the man "extracts" the vital components, meaning the essence of the semen, in order to inject them into his body. The remaining fluid that remains after the extraction is generally worthless (according to the opinion of the ancient Taoist sages, this semen is no longer useful for reproductive purposes).

The man ejaculates this remaining fluid and thereby experiences the familiar and intimate feeling of elation related to ejaculation.

Exercise Sequence for the Extraction Technique:
1. The man works himself into an intensity of 98 or 99% until he is just before the point of one more thrust leading him to ejaculation (100%).
2. Precisely at this moment, he performs the anal-sphincter contraction of the male Deer Exercise (tensing of the anus and pelvic floor, as well as holding his breath). This act causes the intensity to diminish to 60 to 70%, just as the man desires. Then he can continue his activities again with long and short thrusts.
3. This technique of holding back should be done 5 to 8 times in a row. Only then should the man decide to ejaculate. He then ejaculates, but only the remaining fluid comes out. So he can ejaculate without having to fear that he will lose some of the life-sustaining components of the semen.

Effects:

- With the technique of holding back or extraction, he learns to control the prostate gland and not allow any stimulation above 98 to 99%.
- By contracting the anal-sphincter muscles and the pelvic floor, the prostate gland is emptied. However, this occurs in the opposite direction than for normal ejaculation. Instead of shooting out, the semen moves inward and upward to the brain in order to nourish it. This is called "injaculation."
- Since the male Deer Exercise used during the extraction technique also stimulates the circulation in the area of the pubic bone, the semen is carried into other areas of the body through the blood and nourishes the organs, glands, nerves, and other parts of the body.
- At the same time, the man has the feeling of an extensive and progressive orgasm since the extraction technique stimulates the contractions. His partner feels the pulsating of the penis and is delighted by it.
- The technique of extraction makes it possible for the man and woman to not only have an unlimited higher orgasm; it also has a healing and beneficial effect on both of them, whereby the beneficial effect on the man is in the foreground here.

The ten forms for the well-being of the woman and benefit of the man in the retention of the semen energy:

Number of retentions of the semen energy by the man	Increases the body's own powers of self-healing, as well as strength, vitality, and endurance
When the semen energy is **held back once**	ntensifies the semen energy, strengthens the body and the vital energy **House of the Semen Essence**
When the semen energy is **held back twice**	Strengthens the eyes, nose, and ears **House of Growth = thyroid gland**
When the semen energy is **held back three times**	Increases the powers of resistance, strengthens the body's immune system, and slows the aging process **House of Water = kidneys**
When the semen energy is **held back four times**	Strengthens the endocrine system and refills the energy reserves: sexual glands, adrenal glands, pancreas, thymus gland, thyroid gland, pituitary gland, and pineal gland **House of the adrenal glands**

When the semen energy is **held back five times**	Improves circulation, prevents stroke and heart attack, as well as phlebitis **House of the Heart = thymus gland**
When the semen energy is **held back six times**	Supplies the bones with energy, prevents arthritis and bone atrophy **House of Water = kidneys/bladder**
When the semen energy is **held back seven times**	Strengthens muscles, tendons, and ligaments and increases their elasticity **House of Water = kidneys/bladder** **House of the Heart = thymus gland**
When the semen energy is **held back eight times**	Develops and strengthens the aura, as well as the "sixth sense" for extrasensory perceptions **House of Intelligence = pituitary gland** **House of the Mind = pineal gland**
When the semen energy is **held back nine times**	Heals all diseases of the body and mind, promotes unlimited health and longevity **House of the Mind = pineal gland** **House of Intelligence = pituitary gland** **House of Growth = thyroid gland** **House of the Heart = thymus gland** **House of Transcendence = pancreas** **House of Water = adrenal glands** **House of the Semen Essence = sexual glands**
When the semen energy is **held back ten times**	Spiritualizes the man since the pituitary gland and the pineal gland are now completely filled with new vital energy. **House of the Mind**

This description of the one to 10 retentions with the effects on the man comes from the book Su-Nue Ching of the ancient Chinese diagnosis and therapy procedure of Taoist Medicine. The man should therefore be encouraged to practice this extraction technique since the more he holds back during the sexual act with his partner, the healthier his organism will become. Consequently, it is supplied with more energy and nutrients, which in turn gives him strength and endurance, beauty and security.

Please note: The healing effect of retaining the semen energy also occurs when the man masturbates. However, it is more pleasurable and better to use this extraction technique during the sexual act with a partner since reality is much more effective than the imagination.

BAI-HUI
"Meeting point of all meridians"
(Du Mai 20)
of the crown point

6. YUEZHEN
"Jade Pillow"
(Bladder 9) right & left
on back of head
1 inch above the hairline

5. DAZHUI
"Big Hammer"
(Du Mai 13)
between the 1st and 2nd
thoracic vertebrae

4. MINGMEN
"Gate of Life"
(Du Mai 5)
between the 1st and 2nd
lumbar vertebrae
opposite the navel

Brain

8. YINTANG
"Upper Cinnabar Field"
(PAM 3)
between the eyebrows,
at the root of the nose

9. TANZHONG
"Middle Cinnabar Field"
(Ren Mai 17)
on the sternum,
between the nipples—
in the 4th ICR

1. SHAO DANTIEN
"Lower Cinnabar Field"
(Du Mai 3)
One hand's width
beneath the navel

PC muscle   **PC muscle**

2. HUIYIN
"Meeting point of yin"
(Ren Mai 1)
in the center of the perineum
between sexual organs & anus

THE SEVEN SEMEN ENERGIES

According to the classifications of the ancient Chinese healing wisdom, which are now also known in the West, the male semen consists of "seven semen energies." The healing power of these seven semen energies was already praised in ancient times since they strengthen and nourish the endocrine gland system, and therefore also the immune system.

The **"seven semen energies,"** which are supplied again to the organism through the extraction technique

Pineal gland produces	Shizandra	Lack = Weak memory
Pituitary gland produces	Elettaria	Lack = Hormonal problems
Thyroid gland produces	Plantago	Lack = Immune weakness
Thymus gland produces	Rubus	Lack = Heart problems
Pancreas produces	Lycium	Lack = Diabetes problems
Adrenal glands produce	Cuscuta	Lack = Kidney weakness
Sexual glands produce	Siltinum	Lack = Potency problems

Already in the year 1965, Dr. Takuchi Shotai from Tokyo studied the "seven semen energies." The results of his research work and the effects of the energies on the sex drive shocked the Japanese public. What had occurred?

The extracts of the "seven semen energies" of Siltinum, Cuscuta, Lycium, Rubus, Plantago, Elettaria, and Shizandra were tested on 75 married couples with ages ranging from 50-80 years. The couples were physically and mentally healthy, but all had lost their desire for sex and had not had sexual contact for years.

Just 2 weeks after taking these semen extracts, 20 couples had already had sexual contact. Four weeks later, 50 couples had sexual contact. After 18 weeks, a total of 70 couples now had sexual contact on a regular basis. Because of the strict Japanese customs, this practice was severely rejected at that time. Even today, these semen extracts are secretly sold in Japan and America, and even in Europe.

Through the Taoist inner exercises, primarily the male Deer Exercise of anal-sphincter contractions with the tensing of the PC muscle, the "seven semen energies" are reactivated and sexual performance is restored. However, this simple regeneration of the endocrine system's willingness to perform must be practiced on a daily basis since the proverb applies here as well: practice makes perfect!

Please note: When too much semen energy has been lost, the restoration of the "seven semen energies" may be delayed over a longer period of time, which considerably reduces the related vitality and weakens the man's vital force in the long run.

THE MYSTERIOUS ACUPRESSURE POINT JEN-MO

Technique for Suspending and Reversing the Ejaculation

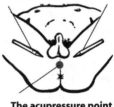

**Moxa therapy
(with herbal cigars) beneath the testicles
for erectile disorders**

**The acupressure point
Jen-mo**

THE JEN-MO TECHNIQUE FOR PROTECTING THE SEMEN

Knowing where, how, and when to press the jen-mo point naturally requires a certain amount of practice. It should be pressed with exactly the right amount of pressure—not too much and not too little. Initially practice this during masturbation until you are certain you can find this point. Pressing the jen-mo point is actually quite simple. With a bit of practice, you can learn to press it so discreetly that your partner won't even notice.

- Just before you ejaculate, simply reach around your thigh and find the point. Press it firmly enough to prevent the semen from exiting the prostate gland.

- If you press too close to the testicles, the semen will get into the bladder and be lost the next time you urinate. If there are repeated failed attempts, the semen will irritate the bladder, which can lead to an inflammation of the bladder.

- However, if you press too close to the anus, the emission will not be stopped. In both cases, this exercise will become useless for you.

In order to avoid the loss of semen, the canals at the base of the prostate gland must be closed with the pressure of the finger. The semen ejaculate can only be withdrawn and absorbed by the blood when this is done.

Important note:
A special acupressure point is located between the anus and the scrotum. This mysterious point, the "Flowing Together of the Yin," where the Servant and the Governor Vessels unite, is called the jen-mo "Conception Meridian" or also the "Conception Vessel." If you press it with three fingers, it feels like a small indentation.

If the jen-mo point is pressed directly before the seminal emission, ejaculation can be reversed without the seminal emission occurring. By means of this technique, a man is much more capable of "injaculating," meaning that he transforms his semen and achieves a more intensive orgasm without losing the semen. At the same time, the semen is withdrawn completely from the full prostate gland and absorbed by the blood. The semen energy rises upward through the meridians, which begin at this point, instead of leaving the body (which is the case for normal ejaculation).

In this way, the man feels all the pleasant sensations that accompany the prostate contractions during ejaculation, but without losing the positive semen energy. However, he should only press this jen-mo point until the orgasm or the resulting transformation of the semen has been completed.

Even beyond the climax of the orgasm, the man should continue to masturbate and apply pressure to the jen-mo point until the pleasant sensations accompanying the prostate contractions have passed.

With this technique of the jen-mo acupressure, there is no failure since it has the great advantage of the man maintaining the erection of his "brave warrior" much longer and continuing the love play until the completion of the female orgasm. This method is also said to avoid unwanted pregnancy of the partner.

Please note: If you have an inflammation of the prostate gland, you must see a physician and receive treatment before you can begin learning the jen-mo technique of interrupting the seminal emission. However, you can bridge the time period until your recovery from the disorder by practicing the PC-muscle tensing of the male Deer Exercise, which will accelerate the healing process.

HOW THE JEN-MO TECHNIQUE WORKS

Once you have used the jen-mo technique and successfully prevented ejaculation, you can use a test to determine whether the semen has returned to the blood circulation or ended up in the bladder. Urinate into a jar for this purpose. A milky urine means that the semen has reached the bladder. After one to two hours, this will be more clearly visible since the semen ejaculate will sink to the bottom of the jar and the clear urine will be above it.

> Men who eat primarily alkaline foods often have bubbly urine. If semen gets into the bladder, the urine will bubble even more intensely.

> During normal ejaculation, meaning that you do not press the jen-mo point or interrupt it by using the anal-sphincter contractions of the male Deer Exercise, about 1/3 of the ejaculate will reach the bladder.

Both techniques of interrupting the ejaculation are not just theoretical in nature. They show the direct, highly stimulating results of a continued will to perform that is demonstrated not only in sexuality but also in the rejuvenation of the man practicing these techniques. The Taoists call this procedure of giving the creative force from their sexual glands back to their body "rebirth."

Many men and even women think that it is unnatural to stop ejaculation, even if there are such positive reasons for doing so. On the level of human consciousness, ejaculation must seem as natural as death. It is said that the man dies a "little death" during each ejaculation. Yet, on the higher level of consciousness, everything that we humans consider unnatural has a natural and necessary reason.

If we want to decide in favor of nature and longevity, then we must prevent ejaculation and menstruation according to the Taoist principles—unless we want to conceive a child.

INJACULATION FOR PROLONGING
AROUSAL AND LIFE

How can such simple techniques like pressing the jen-mo point and performing the male Deer Exercise have such a profound effect on the organism?

The prostate gland contracts and then again expands during a normal orgasm with seminal emission. When a man presses the jen-mo point, he can determine how quickly the prostate gland empties itself. This can occur in fractions of a second during a normal orgasm. When the Taoist technique of finger pressure is used on the jen-mo point, this emptying can be extended for up to five minutes, which also results in a longer-lasting, more intensive orgasm of up to five minutes.

However, even more important than the extended and more intensive orgasm is the fact that the energy and nutrients of the semen—which contain vital substances such as protein, vitamins, minerals, and amino acids, according to scientific studies—are conserved for the body. When this technique is used, the semen does not reach the bladder or the urethra. Instead, the ejaculate initially remains in the prostate gland. From there, the semen is taken into the blood circulation, rises up into the body, and is distributed to the seven glands of the endocrine system, which it supplies with energy. It gives the entire body vital energies and nutrients, activates the skin, lubricates the joints, strengthens the nerves, and is therefore an excellent preventive remedy against diseases such as multiple sclerosis.

In acupuncture, the jen-mo point is called the "First Conception Meridian." It is an energy door through which the male body continuously leaks energy to the surrounding world. Not even abstention can seal this leak. However, through the Taoist closing techniques such as pressing the jen-mo point or the exercise sequence of the male Deer Exercise, it is possible to close this unheeded leak and therefore prevent vital energies from being lost involuntarily.

> There is also a Taoist sitting position for this purpose in which the heel of one foot is pressed against the jen-mo point, which also closes the energy leak. Even in the West, this seated posture is described as an important technique. Sitting on the ishium is not only recommended for stabilizing the entire spinal column: the pressure on the jen-mo point as the connective point between the two legs also closes the entrance door to the energy leak. This can be supported by also performing the closure of the anus and pelvic floor in a varied sequence (contract 7 times for each gland = a total of 49 repetitions).

The tip of the tongue is an additional, important point through which energy is lost. Consequently, the Taoists recommend placing the tip of the tongue on the gums and bending it backward to stop the flow of energy in the body during meditation and even situations that threaten to become stressful, for example.

THE JEN-MO POINT
AS A BIRTH-CONTROL METHOD

Women should also be aware of the fascinating effect of the jen-mo technique since it can help a woman and her partner to achieve undreamed-of heights during sexual intercourse. When a woman presses this stimulation point immediately before the man's orgasm, this increases the desire of both partners many times over.

However, even in ancient China, the technique of pressing the jen-mo point had the function of aiding in family planning and preventing unwanted pregnancies. The ancient Taoist writings tell us that farmers were mainly happy about the birth of new family members because that meant additional workers. It was a special blessing to conceive many children without having to pay particular attention to their health and education.

The Yellow Emperor, his ministers and army leaders, bodyguards, and all of the aristocracy at the emperor's court behaved in exactly the opposite manner. For them, a marriage that was appropriate for a person's rank, the intelligence and legitimacy of a child, the necessity of a son and heir, as well as his medical care and higher education, played a much more important role. All of the members of the Chinese aristocracy made use of the jen-mo point and both techniques of the male Deer Exercise for family planning in order to prevent pregnancies that were unwanted, unnecessary, illegitimate, or at the wrong time. Protection of the semen was a deep-rooted conviction. A couple's own flesh and blood should not have to suffer because of the parent's lust, foolishness, or mistakes.

This is why Yian, a Taoist physician from the Han Dynasty, wrote the following:

"The masculine (= the semen) is from the yang. However, the yang is quick to become aroused (= erection) and yields just as quickly (loss of the ability to have an erection). The feminine (= the jade gate) is from the yin. However, yin is only aroused slowly ("letting the water steam") and takes just as long to satisfy ("the nine steps of the female orgasm"). Yet, while yin is present in an excessive amount and has endurance, yang is limited and vulnerable (= loss through ejaculation). For these reasons, controlling the ejaculation by pressing the jen-mo point is one of the alternatives for maintaining health and longevity.

These correlations are also reflected in the higher life expectancy of women, who live an average of 5-15 years longer than men. The key bringing imbalances back into equilibrium lies in the proper regulation of the relationship between the two sexes: between fire (man) and water (woman), the path of yin and yang that shows us how we can promote health and longevity through sexuality.

The jen-mo acupressure point is one of the most important aspects for transforming the man's semen energy. Only in the advanced stage is it replaced by the PC-muscle tensing of the anal sphincter and the pelvic floor as a much greater control of reversing the semen. The technique of the jen-mo point is just as valuable as it is pleasurable; however, it is soon left behind as "beginner's experience" once a man has learned the advanced techniques such as the Deer Exercise.

THE ADVANTAGES OF INJACULATION

We can assume that both the female and the male readers are now asking: How can sex without the man's ejaculation be any fun at all! The Yellow Emperor also asked the same question when his advisers called upon him to begin with the practice of ejaculation control. Following the Yellow Emperor's question on this point, the following conversation arose between Beng-Ze and the Rainbow Girl, which has been recorded in the Taoist document "Secrets of the Jade Chamber."

Rainbow Girl: It is generally supposed that a man derives great pleasure from ejaculation. But when he learns the Tao he will emit less and less, will not his pleasure also diminish?

Beng-Ze: Far from it. After ejaculation a man is tired, his ears are buzzing, his eyes heavy and he longs for sleep. He is thirsty and his limbs inert and stiff. In ejaculation he experiences a brief second of sensation but long hours of weariness as a result. And that is certainly not a true pleasure. On the other hand, if a man reduces and regulates his ejaculation to an absolute minimum, his body will be strengthened, his mind at ease and his vision and hearing improved. Although the man seems to have denied himself an ejaculatory sensation at times, his love for his woman will greatly increase. It is as if he could never have enough of her. And this is the true lasting pleasure, is it not?

Please note: This last sentence contains an especially subtle and important observation. A man who constantly keeps his testosterone level high and increases his supply of sperm and other components of the masculine essence by practicing ejaculation control will experience a considerable strengthening of the love and affection he feels for his wife. He will also develop the ability to give into this loving desire time and again.

In the Taoist art of love, the emphasis is not placed upon romantic love, but the right technique. This is almost like sporting competition: Winning alone is not enough—both teams must be "in shape" through practice and they must know the rules of the game. However, the Taoist image of sex as a battle, the "battlefield covered with flowers," in no way corresponds with what the West likes to call the "battle of the sexes." This latter formulation indicates a fundamental conflict of opposing views and a vehement struggle for sexual superiority that extends beyond the bedroom. By way of contrast, the Taoists mean the practical, tactical aspects of actual sexual intercourse—which they call the "bedroom strategy."

In the erotic novel *The Prayer Mat of the Flesh* by Li Yu, an author from the Ming Dynasty, we find an amusing description of this martial approach to sexual relationships:

• Apart from the number of participants, are there real differences between the battles that armies carry out with each other and those that take place in bed? In both cases, the most important task of the commander is to get an overview of the terrain and assess the opponent.

• In sexual encounters, the man first turns his attention to the hills and valleys of the woman, while the woman is mostly interested in the size and firepower of his weapons.

• Who will advance and who will retreat? In bed as in war, it is equally important to know oneself and to know one's opponent.

In contrast to battles fought with swords and spears, the women have the advantage over the men. And this is why men must train more for this "battle of love." However, since most men like to think of themselves as stronger than women, they believe their "five-minute blitzkrieg" in bed is completely adequate; most women act satisfied with it but do not actually tell the men what they really want.

In order to truly satisfy his partner and nourish his own essence and energy instead of exhausting it, a man must learn:

- How to prolong the sexual act and repeat it until his partner has experienced complete satisfaction by using the technique of the jen-mo acupressure point in due time before the seminal emission
  - And, in the advanced stage, the technique of the PC muscle (tensing the anal muscles and drawing up the pelvic floor).

The "Plain Girl" calls this method "contact without leaking."

When sexual encounters take place according to the laws of the path, they become a "boundless source of energy" that never dries up and never has an exhausting effect. Moreover, complete abstinence is as harmful for a man's health as an excess of sexual activity.

STATISTICAL STUDIES ON THE JEN-MO POINT

In the course of 15 years (1974 to 1989), 3379 male students in America ranging in age from 19 to 64 years volunteered to participate in a study. Below are some of Professor Stephen T. Chang's interesting research findings:

On the Jen-Mo Point:

1. 73% of the people who learned the technique of pressing the jen-mo point were in their thirties.

2. 85.4% of all participants had an excellent response to it.

3. 12.6% felt no significant difference.

4. 1.96% felt discomfort at times.

One man reported that he felt pain when pressing on the jen-mo point. This man had not participated in the entire seminar on the "Tao of Sexuality" in 1972, but had just attended one hour of instruction, so he had not heard the warning about it. Furthermore, his physician had diagnosed him with a serious inflammation of the prostate gland. When he complained that the pressure on the jen-mo point worsened his complaints, he was advised to immediately stop doing the exercise and first heal his prostate inflammation. Only then should he resume with pressing the point. After his inflammation had subsided, he once again began to press the point and achieved excellent results. Careful examination of the possible causes of the unpleasant sensations revealed that these feelings were based on psychological factors. Continued and regular practice released local tensions, fears and nervousness, and the discomfort disappeared.

On the Male Deer Exercise:

1. The same 3379 people also participated in this study.

2. 78.6% of the men who wanted to hold back during ejaculation were older than 35 years.

3. 91% found the technique of holding back ejaculation to be useful.

4. 8.2% were not satisfied with the results. Almost 1% were afraid to use the technique.

On the Female Deer Exercise:

During the same time period, an additional report was produced. 756 female volunteers ranging in age from 21 to 45 years participated in this study.

1. No one particular age group showed a greater preference for the Deer Exercise than any other age group.

2. 95% of the women felt better after doing this exercise. 5% felt no change. None of the women felt worse afterward.

3. Only 221 women attempted to interrupt their menstrual cycles. Of these, almost 40% were able to completely stop their periods and another 40% experienced a considerable reduction of the bleeding (some had a yellowish or brownish residual discharge). Approximately 20% were not able to influence their menstruation.

4. The 395 women who were able to completely stop their menstrual cycles required three months to do so. About 60% required up to six months and 1% took a year or longer to do so.

EJACULATION
The Coming and Going of the Semen Energy

"The problem with the men of today is that their efforts in sexuality are directed to the leaves and branches instead of the trunk and the roots of love."

SEMINAL DISCHARGE AND ITS EFFECT ON THE HEALTH AND PERSONALITY OF A MAN

1. The task of the prostate gland is to discharge semen, the millions and millions of sperm that carry the female and male DNA code within them. They determine a man's health and longevity, as well as his disposition for illness. Taoist Medicine calls the seminal discharge jing, the "essence of the actual vital strength." This means that the jing is the vehicle of sexual energy that gives form to the material of new life through a type of encrypted message, the DNA code.

2. According to this perspective, ejaculation is a complex process. While the penis is being stimulated, the prostate gland becomes filled with fluid. When it reaches its maximum capacity, it quickly contracts a number of times until it has returned to its normal size.

3. Through these contractions, which the man feels as an orgasm, the fluid is ejected from the prostate gland through the urethra into the penis and out of its tip. Each time it contracts with the subsequent relaxation, the prostate gland draws semen from the seminal vesicles. In this way, a man who practices the "Immortal Breath" (the chi kung exercises of the Deer, Crane, and Turtle) can experience up to 49 contractions. The orgasm consists of such contractions, which is why disorders or complaints of the prostate gland impact its quality.

4. The male sexual glands are the prostate gland and the testicles. The penis is not considered a sexual gland because it is not a gland and actually produces nothing. It is simply the tube through which the glandular secretions flow, an instrument that the sexual glands use for reproduction.

   The testicles produce sperm and hormones; the prostate gland produces the seminal fluid that contains the nutrients, hormones, and vital energy. The two fluids of the testicles and prostate gland form what we call semen—the means of transportation for the sperm.

5. When the normal adult male ejaculates, he loses about one tablespoon of semen. According to the latest scientific studies, this amount of semen contains the nutrients of 2 large steaks, 10 eggs, 8 oranges, 6 lemons, and 5 bananas. It also contains protein, vitamins, minerals, and amino acids—simply everything that the man needs for daily

life. In addition, the semen also contains much vital energy so that each loss of semen means a great deficit of energy and explains the man's exhaustion after ejaculation.

Losing the semen is often called "coming" in colloquial speech, but the more correct expression for it should be something like "going." Just like the erection, the approx. 200-300 million living sperm, hormones, nutrients, vitamins, strength, endurance, even a part of a man's personality and his sense of self-worth, "go" and are lost within seconds in the truest sense of the word. This seminal discharge means a great sacrifice for the man since the physical, mental, and emotional capacities will be extinguished for a longer period of time, just like a burning candle is put out by a bucket of water.

6. After ejaculation, all seven glands are empty, especially the sexual glands, which provide the endocrine system with energy. Taoist Medicine has the following comment on this situation:

"If you go in this direction and focus the sexual energy downward, then you will empty the seven glands. Then you are taking the human path and all humans die before their time (ejaculation = loss of millions of living sperm = reduced life expectancy). A living lion can change into a dead dog within the shortest amount of time, and the human being loses a portion of his youth. However, if you go in the other direction by directing your sexual energy upward through the seven glands, then you can achieve eternal and divine life (injaculation = prolonging of arousal and life)."

Through their observations, the ancient Taoist sages were able to deduce the following:

"If you are at home or traveling in some other place in the world, you will notice that there are many more older yet still attractive women than men. Women, who do not suffer a loss of sexual energy (with the exception of those who have had too many pregnancies), have a life expectancy of up to 15 years longer than men."

Because of this, the ancient Taoist sages sought and found a way for the man to experience an even more pleasurable orgasm without ejaculating and losing his vital energy but maintaining and using it.

If a man is able to injaculate, which means reversing the ejaculation, he can preserve both the valuable vital energy and the erection. The man is then capable of leading the woman through the "nine steps to complete satisfaction."

What is normally called an orgasm in a woman is only the fourth stage in the nine-level sequence of the energetic potential.

HOLDING BACK
THE SEMEN ENERGY

Through the reports on experiences over thousands of years, the ancient Taoist sages discovered that a man should regulate the frequency of his ejaculation. This frequency depends upon the strength or weakness of his ejaculation, as well as his age and general constitution. Moreover, he should never let himself be forced to ejaculate since a man damages his entire endocrine system with each ejaculation. Every man should regulate his semen essence according to his supply of vital energy (see table on page 219 in the chapter on "The Rhythm Theory").

Master Tsu Hse describes the symptoms of a "forced ejaculation" as follows:

• Humming in the ears, tiredness in the eyes, limp limbs, loss of the erection, and a very dry throat, longing for sleep, inadequate breathing, and little desire to move.

• Urge to urinate, morbid appetite, lack of concentration, weak pulse, excessive sweating, bad breath, dizziness, constipation, diarrhea, disinclination to work, aggression, depression, migraine, and premature ejaculation.

He advises holding back the ejaculation by means of the male Deer Exercise (tensing the PC muscle) and has discovered that this practice helps strengthen the vital essence, as well as increasing the ability to hear and see more clearly. Furthermore, he adds that suppressing passion during lovemaking actually increases the man's love for the woman. He feels like he could never get enough of her.

It is best for each man to decide on his own as to whether he wants to ejaculate or hold back his semen by using the male Deer Exercise. A woman should be able to intuitively recognize her lover's physical needs in the same way as she recognizes her own. In no case should she demand that he should also "come" each time that they make love. Instead, she should be prepared to experience their love in a new and different way each time.

All of the ancient Taoist writings emphasize that the other perspective of seeing sex as a race to the climax and to physical collapse has effects that are both limiting on the physical level and harmful on the psychological level. In contrast to this perspective, the East views physical love as the possibility for both partners to experience new heights of ecstasy, of a more advanced and higher quality of orgasm without the loss of semen.

When a man repeatedly fails to achieve the proper rhythm of loving (the 9 x 10 sequence of love and the 108 healing thrusts from the pelvic floor with the tensing of the PC muscle), his vital energy will dry up. The effects of the uncorrected rhythms during lovemaking consist of "forced ejaculation," which quickly leads to the man's exhaustion. As a result, "one-hundred afflictions in the body" can develop over a certain period of time.

The customary, hasty, and forced method of sexual intercourse—for which there is no preparation and in which the woman usually plays a passive role—is equally unsatisfying for both the man and the woman, as well as damaging on the physical and mental/emotional level. Instead of demonstrating affection, this method frequently even causes alienation and separation.

Although the woman has no semen to preserve, she does—just like the man—have an enormous potential of passion. When this passion is properly directed, it can heal sensitive nerves, vitalize the blood, and regenerate the tissue. Through the deeper, genuine unification that represents the innermost feelings of the heart, the man and woman can relieve or heal physical complaints.

The method of the proper rhythm and the occasional retention of the semen energy have a therapeutic value that is matched by hardly any other pharmaceutical remedy or other system of healing. Both the man and the woman can benefit greatly from it when they learn to control their physical orgasms by means of the male and female Deer Exercise. However, it is in no way necessary, and not even advised, to refrain from every ejaculation over an indefinite period of time since a balanced sexual relationship includes giving and taking.

THE SEVEN ENDOCRINE GLANDS
SOURCE OF IMMUNE DEFENSE

We can imagine all seven glands of the endocrine system to be like vessels that are connected with each other through a series of arteries or tubes. In terms of the supply of vital chi, each vessel or gland is dependent on all the others.

When the first vessel, the "House of the Semen Essence," is filled with vital energy, this vital energy is slowly distributed through the arteries or tubes to the other six vessels of the endocrine system. This distribution occurs from bottom to top, as shown in the illustration on page 242.

While the Taoist scholars have already handed down a great wealth of knowledge about the structure, nature, and tasks of the endocrine system and the immune system, modern Western science is only now starting to explore endocrinology (theory of the endocrine system of seven glands). Unfortunately, this is a relatively new medical field of expertise and there is still much research to be done to understand the secret of Taoist Medicine; the latter has the advantage of thousands of years of experience in understanding the endocrine system by comparing it to the rest of nature.

It is not surprising that a condition of weakness or susceptibility to disease develops when one of the seven glands suffers a loss of energy for some reason or another. The sexual glands are then given the task of not only creating a balanced flow of energy to compensate for this weakness, but they also attempt to strengthen the weakened flow of energy so that the maximum possible amount of energy is restored to the body.

The sexual glands form the basis of the gland system, the foundation upon which all of the other glands rest. All seven glands mutually support each other in an ascending order. When the first six houses are not filled to the brim with vital energy, it is not possible to fill the "seventh house," the House of the Mind, with vital energy. So it is also understandable that a chronic deficiency and imbalance will be created in the body when one of the components of the gland system, such as the uterus or prostate gland, is surgically removed. Because of this, all of the available possibilities are exhausted in the ancient Chinese diagnosis and therapy procedure of Taoist Medicine before the decision is made to do surgery, especially operations on the sexual glands. Unfortunately, instead of learning from the Taoist sages, Wes-

Vessel G:
The House of the Mind—pineal gland
(The pineal gland influences the other glands in a very direct way by means of the hormones that are produced and secreted here. We can communicate on a spiritual level through this gland since it is related to consciousness and intuition.) The new energy cycle begins, and this is how we should imagine our endocrine circulation.

Vessel F:
The House of Intelligence—pituitary gland
(The pituitary gland rules the memory, wisdom, intelligence, and thought.) It asses its energy on to:

Vessel E:
The House of Growth—thyroid gland
(The thyroid gland maintains the cellular metabolism in the body and controls growth. It is also connected with the respiratory system.)

Vessel D:
The House of the Heart—thymus gland
(The thymus gland governs the heart and circulation.)

Vessel C:
The House of Transcendence—pancreas
(The pancreas monitors digestion, blood-sugar level, and body temperature.)

Vessel B:
The House of Water—adrenal glands
(The adrenal glands support the kidneys, bones, bone marrow, and spinal column.)

Vessel A:
The House of the Semen Essence—sexual glands
(The sexual glands—the prostate gland and testicles in the man and the ovaries, uterus, vagina, and breasts in a woman—are responsible for hormonal secretions, sexual energy and reactions, as well as reproduction.)

tern medicine continues to think of the individual glands as organs that are independent and therefore treated separately from each other.

In the Taoist Medicine for human health and longevity, removing a gland is virtually considered a "crime" since the entire organism is robbed of its energetic equilibrium as a result. In a sense, this act opens "Pandora's box." When a part of the body that has become inflamed is cut out of it, this is like throwing out the fire alarm because we don't want to hear the

242

siren each time things start to burn (Stephen T. Chang). This type of alarm system, which Mother Nature has created for us human beings, includes the tonsils, which are on the front lines of our organism's immune defense system. These are the first components to be attacked by harmful germs and they react with inflammation to warn the human being. When they are criminally removed through surgery, they can never again serve in their warning function as an alarm sign for the organism.

In the case of a surgical removal of a gland, the Taoist "inner exercises" are a life-saving measure for assuming the function of the removed gland since they continually supply the body with energy and hormones and protect it from additional weakening.

Through the healing inner exercises of Taoism, the system of the seven glands is supplied with new vital energy. It is balanced and the energy optimally increased, which also strengthens the immune defense. This is the Taoist path of overcoming existing weaknesses and healing ourselves, as well as also using the higher order of the vital energy to open our mental/spiritual center (Stephen T. Chang).

Only a person with strong sexual glands will not age since these act like a "wheel of life." Only when this wheel of life turns smoothly can health disorders be avoided in the organism and there will be no interference in the continuously growing cellular processes of the body.

MALE AFTERPLAY FOLLOWING EJACULATION

The Meridian Massage of the Penis for Strengthening the Erection and Desensitization

In order to maintain the future erections of the penis, the Taoist masters recommend the use of male afterplay following ejaculation. This practice is also called "Milking the Jade Stem" (also see page 79 ff.).

1. Desire and energy also fade after the seminal discharge. The penis quickly retracts and remains flaccid and soft. This powerless state of the penis continues for a much longer time than the aroused state since the force that created the retreat is stronger than the erection. With increasing age, the penis develops a tendency to be flaccid, which makes it more difficult to have an erection.

2. The man should therefore create lasting, favorable conditions to maintain the aroused state of the penis for a long time. Maintaining the erection is an ancient Taoist secret and is called "male afterplay." In this way, the man may never in his life have to suffer from the consequences of an impotent member.

3. The effectiveness of male afterplay depends on two factors: the physiological reaction and the psychological feedback.

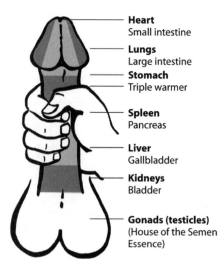

Heart
Small intestine

Lungs
Large intestine

Stomach
Triple warmer

Spleen
Pancreas

Liver
Gallbladder

Kidneys
Bladder

Gonads (testicles)
(House of the Semen Essence)

Milking the penis
Push the shaft of the penis with your hand from the start of the testicles to the bottom of the glans as if you were milking it. In this way, the blood reaches the glans, enlarges it, and strengthens the erection. The ideal mushroom form of the penis can be achieved in this manner. Repeat this milking process of the penis every day in the early morning and late evening 81 times with the right and the left hand.

Please note: Milking the penis applies only to the shaft. Do not touch the glans. This method should be done after the end of every sexual act with or without ejaculation.

4. As a countermeasure to the physiological retreat after completed intercourse, the man can work and "milk" the shrinking penis with his hand. Pulling and manipulating loosens the tissue and makes it easier for it to swell up. A trained penis has no problem absorbing larger amounts of blood, making it easy for erections to occur.

5. Every swelling process makes it easier for the next one to occur. In order to counteract the psychological retreat, a man should not tell himself that everything is over after the seminal discharge. If physical exhaustion occurs at the same times as this suggestion, the negative approach will gradually overrule the man's natural ability and lead to impotence.

6. Male afterplay following ejaculation can help the man to overcome and eliminate all of the insufficient functions.

ANCIENT CHINESE ACUPUNCTURE POINTS FOR SPERMATORRHEA

The term "spermatorrhea" describes a nightly seminal emission, with or without accompanying dreams.

As I once observed a Chinese physician treat five different men with this affliction, I saw that—as he asked questions and used the meridians and sensitive acupuncture points as reference points for the diagnosis—each of these men had more physical than psychological reasons for the spermatorrhea. In one case, the patient was pale, emaciated, and had a weak pulse. Another suffered from intense heart palpitations and complained of insomnia, weakness, and lack of appetite. His face was also emaciated. The third man could no longer think coherently and had a weak pulse. The other two were obese, yet had no appetite. Although no two of them were completely alike, the same acupuncture and acupressure treatments were used successfully on all of them.

Treatment Instructions for Spermatorrhea

A	B	C	D	E
Sp-2	CV-3	St-36	Bl-12	Ki-12
Sp-6	CV-4		Bl-15	
Sp-8			Bl-21	
Sp-9			Bl-23	
			Bl-31	
			Bl-38	
			Bl-47	
			Bl-50	
			Bl-67	

Ancient Chinese Acupressure Points for Spermatorrhea

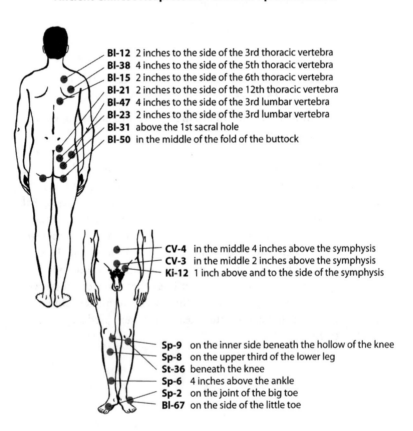

Bl-12 2 inches to the side of the 3rd thoracic vertebra
Bl-38 4 inches to the side of the 5th thoracic vertebra
Bl-15 2 inches to the side of the 6th thoracic vertebra
Bl-21 2 inches to the side of the 12th thoracic vertebra
Bl-47 4 inches to the side of the 3rd lumbar vertebra
Bl-23 2 inches to the side of the 3rd lumbar vertebra
Bl-31 above the 1st sacral hole
Bl-50 in the middle of the fold of the buttock

CV-4 in the middle 4 inches above the symphysis
CV-3 in the middle 2 inches above the symphysis
Ki-12 1 inch above and to the side of the symphysis

Sp-9 on the inner side beneath the hollow of the knee
Sp-8 on the upper third of the lower leg
St-36 beneath the knee
Sp-6 4 inches above the ankle
Sp-2 on the joint of the big toe
Bl-67 on the side of the little toe

Additional Therapies

Affliction	A	B	C	D	E
Frigidity	Ki-7	St-29 St-6	St-1	GV-4	
Lack of desire	Li-8	SI-5	TW-4	CV-1 CV-2	
Male sterility	Sp-5	Bl-32 Bl-33	Ki-5	TW-10	
Painful penis	Lu-7	St-29 St-30	Sp-6	Bl-47 Bl-50	
Premature ejaculation	St-27	Bl-23	LI-4	TW-10	Ki-5

Ancient Chinese Acupressure Points for Premature Ejaculation

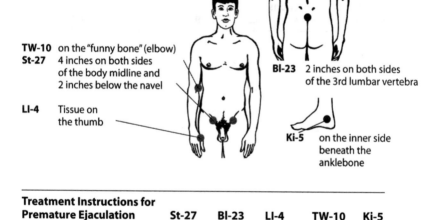

TW-10 on the "funny bone" (elbow)
St-27 4 inches on both sides
of the body midline and
2 inches below the navel

LI-4 Tissue on
the thumb

Bl-23 2 inches on both sides
of the 3rd lumbar vertebra

Ki-5 on the inner side
beneath the
anklebone

Treatment Instructions for Premature Ejaculation	St-27	Bl-23	LI-4	TW-10	Ki-5

TW = **Triple warmer, which influences the nerves, lymph glands, and endocrine system ("seven glands").**

Ancient Chinese Acupressure Points for a Painful Penis

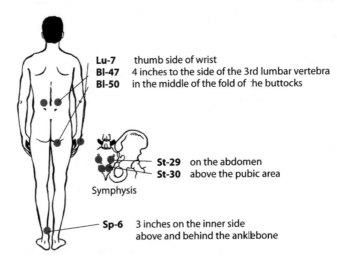

Lu-7   thumb side of wrist
Bl-47   4 inches to the side of the 3rd lumbar vertebra
Bl-50   in the middle of the fold of the buttocks

St-29   on the abdomen
St-30   above the pubic area

Symphysis

Sp-6   3 inches on the inner side
above and behind the anklebone

Treatment Instructions for a Painful Penis	Lu-7	St-29	St-30	Sp-6	Bl-47	Bl-50

THE NINE-TIMES-TEN LOVING PENIS THRUSTS
The 9 x 10 Sequence of Love

"A man must encounter the daily challenges of lovemaking with the courage of a brave warrior since whoever brings together movement, breath, and semen becomes indestructible."

Acupuncture points, meridian pathways, and nerve endings from the entire body run through the penis and the vagina, as well as the hands and feet. We use the term reflex zones for the areas of the body in which the nerve cords end. They can be activated in order to stimulate the respective organs. The foot reflex-zone massage is now familiar to most people The "Nine Thrust Sequence" during the sexual act is just as beneficial, but a much more pleasurable reflex-zone massage.

As mentioned above, the reflex zones of the penis and vagina are directly connected with the various organs. This is best seen in relation to the lung reflex zones on the penis. If this area alone is stimulated, the man begins to breathe and moan intensely. Heavy breathing or moaning is the apparent indication of a connection between the reflex zones and the organs. Using this example, we can deduce how the other reflex zones and organ connections function. During the sexual act, the penis may not be evenly massaged. The explanation for this is that the folds in the vaginal canal prevent an even contact between the penis and the vagina, which means that certain areas will be more stimulated than others. But with the 9 x 10 Sequence, both the penis and the vagina are massaged evenly.

However, for many men—at least at the beginning—it will be difficult to just get through the first sequence since the arousal is overwhelming for both sexual partners. In this case, the man can shorten the sequence, vary the individual series, or repeat the same sequence more than once. When he has the feeling that he can continue, then he should. He can experiment with it until he has found his own rhythm and knows what feels best to him and his partner. He can take a very flexible, non-mechanical approach to these series of movements; they can all be easily adapted to the individual needs.

An additional advantage of the 9 x 10 Sequence is that when it is used together with the Deer Exercise (tensing of the PC muscle with Crane Breathing) and holding back the semen, an even more enjoyable orgasm will result:

1. The simultaneous massage of the head and shaft of the penis automatically delays the orgasm and prolongs the sexual act considerably.

2. The stimulation of the shaft of the penis, which triggers the urge to ejaculate, is compensated for by the stimulation of the glans, which tends to have the opposite effect.

3. The man and the woman individually determine the movement rhythm during the nine series. However, a slow rhythm is the most pleasant and beneficial. Furthermore, it has the advantage for both sexes that the healing energies can better flow through the entire body. When the penis has withdrawn almost completely from the vagina, but without leaving it, the vagina instinctively contracts in order to hold onto the penis. This is an automatic reaction that stimulates the ability of the woman to wait until she can hardly anticipate the return of the penis.

4. In order to increase the pleasure even more, the woman can intentionally tense and tighten her vagina—as in the Deer Exercise. This creates additional friction, stimulation, and, above all, pleasure. The couple should assume a comfortable position that primarily gives the man control. Some couples prefer the so-called "missionary position" for this purpose.

> The man now begins to alternate between shallow and deep thrusts: first nine times flat—with only the glans penetrating the vagina—and then once deep (with the entire penis). This is followed by eight shallow and two deep thrusts, then seven shallow and three deep thrusts, etc., until he only does one shallow thrust and nine deep thrusts. Overall, these are nine series of ten shallow and deep thrusts each = a total of ninety thrusts.

5. If the man succeeds in performing the 9 x 10 Sequence without ejaculating, then he can start and complete a second series, etc.—the more, the better for his partner.

6. The man should repeat the 9 x 10 Sequence three times in a row (for a total of 270 penis thrusts) and attempt not to ejaculate in the process.

> With the help of tensing the PC muscle, it will be much easier for the man to postpone his ejaculation and the associated orgasm as long as possible, which brings increased sexual activity with it.

> With this same ability of contracting the PC muscle and the pelvic floor, the woman can tighten the vaginal area and achieve a faster and more intensive orgasm, which can be repeated up to 9 times.

7. Especially at the beginning, it is understandable that these "Nine Times Ten Loving Penis Thrusts" may cause a man increased problems when he makes the first attempts at desensitizing his penis and simultaneously sensitizing his partner's vagina since it is very difficult to control the sexual arousal of both partners.

8. However, the man should not let himself be diverted from his three-series repetitions of the 9 x 10 Sequence. He should firmly attempt to perform them since this is the only way for him to find his personal rhythm and adapt it to his individual needs.

The 9 x 10 Sequence and Its Effects

1. Nine shallow penis thrusts = only the glans penetrates the vagina; one deep thrust of the penis—the entire penis penetrates the vagina: The woman sighs, breathes heavily, and saliva collects in her mouth. Strengthening of lungs and large intestine.

2. Eight shallow thrusts, two deep thrusts: The woman sticks her tongue out while the man kisses her. The tongue corresponds with the House of the Heart. Strengthening of the heart and circulation, activation of the sexual energy.

3. Seven shallow thrusts, three deep thrusts: The woman's muscles become activated, she embraces the man and holds him tight with both arms. Stomach/spleen/pancreas are stimulated and the digestive tract is activated.

4. Six shallow thrusts, four deep thrusts: The woman's vagina begins to pulsate, the fluids flow and cover the penis. The kidneys and bladder begin their energy cycle.

5. Five shallow thrusts, five deep thrusts: The woman's limbs and joints become soft and flexible. She begins to scratch and bite the man. This stimulation makes the bones firmer and promotes the growth of the bone marrow.

6. Four shallow thrusts, six deep thrusts: The woman's body convulses and writhes like a snake while she winds her arms and legs around the man and squeezes him. Liver, gallbladder, and nerves begin their energy cycle.

7. Three shallow thrusts, seven deep thrusts: The woman's blood begins to surge through her veins and she wants to touch and feel the man everywhere. The heart and circulation increase their activities in order to also pump the blood to distant capillaries and achieve the highest level of stimulation.

8. Two shallow thrusts, eight deep thrusts: The woman's muscles relax completely. She bites even harder and reaches for the man's nipples. The woman's muscles achieve their higher level of stimulation through this relaxation.

9. One shallow thrust, nine deep thrusts: The woman achieves her absolutely most intensive orgasm and relaxes completely. She now totally abandons and opens herself to the man. The bodies of both the man and the woman are now charged with energy.

Effects in the Order of the Seven Energy Centers
(ascending energy)

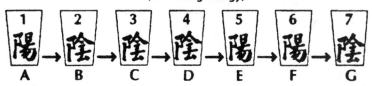

1	2	3	4	5	6	7
陽 →	陰 →	陰 →	陰 →	陽 →	陽 →	陰
A	B	C	D	E	F	G

7. House of the Mind	= pineal gland	yin form
6. House of the Intelligence	= pituitary gland	yang form
5. House of Growth	= thyroid gland	yang form
4. House of the Heart	= thymus gland	yin form
3. House of Transcendence	= pancreas	yin form
2. House of Water	= adrenal glands	yin form
1. House of the Semen Essence	= sexual glands	yang form

A: End of the 1st energy cycle = 90 penis thrusts
B: End of the 2nd energy cycle = 180 penis thrusts
C: End of the 3rd energy cycle = 270 penis thrusts
Etc.

Thrusts with the jade stem and activation of the triple warmer (nerves, lymph glands, and endocrine system are defined as the triple warmer).

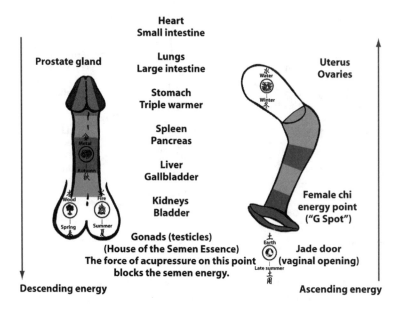

Heart
Small intestine

Prostate gland

Lungs
Large intestine

Uterus
Ovaries

Stomach
Triple warmer

Spleen
Pancreas

Liver
Gallbladder

Female chi
energy point
("G Spot")

Kidneys
Bladder

Gonads (testicles)
(House of the Semen Essence)
The force of acupressure on this point
blocks the semen energy.

Jade door
(vaginal opening)

Descending energy

Ascending energy

253

The Yin Sequence

Yin sequence = shallow thrust

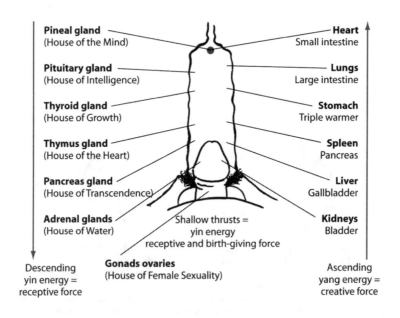

9 times	🦪🦪🦪🦪🦪🦪🦪🦪🦪
8 times	🦪🦪🦪🦪🦪🦪🦪🦪
7 times	🦪🦪🦪🦪🦪🦪🦪
6 times	🦪🦪🦪🦪🦪🦪
5 times	🦪🦪🦪🦪🦪
4 times	🦪🦪🦪🦪
3 times	🦪🦪🦪
2 times	🦪🦪
1 times	🦪

Pineal gland (House of the Mind)

Pituitary gland (House of Intelligence)

Thyroid gland (House of Growth)

Thymus gland (House of the Heart)

Pancreas gland (House of Transcendence)

Adrenal glands (House of Water)

Heart Small intestine

Lungs Large intestine

Stomach Triple warmer

Spleen Pancreas

Liver Gallbladder

Kidneys Bladder

Shallow thrusts = yin energy receptive and birth-giving force

Descending yin energy = receptive force

Gonads ovaries (House of Female Sexuality)

Ascending yang energy = creative force

The vagina is a melting pot, a vessel of transformation. In this wonderful golden cave, the yin and yang essences connect with each other, transform themselves, and nourish the couple. This process takes place on both the physical and the subtle level.

The Yang Sequence

Yang sequence = deep thrust

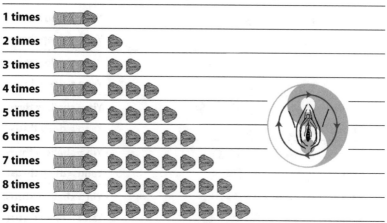

1 times		
2 times		
3 times		
4 times		
5 times		
6 times		
7 times		
8 times		
9 times		

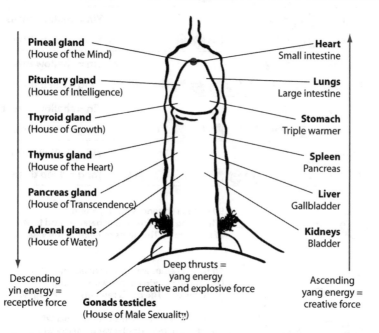

All of the Taoist bedroom arts are aimed at extending "The Visit of the Ambassador (= penis) in the Heavenly Palace" as long as possible by teaching the man the proper rules of behavior and equipping him with the correct references of a master lover.

The 9 x 10 Sequence

Yin sequence = shallow thrust yang = deep thrust

9 times	🍆🍆🍆🍆🍆🍆🍆🍆🍆	**Yin = shallow thrust**
1 time	🍆	**Yang = deep thrust**
8 times	🍆🍆🍆🍆🍆🍆🍆🍆	**Yin = shallow thrust**
2 times	🍆 🍆	**Yang = deep thrust**
7 times	🍆🍆🍆🍆🍆🍆🍆	**Yin = shallow thrust**
3 times	🍆 🍆🍆	**Yang = deep thrust**
6 times	🍆🍆🍆🍆🍆🍆	**Yin = shallow thrust**
4 times	🍆 🍆🍆🍆	**Yang = deep thrust**
5 times	🍆🍆🍆🍆🍆	**Yin = shallow thrust**
5 times	🍆 🍆🍆🍆🍆	**Yang = deep thrust**
4 times	🍆🍆🍆🍆	**Yin = shallow thrust**
6 times	🍆 🍆🍆🍆🍆🍆	**Yang = deep thrust**
3 times	🍆🍆🍆	**Yin = shallow thrust**
7 times	🍆 🍆🍆🍆🍆🍆🍆	**Yang = deep thrust**
2 times	🍆🍆	**Yin = shallow thrust**
8 times	🍆 🍆🍆🍆🍆🍆🍆🍆	**Yang = deep thrust**
1 time	🍆	**Yin = shallow thrust**
9 times	🍆 🍆🍆🍆🍆🍆🍆🍆🍆	**Yang = deep thrust**

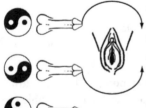

90 thrust sequences = yang energy
(Thrusting forward with exhalation and tensing of PC muscle). The penis remains in the vagina.

90 thrust sequences in a clockwise direction
(Exhalation) = yin energy with tensing of PC muscle. The penis remains in the vagina.

90 thrust sequences in a counterclockwise direction. (Exhalation) = yang energy with tensing of PC muscle

90 thrust sequences = yin energy (thrusting forward with inhalation and tensing of PC muscle). The penis remains in the vagina.

The Energy cycle of the vaginal clock around the labia with its 12 pressure points is stimulated by the 9 x 10 loving penis thrusts as follows:

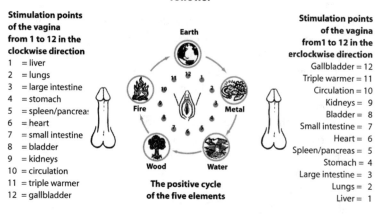

Stimulation points of the vagina from 1 to 12 in the clockwise direction

1 = liver
2 = lungs
3 = large intestine
4 = stomach
5 = spleen/pancreas
6 = heart
7 = small intestine
8 = bladder
9 = kidneys
10 = circulation
11 = triple warmer
12 = gallbladder

Earth

Fire

Metal

Wood

Water

The positive cycle of the five elements

Stimulation points of the vagina from 1 to 12 in the erclockwise direction

Gallbladder = 12
Triple warmer = 11
Circulation = 10
Kidneys = 9
Bladder = 8
Small intestine = 7
Heart = 6
Spleen/pancreas = 5
Stomach = 4
Large intestine = 3
Lungs = 2
Liver = 1

HARMONY BETWEEN THE SEXUAL ORGANS

A couple's love life is only perfect when the penis and vagina fit together exactly. When there is such total harmony, many problems can be prevented since a woman can only be satisfied completely by a man in this way.

It is important that the man can fulfill the tasks intended for him by Mother Nature since the penis conducts the creative yang energy directly to the woman through the vagina (yin energy = receptive force). Mother Nature has selected the man to "serve" the woman in sexuality and give her satisfaction. The woman can only open herself and receive the love of the man during orgasm. This is the secret of two people living together, and the man will receive the unconditional love of the woman as the most beautiful gift.

EXAMPLES FOR THE HARMONY OF THE PENIS AND THE VAGINA

1. If the man's penis is shorter than the woman's vagina, he may not be able to penetrate her completely in order to give her total satisfaction. However, the same man can make a woman with a shorter vagina very happy.

2. If the man's penis is longer, he will inevitably cause pain for a woman with a shorter vagina, but will fit wonderfully with a woman whose vagina is just as long.

3. This contradicts the superstition, widespread in the Western world, that the length of the penis is a decisive factor.

4. The harmony of the penis and the vagina is the decisive factor for the physical harmony of a couple. Only when both of their reflex zones are connected will the mutual orgasm be harmonized with an even reaction.

5. In addition, the complete harmony between the penis and vagina also serves as therapy for blockages of the meridians and reflex zones such as:
   • Kidneys/bladder
   • Liver/gallbladder
   • Stomach/spleen/pancreas
   • Lungs/large intestine
   • Heart/small intestine, circulation/triple warmer
   And the entire endocrine systems with:
   • Sexual glands
   • Adrenal glands
   • Pancreas
   • Thymus gland
   • Thyroid gland
   • Pituitary gland
   • Pineal gland
   And the nervous system and lymphatic gland system.

The sexual activity in the man and woman is dependent upon the size, form, and strength of their sexual organs (penis and vagina). While all three of these aspects are important in the East, people in the West seem to believe that just the size of the female and male sexual organs are significant in the sexual act.

Taoist discourses on lovemaking between the man and the woman categorize both sexual organs according to their dimensions in three classes. They recommend coming as close as possible to the complete harmony between the penis and the vagina. According to their "fit," sexual unions are either equal or unequal. Through the use of various positions, insufficient anatomical harmony between the penis and the vagina can be balanced to a certain degree.

● Widely opened positions create space for a large penis so that it can even penetrate a small jade door.

● The skillful use of pillows to raise the woman's buttocks helps the man with a small penis to penetrate more deeply.

On the basis of their thousands of years of experience, the Taoist sages came to the conclusion that the form and hardness of the penis that Mother Nature has given a man are only external signs and not evidence of his overall active masculinity. The skill that ensures a woman will enjoy his way of loving her is expressed inwardly.

When a man and a woman truly love each other, whether their sexual organs are long or short, fat or thin is completely inconsequential. People in the West, and not just the East, should know by now that a thick penis is often much worse for a woman than a long, thin one that is firm and stiff; and a firm, stiff penis that is thrust in and drawn out in a coarse manner is worse than one that is moved with care and tenderness.

When a couple is in harmony, then their sexual organs will adapt to each other during the course of the partnership. It is rarely necessary to use artificial aids to compensate for the different sizes of the sexual organs. However, one very important point is that the proper emphasis is placed on foreplay. This is a great help in harmonizing sexuality and the relationship of the partners. When you are considerate of your partner, then the very embarrassing question of sexual standards and fits will come to an end and no longer have any significance.

SPECIAL STRENGTHENING METHODS FOR THE SEXUAL ORGANS

In the ancient Taoist texts, which were accessible only to the imperial household and the respective officials and bodyguards, medical formulas were developed to either increase or decrease the size of the male and female sexual organs. These writings point out that the desired effect can be achieved through the following methods:

• Use of ointments, compresses, powders, and drinks made of plants, tree bark, and mushrooms, and various organic and inorganic substances.

• Specific massages of the abdominal organs (milking, squeezing, and desensitizing).

- Special energetic chi kung exercise variations (Deer, Crane, and Turtle with tensing of the PC muscle).

Wu Hsien, a Taoist master of the Han Dynasty (206 B.C. to 219 A.D.), described the longevity exercises of the Deer (tensing of PC muscle), the Crane (inhaling into the abdomen with tensing of PC muscle), and the Turtle (further inhalation and drawing the breath up into the overextended neck to the back).

Use of these sexual energy exercises provides not only the endocrine system, the lymphatic gland system, and the nervous system with new chi energy, but also increases circulation in the penis and vagina. This makes a small penis larger, the vagina tighter and firmer, and strengthens the necessary contractions.

The Immortal Breath

The chi kung exercise series that is called the "Immortal Breath" should be done as follows:

- In order to enlarge an unusually small and weak weapon (= penis), the man should stand at shoulders' width facing the East in the early morning hours, when the yin force is declining and the yang force is increasing and first inhale and exhale calmly nine times.
- After this brief meditation phase, he should inhale deeply 49 times (7 x 7 = 49, activation of the seven glands, seven breaths for each gland), bringing the breath from the abdomen up into his overextended neck and into the head.
- Immediately afterward, the man should rub the palms of his hands together until they are burning hot. Then he should hold his jade stem with his right hand and concentrate his mind. With the left hand, she should rub his navel region in circles and let the palms rotate 81 times to the left in a counterclockwise direction (= cosmic energy). Then he should rub his navel center (bladder, pubic bone) in the same way with his right hand but now 81 times to the right in a clockwise direction (= human energy).
- Then he should rub his jade stem between his palms 49 times, as if he were trying to make wool into yarn. Then he should milk his jade stem 49 times and squeeze it 49 times. In conclusion, he should desensitize the jade stem by hitting it back and forth between his thighs 49 times.

THE THREE TYPES OF MALE SEXUAL ORGANS

The Taoists speak of three types of male sexual organs according to their dimensions, making it possible for any man to classify his "weapon" in the appropriate category.

1. The Rabbit—Jade Stem

When completely aroused, this is a penis that is no longer than 6 fingerwidths = about 5 inches long. A man with such a penis normally has a short stature, but is well proportioned with a calm disposition. His semen is usually whitish and associated with the lungs, large intestine, stomach, and spleen/pancreas. He is considered a man of small dimensions.

2. The Bull—Jade Rod

When completely aroused, this is a penis that is no longer than 9 fingerwidths = about 7 inches long. A man with such a penis is usually robust, with a high forehead, large eyes, and restless temperament. His semen is mother-of-pearl in color and usually salty. It is associated with the heart, small intestine, bladder, and kidneys. He is always prepared to make love and is considered a man of medium dimensions.

3. The Horse—Jade Hammer

When completely aroused, this is a penis that is no longer than 12 fingerwidths = about 10 inches long. The owner of such a supernatural tool is normally large, strong, muscular, and has a powerful voice. His nature is voracious, greedy, lascivious, passionate, rash, and lazy. He walks slowly and has little interest in lovemaking—unless he is very suddenly overcome with a desire for it. His semen is very abundant and tends to be tart. It is associated with the circulation/sexuality, triple warmer, gallbladder, and liver. This is a man of large dimensions.

Wise Taoist Sayings About Sexual Love

An ancient Taoist proverb says that a man whose jade stem is very long (more than 12 fingerwidths) will always be poor. A man whose jade stem is thick will suffer distress and affliction. A man with a thin and slender penis will have good fortune, and a man whose jade stem is short may even turn become a king.

The Su-nu-miao Lun, an ancient Taoist manuscript, saying the following about these matters:

Men are born with as many different weapons (= sexual organs) as faces. This all depends on Mother Nature and is influenced by the movement arts.

 A considerable number of small men have long weapons.

 Some large men have small weapons.

 Thin, weak men often have thick, hard weapons.

 Large, well-built men often have small, weak weapons.

THE THREE TYPES OF FEMALE SEXUAL ORGANS

The quality of the female sexual organ does not depend upon the type of woman or her position but how it is used. High, medium, and low all possess desirable qualities as long as a woman knows how to use them.

A woman of the medium type is suited for love any day of the year and in any position (Su-nu-miao Lun). The best among these women is the one who comes from a spiritual family. She is endowed with favorable signs and free of the "four defects" of the sexual organs.
• She has no menstrual flow
• She has no unpleasant odors
• She is not ill
• When she is filled with sexual desire, she feels no shame or reserve in being together with her partner.

In the Taoist tradition, the three types of female sexual organs are differentiated in relation to their dimensions:

1. **The Deer—Jade Door**
   This is a vagina with a depth of no more than 6 fingerwidths = about 5 inches long. A woman with such a vagina usually has a soft, girlish body and is well proportioned with good breasts and solid hips. She eats moderately and surrenders to the joys of lovemaking. Her mind is very active. The secretion of her jade door has the pleasant perfume of the lotus flower. She is considered a woman of small dimensions.

2. **The Mare—Jade Gate**
   This is a vagina with a depth of 9 fingerwidths = about 7 inches long. A woman with such a vagina usually has petite body. The breasts and

hips are wide and her navel region is raised. She has well-proportioned hands and feet, a long neck, and a retreating forehead. The throat, eyes, and mouth are wide, and her eyes are very beautiful. She is very versatile, tender, and graceful. She loves the good life and much peace and quiet. She does not climax easily, and her love juice is perfumed like a lotus. She is considered a woman of medium dimensions.

3. The Cow Elephant—Jade Courtyard

This is a vagina with a depth of 12 fingerwidths = about 10 inches long. Such a woman usually has large breasts, a wide face, and rather short limbs. She is voracious and very noisy. Her voice sounds hard and brusque. This woman is very difficult to satisfy, but her love juice is quite abundant and smells like the secretions of an elephant in heat. She is considered a woman of large dimensions.

COMBINATION POSSIBILITIES IN SEXUAL UNION

The combinations of male and female sexual organs result in nine different possibilities of sexual union:

- There are three equal unions between people with the corresponding dimensions of sexual organs.
- There are six unequal unions in which the size of the sexual organs does not correspond.

This results in a total of nine types of sexual unions between a man and a woman. There are never sexual problems in equal unions, but various positions should be used to compensate in unequal unions.

Harmonious union between man and woman:	Disharmonious or difficult union between man and woman:
• 1. Rabbit with Deer	• 1. Rabbit with Mare
• 2. Bull with Mare	• 2. Rabbit with Cow Elephant
• 3. Horse with Cow Elephant	• 3. Bull with Deer
	• 4. Bull with Cow Elephant
	• 5. Horse with Deer
	• 6. Horse with Mare

The Sex Life

There are all types of statistical surveys today—naturally also about how satisfied people are with their sex lives. In Europe, it is surprising to discover that the French (who happen to have a very good reputation in this respect) only rank—just like the Germans—right below the European average. Even more surprising is that fact that the Swiss are most satisfied with their sex lives. Why is that?

Calorie Chart for Love Play

This is how many calories you burn:

Greeting someone with a kiss	1 cal.
Warm embrace	3 cal.
Passionate kiss	5 cal.
Wild smooching	115 cal.
Stage fright before going to bed	60 cal.
Freeing partner from clothing	82 cal.
Intensive fooling around	100 cal.
Foreplay with pounding heart	50 cal.
Fleeting love play	15 cal.
Sighing and giggling	7 cal.
Petting, intense and skillful	34 cal.
Passionate love play until the earth moves, the bells ring, and sparks fly	300 cal.
Double Rittberger	180 cal.
Jump from closet into bed	40 cal.
Love play under the shower	63 cal.
Searching for a towel	63 cal.
Moving to unused side of bed	14 cal.
Satisfied grunts of thanks	1 cal.

Conversion: 100 cal. = 400 joule

The most pleasant way to lose weight naturally.

SALIVA, HEAVENLY WATER
OF THE LIFE FORCE

The ancient Taoist sages particularly valued saliva, which is called the "Heavenly Water" or even "The Dragon Churns Up the Sea". It calls to mind not only the animal reflex of licking the wound or the way that cats clean themselves, but also that our ancestors cleaned wounds with saliva and made them sterile in this way. Because of its composition, saliva is alkaline and best suited for disinfection, even today.

Moreover, the Taoists had the custom of spitting in their hands before they rubbed them warm and began massaging their faces with them. The use of the saliva can also have negative purposes, such as spitting in someone's face to insult them or jinxing something by spitting on the ground.

Taoist physiology differentiates between two types of saliva:
- The thick saliva that is secreted by the kidneys and contains the chi (jing) inherited from the parents, which is stored in the kidneys. This saliva is "full of the vital essence" of the individual, meaning it is full of power. Consequently, the Taoists warn against spitting thoughtlessly since this can lead to a loss of vital energy.
- The jing contained in the saliva, meaning the yin or yang force of the woman or man, is exchanged during kissing (50% when the lips touch, 100% energy exchange during French kissing). This vital force is freed particularly in the moments when the energy is flowing more intensely, especially during the orgasm.

In the Taoist exercises of Sticking Out the Tongue, Clenching the Teeth, and Chattering the Teeth, as well as Brushing the Teeth with the Tongue, which should be done immediately after meals, the energy of the thick saliva is used to transport it to the "Sea of Energy" (= lower Dantien). All of the breath exercises in Taoist chi kung should always be started with the "Exercise of the Heavenly Water" in order to activate the "Sea of Energy."

Therapeutic Application Before Breakfast
The morning, when the stomach is still empty, is the best time to start with the saliva exercise of the Heavenly Water ("The Dragon Churns Up the Sea") in order to cleanse and detoxify the mucous membranes of

the esophagus. Before beginning this exercise—and also before a sexual encounter—it is advisable to rinse the mouth with saltwater since salt corresponds with the taste quality of bladder and kidneys and is associated with the element of water (House of the Semen Essence). The salty taste stimulates the bladder and the kidneys, as well as the secretion of the thick saliva in the mouth that is responsible for the disinfection of the mucous membranes (alkaline reaction).

Please note: At the beginning of the Heavenly Water exercise, especially when the stomach is empty, nausea may occur because of the reflex zones of the gums (especially when the gums are not in good shape). At the beginning, the saliva will be more firm and sticky, which is noticeable when speaking, but these initially unpleasant qualities quickly disappear.

Also remember that these techniques of sticking the tongue out, clenching the teeth, chattering with the teeth, as well as cleaning the teeth with the tongue, should be done after every meal, if possible.

Your stomach will thank you for this!

TAOIST PRACTICES FOR STIMULATING THE SALIVARY GLANDS AND PROTECTING THE TEETH

TAPPING THE TEETH

On a 4-meter high and 10-meter long fresco in Grotto 196 of the world-famous Thousand Buddha Grotto of Tun-huang in China, an old but healthy and sprightly man who looks like a monk is depicted. He sits on the ground, holding a water bottle in his left hand and is sticking the index finger of his right hand into his mouth—a realistic depiction of someone brushing his teeth. This fresco shows that dental hygiene was important even 1500 years ago. Further evidence of this fact has been discovered in archeological excavations, a toothbrush from the Liao Dynasty that is more than 1000 years old and made of animal bones. In oracle inscriptions that are more than 3,000 years old, tooth decay is already described as a general malady.

In the oldest classical medical work of China from the period of the Fighting Realms (475-221 B.C.), the Huang Di Nei Jung ("Canon of the

Yellow Emperor on the Inner Diseases"), the physiological characteristics of normal teeth are described. Since the period of the Fighting Realms, the Chinese have developed a series of techniques for tooth care, such as tooth tapping, in addition to rinsing the mouth and cleaning the teeth with "toothpaste" after meals and before going to bed.

 "Tapping the Teeth" means tapping the upper and lower teeth against each other. More than 1500 years ago, Ge Hong, a scholar of the Jin Dynasty who was involved with the maintenance of good health, wrote this in his book Bao Pu Zi ("Book of the Master Bao Pu"): "The teeth will never be lost if they are tapped 360 times every morning." In China, there are many elderly people who have the habit of clenching their teeth during urination and defecation. Clenching the teeth together massages the roots of the teeth, promotes the local blood circulation, and improves the supply of nutrients, which contributes to strengthening the set of teeth. Since the teeth are the beginning of the digestive system, a healthy set of teeth affects the well-being of the entire body. This is the secret of longevity through tapping the teeth.

The traditional practice of tapping the teeth consists of the following steps:

- Either in the morning right after getting up or in the evening before going to bed, first tap the molars against each other. Then tap the incisors, and finally the canine teeth. This must be done consecutively because they are not all on the same level.
- After tapping the teeth, stroke the tongue across the gums of the entire set of teeth and the mucous membranes of the cheeks in order to stimulate the secretion of saliva. Then gargle several times with the saliva and swallow it. Traditional Chinese Medicine believes that the saliva, as a bodily fluid, should not be spit out—as long as there is no formation of mucous present.
- Next, massage the gums with the tongue. This promotes good circulation in the gums.
- Finally, clench the teeth and inflate the cheeks to increase the secretion of saliva. Gradually swallow the saliva. This exercise, which is meant to protect the teeth, can be repeated 40-50 times within a period of ten minutes. In doing so, frequent repetitions naturally produce better results.

ADDITIONAL TECHNIQUES FOR TEETH, GUMS, AND SALIVA

In addition to the other regions of the face, we must also concentrate on the mouth, teeth, and gums. These areas need to be stimulated so that they remain strong and healthy. We continuously use our mouth, our teeth, and our gums—and show them to other people—when we talk, breathe, eat, drink, or even kiss. In order to keep this area healthy and

Reflex zones of the tongue

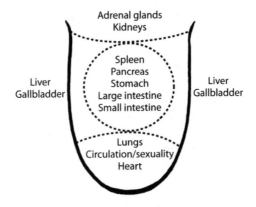

prevent diseases of the teeth and gums (gingivitis), the Taoist sages selected the following exercises:

1ST EXERCISE:
STICKING OUT THE TONGUE (Repeat 9 times)

2ND EXERCISE:
CLENCHING THE TEETH (Repeat 9 times)
and tapping the teeth (Repeat 2 x 36 times)

The body normally becomes slack after sexual intercourse and orgasm, as well as after the bowel movement, and is then especially susceptible to colonization through pathological germs. In these situations, tapping the teeth or clenching the teeth can be helpful in protecting the body and increasing the natural powers of resistance.

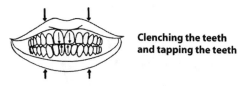

Clenching the teeth and tapping the teeth

1. Keep your jaws pressed together so that the teeth are on top of each other.

2. Clench your teeth and grind with the lower and upper jaws so that the jaw muscles bulge out at the temples.

3. Afterward, relax the muscles and repeat the exercise 9 times.

4. In conclusion, tap your teeth on top of each other for a total of 2 x 36 times.

Effects:

This exercise strengthens the teeth and the gums, tones the jaw muscles, and improves the circulation to the tissue of the gums. In addition, it moves the energy into the head and directs the mental attention inward.

3ʳᵈ EXERCISE: BRUSHING THE TEETH WITH THE TONGUE

1. Start by circling the tongue around the gums and the teeth 9 times in a clockwise direction and 9 times in a counterclockwise direction.

2. Then let the tip of the tongue ("Bud of the Heart") circle along the inside of the teeth 9 times in both directions. This promotes the secretion of saliva when the tongue touches the upper incisor teeth.

3. Collect a large amount of saliva (let your mouth fill with saliva while moving your tongue as if you wanted to spit it out). Rinse your mouth with this collected amount of saliva by swishing it back and forth like mouthwash.

4. Divide the collected saliva, which is very alkaline, into three equal parts that you swallow one after the other. Concentrate on how it sinks into your lower Dantien, which is one hand's width below the navel, in order to gather the vital force of chi in this "Sea of Energy."

5. You can visualize this process as connected with a beam of light that is swallowed together with the Heavenly Dew (= the alkaline saliva).

Brushing the teeth with the tongue

**Merging the
conception vessel
with the governor vessel**

Effects of the Tongue Massage:
- This exercise stimulates the important function of saliva secretion under the tongue. One part of the saliva is secreted by the pituitary gland, which has a rejuvenating effect, activates the thyroid gland, and cleanses the sexual glands.
- The highly effective enzymes that are contained in this salivary secretion contribute to the elimination of bad breath since they digest the bacteria in the mouth and stomach.
- Since the tongue muscle is directly connected with the heart muscle, this exercise also has a relaxing effect on the heart.

4TH EXERCISE:
PRESSURE-POINT MASSAGE OF THE GUMS

We can press a total of eight acupressure points, located above and below the upper and lower lips, to stimulate the meridians that supply energy to the mouth, teeth, and gums. This exercise should be done after Tapping the Teeth.

**Pressure points
for gum acupressure**

Firmly and evenly press each of the 8 acupressure points illustrated here for a total of 9 times. Afterward, rub them briefly in order to energetically charge each of the respective points.

CLOSING REMARKS
Summary of the Taoist Bedroom Secrets

Through this depiction of the ancient Chinese diagnosis and therapy procedure, you have now learned the basic secrets of Taoist bedroom practices. Sexuality has always been a recurrent topic between the sexes that is probing and sometimes even unpleasant. There has been knowledge about sex at a mature in old age for more than 8,000 years, but the fear of failure was never a topic of concern. The miracle-working methods of rejuvenation and prolonging life were made available to the Chinese emperors by the Taoist monks, who in turn were provided with food, shelter, and protection.

Sex is an important component of life for all of us. It gives us strength, vitality, health, desire, and pleasure. Sexuality is therefore much too precious to be used in the wrong way or even abused. This is why Mother Nature responds with a strict checks-and-balances system so that sexual misuse is punished with disease, weakness, loss of libido, and even serious mental damage.

This is why the Taoist monks, who were permitted to live their sexuality in a heterosexual way, created the respective energy exercises and sexual techniques in order to use the ability of their sexual energy to conceive healthy children or to transform it for other purposes. The latter means the ability to unite with the current of life, as well as becoming relaxed and calm despite life's mishaps, in order to receive an understanding for the laws of life.

When this occurs, you can attune yourself to the mysteries of life. You can even connect with this energy and become a valuable part of the greater whole in a very conscious manner. Then you will be able to free yourself from the feeling of the fateful pain of life. Your independence will be improved and strengthened in terms of your sexuality, as well as in daily life.

By recognizing and understanding your own sexuality, you can even predict your future and be your own "healer" or psychological adviser. If, up to now, you have experienced mainly pain and disappointments in your relationships, you can now develop and understand the true ability to love and live, as well as how other people fit into the larger plan of your life. You can let everything happen in the way that you desire it to happen and can visualize it in your mind.

If you now openly confront the life stream of sexuality, life will also move with you. Success and happiness will flow to you, which will ultimately promote your courage to take action. Failures will occur less frequently and lose their effects since energy will continuously flow to you with the Taoist exercise forms and help you gain power and influence.

Love and you will be loved! Love is a mathematical equation in which both sides correspond—you and your sexuality. If you accept sexuality for what it really is, namely the union of spiritual and physical love, then this love will change you so much that you will experience yourself as a new human being. Sexuality is the love between the body, mind, and soul—and this love gives all of us the strength to do miracles, if we only are willing. It is never in vain. Even if it is not returned, it still will come back to us to warm and lift up our own heart since each of us is an extraordinary and loving personality.

So tell yourself every day: "I greet this day from a heart full of love, and I will succeed at everything." In silence, say to yourself: "I love sexuality and am no longer afraid of it."

During the first weeks of studying the Taoist bedroom secrets and working with the energy exercises and sexual practices described here, you will notice a gradual change in your behavior and your attitude toward the surrounding world. In your immediate and familiar environment or even in more random encounters you may hear comments like: "What's going on with you all of a sudden?" or "You seem so different!".

When these types of experiences occur more frequently, you will know that the Taoist bedroom secrets primarily involve your personality and, secondly, harmonize your yearning for sexual experiences. All of this will become increasingly solid, deep, and well-developed in the course of time. Furthermore, you will achieve an energetic high of undreamed-of dimensions with the Taoist chi kung exercises. Greet this harmonious sexuality from a heart full of love since it is the greatest secret for health and longevity, despite all of the perils of living taking action.

Sexuality can be compared to a fuel. If we can take advantage of this fuel, we can obtain from it the strength to soar up into the higher regions. But if we hesitate in using this fuel because we are ignorant, negligent, or weak, we will turn to ash and be drawn downward by our falsely practiced sexuality. Sexuality and love come from God, and everything that is manifested as energy through human beings (such as semen energy) is a divine energy in accordance with its origins.

We can also compare this energy to electricity: Electricity is a form of energy, the nature of which remains unknown to this very day, yet it still exists and functions. If it is conducted through a lamp, it becomes light; conducted through a hotplate, it turns into heat; when it goes through a magnet, it turns into magnetism; when it goes through a ventilator, it becomes movement, etc.

In the same sense, there is also cosmic energy—chi, as the ancient Chinese wisdom of healing calls it—which, according to the organ of the human being in which it manifests itself, assumes one or another form of expression. If this energy flows into the brain, it becomes intelligence and the power of discernment. If it flows through the solar plexus, it becomes feeling and sensation. It becomes movement through the musculature, and the energy that flows through the sexual organs turns into attraction to the opposite sex. However, it is still the same divine energy.

Sexuality and love only begin when chi, the divine energy, simultaneously also activates other centers in the human being, namely the endocrine system of the seven glands. At this moment, the body, mind, and soul are unified so that the attraction, the desire to be close to another person, is illuminated and enlightened by the thoughts, feelings, and an esthetic sense of beauty. This is love in an expanded type of sexuality, which has transformational powers.

With the Taoist energy exercises, you have found a way to connect love and sexuality for your own advantage and for the benefit of your fellow human beings.

From the bottom of my heart, I wish you all the best and much happiness and joy in practicing these energy exercises.

Master Chian Zettnersan

Master Chian Zettnersan

Master Chian Zettnersan has been intensively involved with the Eastern philosophy of Traditional Chinese Medicine, diagnosis and therapy procedure of the fundamental ancient Chinese Medicine, as well as the Asian martial arts, since 1968.

Under the supervision of the Sport College of Cologne, he passed the examination to become a specialized sports teacher for karate-do (martial arts) in 1974.

He has written the following dissertations;

The Path of the Warrior" (hard chi kung = martial art), "Ancient Chinese Energy Exercises" (soft chi kung = art of healing), and "Taoist Bedroom Secrets" (still chi kung = meditation). He was named Professor for the Wisdom of Martial Arts (Renshi).

As a multiple German, International German, and European Karate Master, he has also been the chief judge at national and international championships from 1970 to 1988.

From internationally renowned scholars and physicians of Eastern and Western medicine who were also masters of the various martial arts traditions, he acquired his medical knowledge about the "Eight Pillars of Taoism": the Tao of philosophy and psychology, revitalization (inner exercises), the balanced diet, the forgotten medicinal plants, the art of healing and the martial arts, sexual wisdom and love, numerology, astrology, and the I Ching, as well as geomancy and feng shui (the golden section), and the diagnosis procedure and therapeutic applications of ancient Chinese healing wisdom.

In 1993, Master Chian Zettnersan became an official member of the World Organization for Orthopedics, Traumatology, and Acupuncture at the University of Peking.

Since 1990, he has been the acting president of the German-Chinese Chi kung and Feng-Shui Academy of the Ancient Chinese Diagnosis and Therapy Procedure. As a lecturer and examiner for this academy, he is responsible for training and advanced training in the above-mentioned "Eight Taos".

Contact address:
www.chikung.de
e-mail: info@chikung.de

The masters of the Taoist art of healing and martial arts who trained Master Chian Zettnersan:

1. Professor Fred Johannson, M.D. (USA): grand master of karate, chi kung, and feng shui; specialist for orthopedics, surgery, and neurology.

2. Professor Kim Sun, M.D. (Korea): grand master of karate, chi kung, and feng shui; specialist for orthopedics and surgery.

3. Dr. Nakamura, M.D. (Japan): Professor for clinical medicine and psychology; physician for Western medicine and respiratory specialist, author of several scientific books.

4. Bian Zhizhong (China), chairman of the Chinese research association for traditional Tao chi kung exercises for health and longevity; author of textbook for Taoist exercises.

5. Professor Stephen T. Chang, M.D. (USA), grand master of chi kung and feng shui; Doctor of Philosophy, Religious Studies, and Jurisprudence; lives and teaches in the USA; his publications, such as The Tao of Revitalization, The Tao of Diet, and The Tao of Sexuality are outstanding textbooks on Taoist chi kung.

6. Dr. Koichi Tohei (Japan, Ki No Kenkuykai H.O. Tokyo), grand master of chi kung and aikido; author of special emphasis training and activation of the vital energy chi and its healing powers in the organism; author of numerous aikido books.

7. Professor Dong Haiguan, M.D. (China), grand master of chi kung and feng shui and physician for Traditional Taoist Medicine, orthopedics and chiropractic; master of the Ba-Gua Chuan martial art.

8. Dr. Zhi Chang Li (China): teaches in Munich at the Qigong Institute Li; grand master of qigong and tai-chi master; master of various qigong forms and specialist for motionless qigong.

9. Professor Dr. Shen Zhixiang, M.D. (China): president of the University of Peking for Acupuncture, Orthopedics, and Chiropractic; chi kung and feng-shui master.

10. Professor Wei Guiking, M.D. (China): president of the chi kung masters; president of the University of Nanjing for Orthopedics, Chiropractic, and Acupuncture.

11. Professor Wu Zhiming, M.D. (China): currently at the University of Bayreuth in Germany as lecturer for Chinese and German; specialized interpreter for Traditional Chinese Medicine and Taoist

Medicine; honorary president and first vice-president of the German-Chinese Chi kung and Feng-Shui Academy.

12. Dr. Hiru Tanaka (Japan): Professor for classical medicine and psychology; karate and feng-shui grand master.

13. Professor Dr. Ding Hongyu (China): University of Nanjing; master for chi kung and tai chi chuan.

Additional information from:

Director Gerhard H. Eggetsberger (Austria), Institute for Applied Biocybernetics and Feedback Research in Vienna.

R. L. Wing (USA), author of "The I Ching Workbook", Doubleday ISBN 0-385-12838-X

Daniel Reid (USA), author, studied sinology at UC Berkeley and in Monterey; lived in Taiwan from 1973 to 1988 and intensively studied the source texts of Traditional Chinese Medicine.

Walter Lübeck

The Chakra Energy Cards

Healing Words for Body, Mind, and Soul

For All Forms of Energy Healing and Reiki Treatments

With Healing Symbols from the Great Goddess and Her Angels

Each card has a special healing symbol, which conveys its message directly to the user. The cards spark gentle processes of healing and inspire us in a loving way. Supplemented in the accompanying handbook by helpful suggestions for actions that offer support in resolving and releasing stuck energies. *The Chakra Energy Cards* offer a complete method by themselves, yet they can also be integrated into almost any other spiritual system, especially Reiki. The effect of each card can be optimally complemented with the specific use of the healing gemstones, fragrance essences, and Bach Flowers.

Set (book and card pack) with 192-page handbook and 154 Chakra Energy Cards · $24.95
ISBN 0-914955-72-1

Paula Horan

The Ultimate Reiki Touch

Understanding Energy Medicine

21 Healing Cycles for Complete Self-Empowerment

For the newcomer and advanced Reiki practitioner alike, *The Ultimate Reiki Touch* provides a motherlode of heart-knowledge and a deep and refreshing source of inspiration. It beautifully conveys how to explore and share the essence of Reiki.

So far, it is a most interactive and practice oriented guide. It clearly, yet poetically and respectfully elucidates the mysteries of Universal Life Force Energy. What is even more pertinent, it introduces you to an abundance of easy to follow, yet focused ways to enhance your receptivity for the healing love and compassion inherent in this gentle form of energy medicine.

The Ultimate Reiki Touch will support you in liberating your mind from old dross and help you uncover your innate resources for more enlightened action, based on the skill, openness, and Grace of Universal Life Force Energy.

224 pages · $14.95
ISBN 0-914955-70-5

Master Gao Yun · Master Bai Yin

Qigong Energy Healing

Five Elements Rejuvenation Therapy

The Personal Program to Heal and Strengthen Your Life with Sounds, Diet, Mudras, Timing, and the Five Rejuvenation Exercises

Qigong energy healing means strengthening the life energy with sounds, the right timing and diet, with certain mudras, and with the five rejuvenation exercises. These five elements are the basis for revitalizing the energetic field of the body and mind.

With the help of *Qigong Energy Healing*, everybody can find out his own "qi code", the best time of the day, the right sounds, the mudras, and the vitalizing five elements rejuvenation exercises that correspond to his personal type. These exercises are short, meditation movements that can be performed effortlessly. They cleanse the meridians, so that the qi can flow freely. Also suitable for those who have no previous experience with qigong.

80 pages · full color · $14.95
ISBN 0-914955-69-1

Wilhelm Gerstung · Jens Mehlhase

The Complete Feng Shui Health Handbook

How you can Protect Yourself Against Harmful Energies and Create Positive Forces for Health and Prosperity

The authors are experienced Feng Shui practitioners and consultants. They explain how the invisible energies of Feng Shui can be directly measured and evaluated using a L-rod tensor (single-handed dowser) or pendulum. This means that you can use Feng Shui to understand many health problems by relating them to energy imbalances.

This fascinating handbook provides a wealth of graphics and practical information, which help design every home in such a way that it becomes a source of energy, allowing everybody to relax and re-energize himself. The authors integrate their many years of research and extensive knowledge of energies in the home, and particularly the sleeping area, with the Western science of underground watercourses and grids.

248 pages · $16.95
ISBN 0-914955-60-8

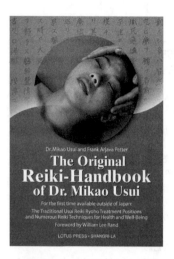

Dr. Mikao Usui and Frank A. Petter

The Original Reiki Handbook of Dr. Mikao Usui

The Traditional Usui Reiki Ryoho Treatment Positions and Numerous Reiki Techniques for Health and Well-Being

For the first time available outside of Japan: This book will show you the original hand positions from Dr. Usui's handbook. It has been illustrated with 100 colored photos to make it easier to understand. The hand positions for a great variety of health complaints have been listed in detail, making it a valuable reference work for anyone who practices Reiki. Now, that the original handbook has been translated into English, Dr. Usui's hand positions and healing techniques can be studied directly for the first time. Whether you are an initiate or a master, if you practice Reiki you can expand your knowledge dramatically as you follow in the footsteps of a great healer.

80 pages · 100 photos · $14.95
ISBN 0-914955-57-8

W. Lübeck · F.A. Petter · W.L. Rand

The Spirit of Reiki

The Complete Handbook of the Reiki System

From Tradition to the Present: Fundamental, Lines of Transmission, Original Writings, Mastery, Symbols, Treatments, Reiki as a Spiritual Path in Life, and Much More

Never before, have three Reiki masters from different lineages and with extensive background come together to share their experience.

A wealth of information on Reiki never before bought together in one place. The broad spectrum of topics range from the search for a scientific explanation of Reiki energy to Reiki as a spiritual path. It also includes the understanding of Dr. Usui's original healing methods, how Reiki is currently practiced in Japan, an analysis of the Western evolution of Reiki, and a discussion about the direction Reiki is likely to take in the future.

312 pages · 150 photos and b/w illustrations · $19.95
ISBN 0-914955-67-5

Herbs and other natural health products and information are often available at natural food stores or metaphysical bookstores. If you cannot find what you need locally, you can contact one of the following sources of supply.

Sources of Supply:

The following companies have an extensive selection of useful products and a long track-record of fulfillment. They have natural body care, aromatherapy, flower essences, crystals and tumbled stones, homeopathy, herbal products, vitamins and supplements, videos, books, audio tapes, candles, incense and bulk herbs, teas, massage tools and products and numerous alternative health items across a wide range of categories.

WHOLESALE:

Wholesale suppliers sell to stores and practitioners, not to individual consumers buying for their own personal use. Individual consumers should contact the RETAIL supplier listed below. Wholesale accounts should contact with business name, resale number or practitioner license in order to obtain a wholesale catalog and set up an account.

Lotus Light Enterprises, Inc.

P. O. Box 1008
Silver Lake, WI 531 70 USA
262 889 8501 (phone)
262 889 8591 (fax)
800 548 3824 (toll free order line)

RETAIL:

Retail suppliers provide products by mail order direct to consumers for their personal use. Stores or practitioners should contact the wholesale supplier listed above.

Internatural

P. O. Box 489
Twin Lakes, WI 53181 USA
800 643 4221 (toll free order line)
262 889 8581 office phone
WEB SITE: www.internatural.com

Web site includes an extensive annotated catalog of more than14,000 products that can be ordered "on line" for your convenience 24 hours a day, 7 days a week.